INDUSTRIAL LOCOMOTIVES

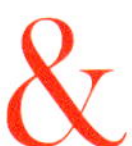

&

RAILWAYS OF THE NORTH EAST

Gordon Edgar

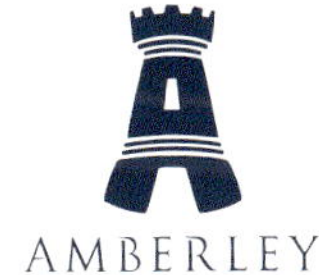

AMBERLEY

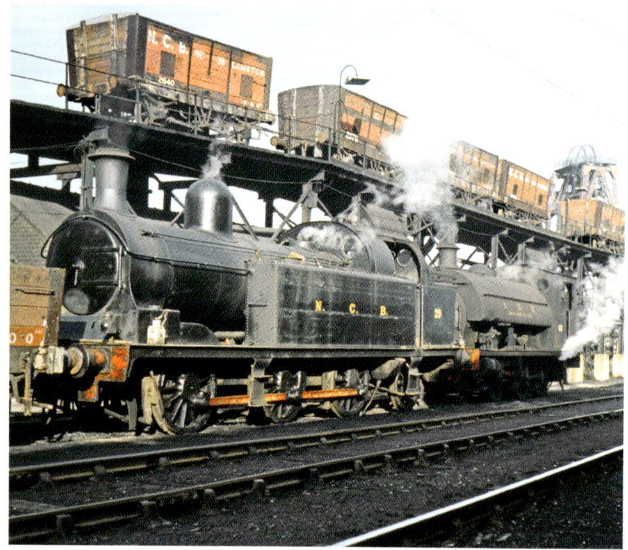

Front cover: Hawthorn Leslie 0-4-0 saddle tank No. 10 (W/No. 3352, built in 1918) with a rake of BR 21-ton hopper wagons alongside the Seaham Harbour Dock Co. Ltd's staiths on 9 July 1966. Unpopular at Seaham, within a year it had been reduced to a pile of scrap metal. (Author's collection)

Back cover: BR Swindon Works 1964-built Paxman 0-6-0 diesel-hydraulic No. 507 (formerly BR Class 14 D9525) passing Ashington colliery with loaded merry-go-round wagons on 25 March 1986. (Author)

Right: Kitson 0-6-2 tank No. 29 (W/No. 4263 of 1904) and Robert Stephenson & Hawthorns 0-6-0 saddle tank No. 63 (W/No. 7600 of 1949) overshadowed by the iconic coaling stage at Philadelphia shed in February 1969. (Jack Patience)

First published 2019

Amberley Publishing
The Hill, Stroud
Gloucestershire, GL5 4EP

www.amberley-books.com

ISBN 978 1 4456 4940 5 (paperback)
ISBN 978 1 4456 4941 2 (ebook)

British Library Cataloguing in Publication Data.
A catalogue record for this book is available from the British Library.

Typeset in 10pt on 12pt Sabon LT Std.
Origination by Amberley Publishing.
Printed in the UK.

CONTENTS

INTRODUCTION & ACKNOWLEDGEMENTS

In this, the eighth book of the regional series examining the industrial railways of England, Wales and Scotland, we review the North East of England, covering a timescale of around six decades – a period when Britain's traditional heavy industries such as coal mining, steelmaking and shipbuilding were rapidly declining. The economic change and influence of global markets saw deep coal mining entirely eradicated in the region by 2005, and steelmaking on Teesside totally decimated, except for certain specialist products. The North East of England, widely acknowledged as the region in which the birth of the railways came about, was dealt a hammer blow and inflicted with swinging cuts and closures more than anywhere else in the country, especially with the disappearance of many private railways that once served those traditional heavy industries, including complex systems inherited from the pre-Nationalisation coal mining concerns such as the Lambton Railway, the Bowes Railway and the Hetton Railway. In fact, the Hetton Colliery Railway of 1822 was the doyen of the North East colliery railways and stretched for 8 miles over Warden Law, south of Sunderland, linking Hetton colliery with the staiths on the River Wear. Indeed, it was the first complete railway engineered by George Stephenson. The railway employed locomotives on the level stretches of line and stationary steam engines on the six inclines. Remarkably, it was around the surviving remnants of this early railway that industrial steam traction was to bow out in County Durham, at South Hetton colliery in 1976. In Northumberland regular steam activity would cease during the following year when, rather appropriately, a former BR wartime-built locomotive, 'J94' Class Austerity saddle tank No. 68078, would bring down the curtain on industrial steam in the North East, at Widdrington Disposal Point.

The end of BR steam in the North East had come about in September 1967, with some locomotives of two pre-Grouping classes, the J27 0-6-0 and Q6 0-8-0, soldiering on right until the very end. But after this time there were still several non-BR steam-worked railway systems of note surviving, along with numerous National Coal Board collieries and byproducts plants still regularly relying on steam traction. It is therefore not surprising that the attention of the steam railway enthusiast was then drawn to this region of the country, where everyday working steam could still be experienced in relative abundance, such as on the remarkable systems at Philadelphia, Derwenthaugh, Ashington and Backworth in the late 1960s. Some of these railways had direct access, or running rights over BR lines, to their own staiths or ports. Away from the collieries, Doxford's shipyard at Sunderland was home to a unique fleet of four-coupled crane tanks, clinging on to a tenuous existence supporting the vulnerable shipbuilding industry.

This shipyard, in the shadow of Sunderland's Queen Alexandra Bridge at Pallion, unsurprisingly proved to be a magnet for steam railway photographers. But sadly, time was quickly running out, and these havens for steam were gradually falling by the wayside one by one, either as a result of dieselisation or following complete closure. Arguably, the most notable loss of all was the former Lambton Railway at Philadelphia, steam bowing out in style there after heavy snowfall in mid-February 1969. Before its demise, if one could bear to draw oneself away from Philadelphia, just 6 miles further east were to be found the remarkable staiths at Seaham, connected to South Hetton and the modern Hawthorn Combined Colliery by the Cold Hesledon self-acting inclines, and having a line along the coast to Dawdon colliery. The Hesledon inclines, the last self-acting inclines to remain in commercial operation in the North East, were examples of many that at one time were in widespread use in County Durham, moving large volumes of coal to staiths on the rivers Tyne and Wear. The most numerous and arguably well-known examples were those integral to the Bowes Railway, connecting mines several miles inland in north-west Durham with Jarrow staiths on the River Tyne. These inclines remained virtually intact until 1968 and the heritage Bowes Railway today maintains two of them, both of which are scheduled ancient monuments. The Bowes Railway also operates a demonstration railway based on Springwell, including the historic Springwell wagon workshops and a fleet of around forty wagons. Further west, the former NCB Bowes Railway's Marley Hill locomotive shed is the home of the Tanfield Railway, which provides steam services and occasionally operates demonstration coal trains between East Tanfield, Causey Arch, Andrew's House and Sunniside. Both heritage railways, located within 5 miles of one another in the Gateshead area, happily keep the tradition alive of former industrial colliery railways of the region and are a recommended visit whenever in the area.

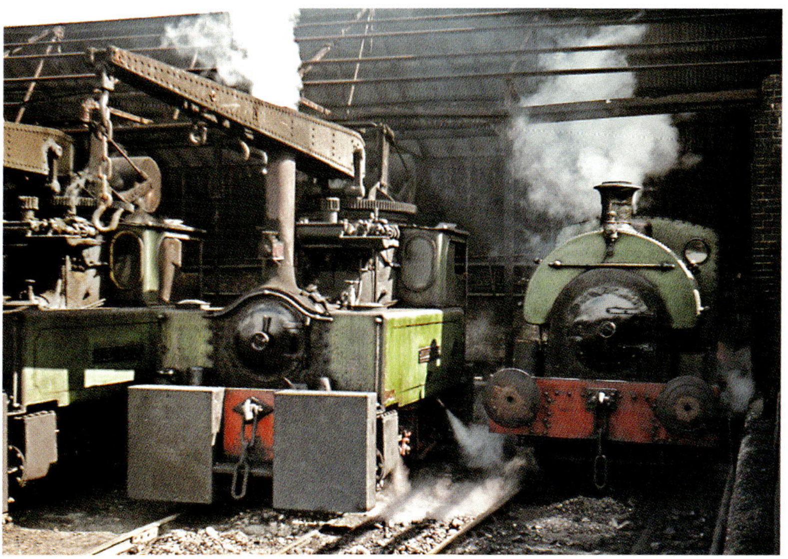

The Doxford & Sunderland Shipbuilding & Engineering Co. employed a fleet of crane tanks and one solitary Peckett saddle tank. This 1968 morning scene features Peckett 0-4-0 saddle tank *General* (W/No. 2049 of 1944) and Robert Stephenson & Hawthorns 0-4-0 crane tank *Millfield* (W/No. 7070 of 1942) preparing to move off shed. (Author's collection)

Of course, this book is not just about steam traction in industry, for the North East was also blessed with numerous other railway delights, such as the Harton Railway south of the Tyne, with its fleet of veteran electric locomotives. There was also a rich diversity of diesel traction on offer, including BR's discarded 'Paxman' Class 14 diesel-hydraulic locomotives and a whole host of other diesel locomotive types at work in all manner of industries. Teesside was excluded from the previous book published in this series, covering Yorkshire, but a selection of its industrial railway heritage is now presented herein.

Noteworthy at Lackenby were the 'tridem' locomotives, and a fleet of General Electric 750 hp six-wheel diesel-electrics, all bearing local names, and more recently the former Norwegian Di8 Class locomotives. At the other end of the scale were the diminutive Robert Stephenson & Hawthorns 'Husky' locomotives, of which only a small number were built.

Maintaining the same format as previous books in this series, this is primarily a photographic album with extended captions. Chapter introductions have been excluded in order to present as widespread a range of historical photographs as possible within the constraints of the 128 pages, the photographs telling their story, with supporting informative captions appended. With such a rich and diverse industrial railway history, it has been a challenging, but nevertheless pleasurable, task to select the images for this book, although the size of such a publication means that unfortunately not everything can be covered. Without the support of other photographers who thankfully sought out and photographed these railways and locomotives before their demise, this book would not have been possible single-handed, and I owe my gratitude to Colin Alexander, Tony Brown, Roy Burt, Kevin Lane, Jon Marsh, Duncan McEvoy, Jack Patience, John Sloane and Richard Stevens for having the foresight to record on film some of the industrial railway treasures once to be found in abundance in the North East. I would also like to record my thanks to the Industrial Railway Society and Colour Rail for permitting the use of some photographs from their archives, as without such support a work of this scope would have been impossible to produce.

In compiling this book, I have consulted numerous works of reference previously published by the Industrial Railway Society, which always prove to be invaluable in researching the history of the locations and the industrial locomotives of the United Kingdom. I would like to extend my gratitude to Adrian Booth, Colin Mountford and John Cowburn for their informative Industrial Railway Society

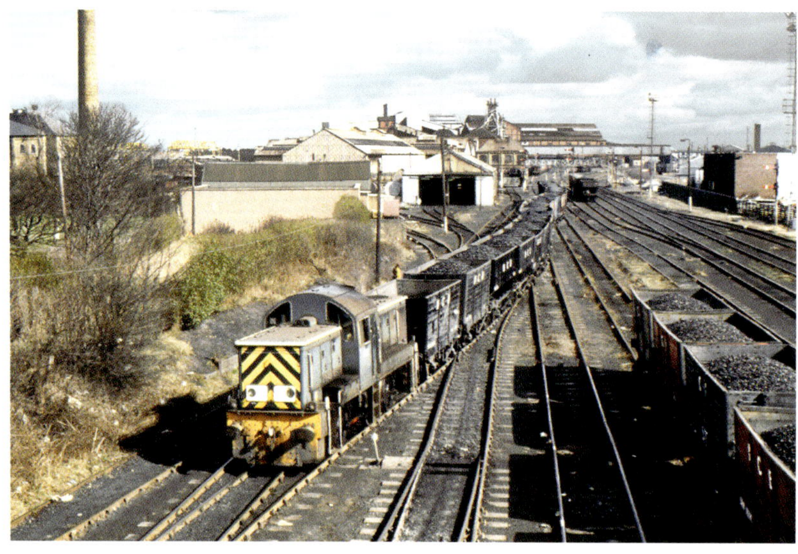

On 25 March 1986, Paxman 0-6-0 diesel-hydraulic No. 507 runs into Ashington sidings with loaded internal hopper wagons. (Author)

publications on Seaham Harbour, the private railways of County Durham and Teesside cast products respectively. I would also like to thank Richard Stevens for reviewing the draft copy, although I accept full responsibility should have any errors crept in. Finally, and by no means least, I would particularly like to pay tribute to my wife Valerie for her support and patience during the extended period that I have been engaged in producing not just this book, but the entire series.

Gordon Edgar
Ripon, North Yorkshire
December 2018

1

PORTS & WAREHOUSING

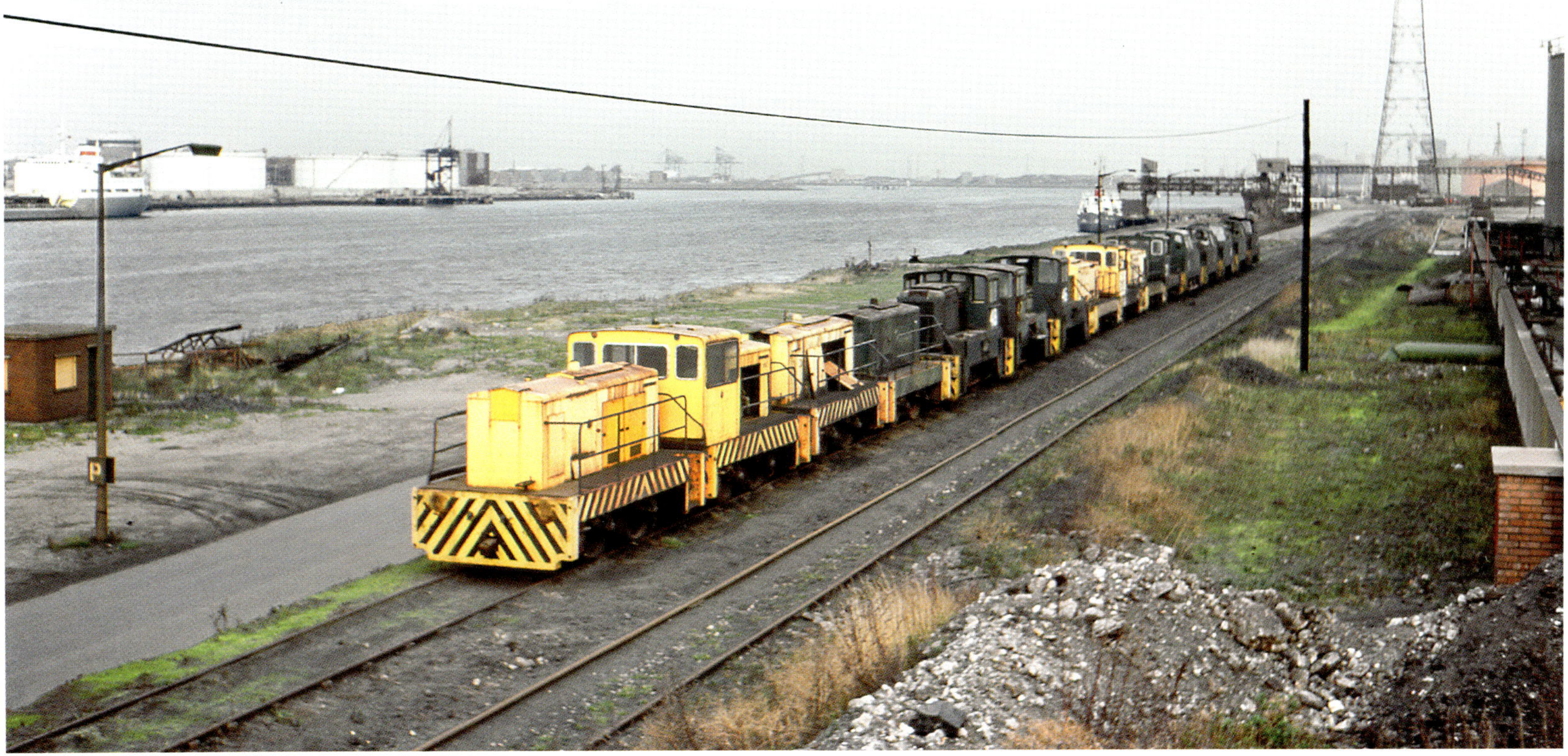

A remarkable line-up of redundant British Steel Corporation (BSC) diesel locos alongside the River Tees, including Thomas Hill articulated 'tridem', Yorkshire Engine and Sentinel locos (*see pages 116–118 for further information on the Teesside works*). The 1969-built Thomas Hill articulated diesel-hydraulic units each had a Rolls-Royce Type C6TFL power unit delivering 278 hp. The driving unit had the provision for attaching a power unit at each end, delivering 834 hp as an articulated loco. (Roy Burt)

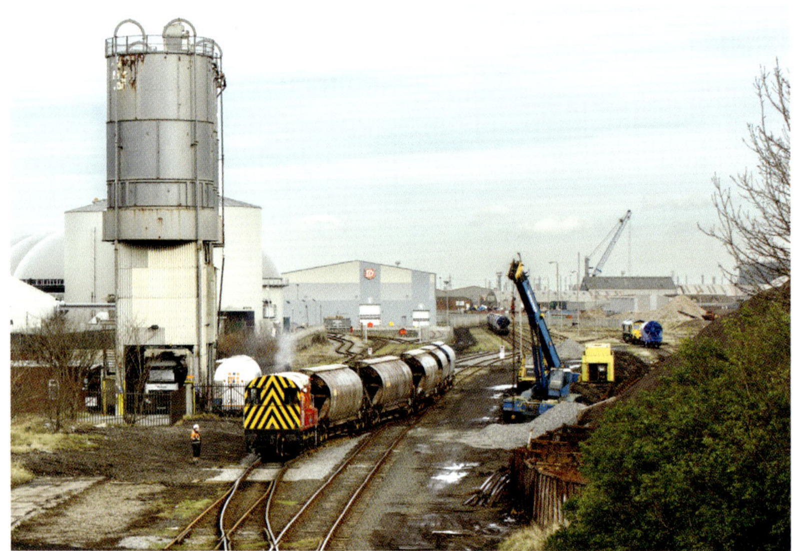

The Middlesbrough-based logistics company of A. V. Dawson Ltd, founded in 1938, provides transport, storage, import and export solutions. To this day the company continues to use rail transportation connecting with its wharf – established in 1973, located on the south bank of the River Tees a quarter of a mile west of the famous Transporter Bridge – and the Ayrton International Railhead & Store, opened in 1988 and offering over 200,000 square feet of rail-connected covered storage. Although initially using a Baguley-Drewry and a Robert Stephenson & Hawthorns 'Husky' loco (*see pages 100 and 109*) in its early industrial railway days from the late 1980s, it now employs former BR 350 hp Class 08 locos to handle mainly inbound products, including automotive steel coil from British Steel Port Talbot, on behalf of Nissan at Washington, and potash/polyhalite from the Boulby mine.

Above: A. V. Dawson Ltd's Class 08 shunter No. 08774 *Arthur Vernon Dawson* (built at BR Derby Works in 1960 as D3942) moves the first consignment of potash wagons of the day into the Ayrton Railhead on 19 February 2016. Freightliner Heavyhaul No. 66564, on the right, had just brought the twelve loaded wagons into the exchange sidings on the 09.34 working from Boulby Carlin How potash mine sidings. (Author)

Right: Baguley-Drewry 204 hp 0-4-0 diesel-mechanical *Eleanor Dawson* (W/No. 2725 of 1963) at A. V. Dawson, Middlesbrough Wharf, on 9 May 1994, with flat wagons used for conveying steel bars for export to Holland. Previously named *Dorothy Lightfoot* during its service at the Bidston Ore Terminal in the Wirral, it was re-named upon arrival in Middlesbrough. (Author)

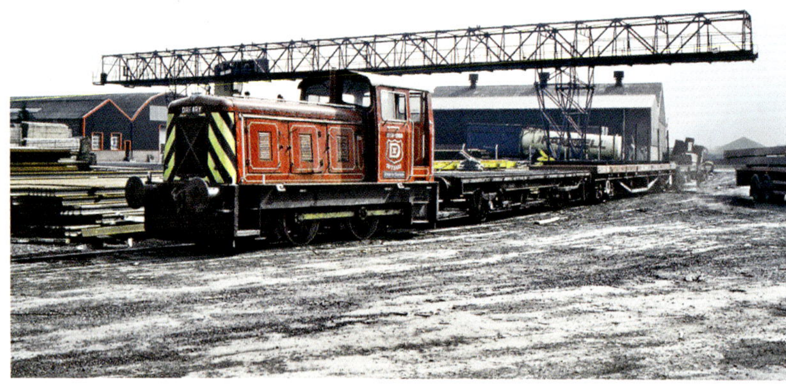

Right: French-built industrial locos working in the UK are rare. This Locotracteurs Gaston Moyse-built four-wheel diesel-electric, No. 2 (W/No. 1364 of 1976), worked at the railhead of Stockton Haulage Co. Ltd in Middlesbrough and was photographed there on 5 September 1994. Named *Autumn Gold*, it handled the steel and general cargo products contracted to this third-party logistics provider, one rail traffic flow in the 1990s being steel for export to Ireland via Stranraer. It survives today as a hire loco for Hartlepool contractor Ed Murray & Sons and has seen use with Liberty Steels at Hartlepool. (Author)

Below: Nine former Norwegian Di8 Class Bo-Bo diesel-electric locos in temporary secure storage at P. D. Ports, Teesport, on 4 April 2016. In the line-up (from left to right) are Nos 817 (8.717), 8.701, 8.712, 8.704, 8.718, 8.703, 8.716, 820 (8.720) and 8.719. From the following day the first, No. 820, was moved by road to British Steel Scunthorpe, followed by the remainder of the Maschinenbau Kiel, Germany, 1996-built 2,110 hp locos over the following ten days. (Author)

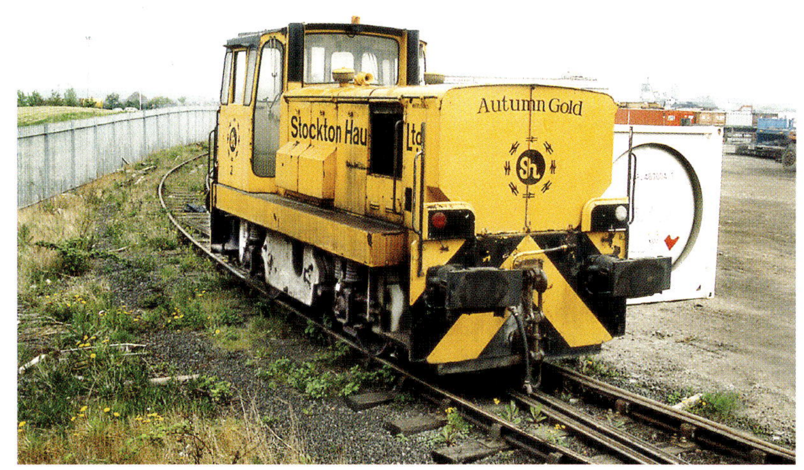

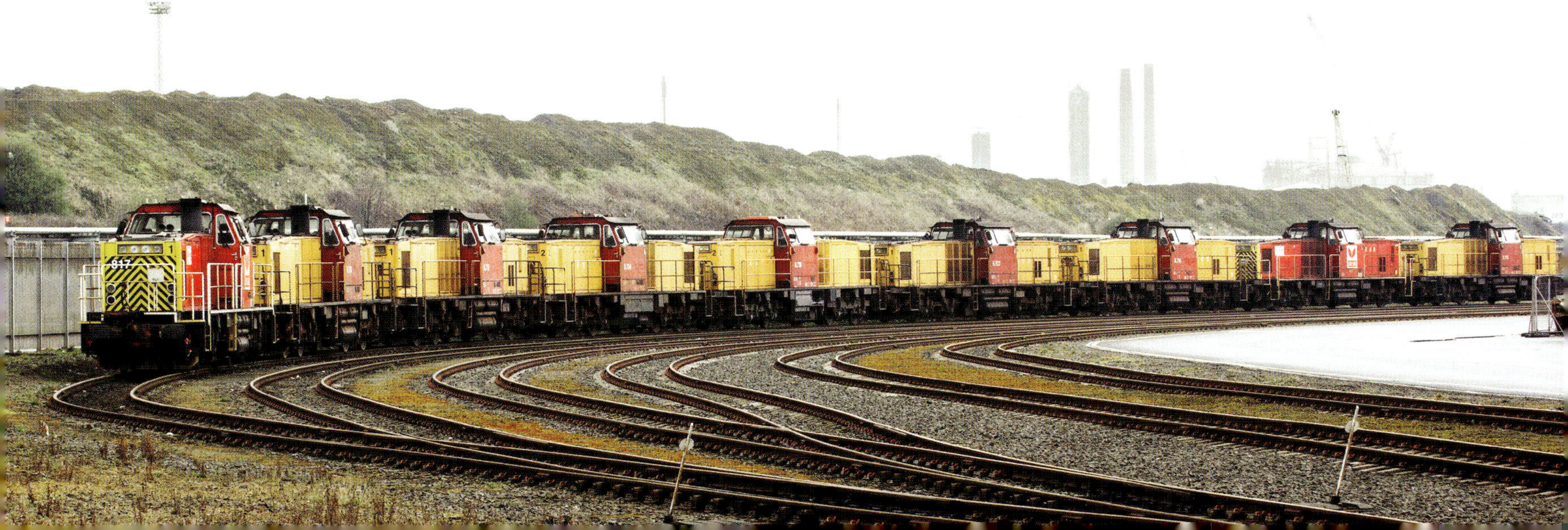

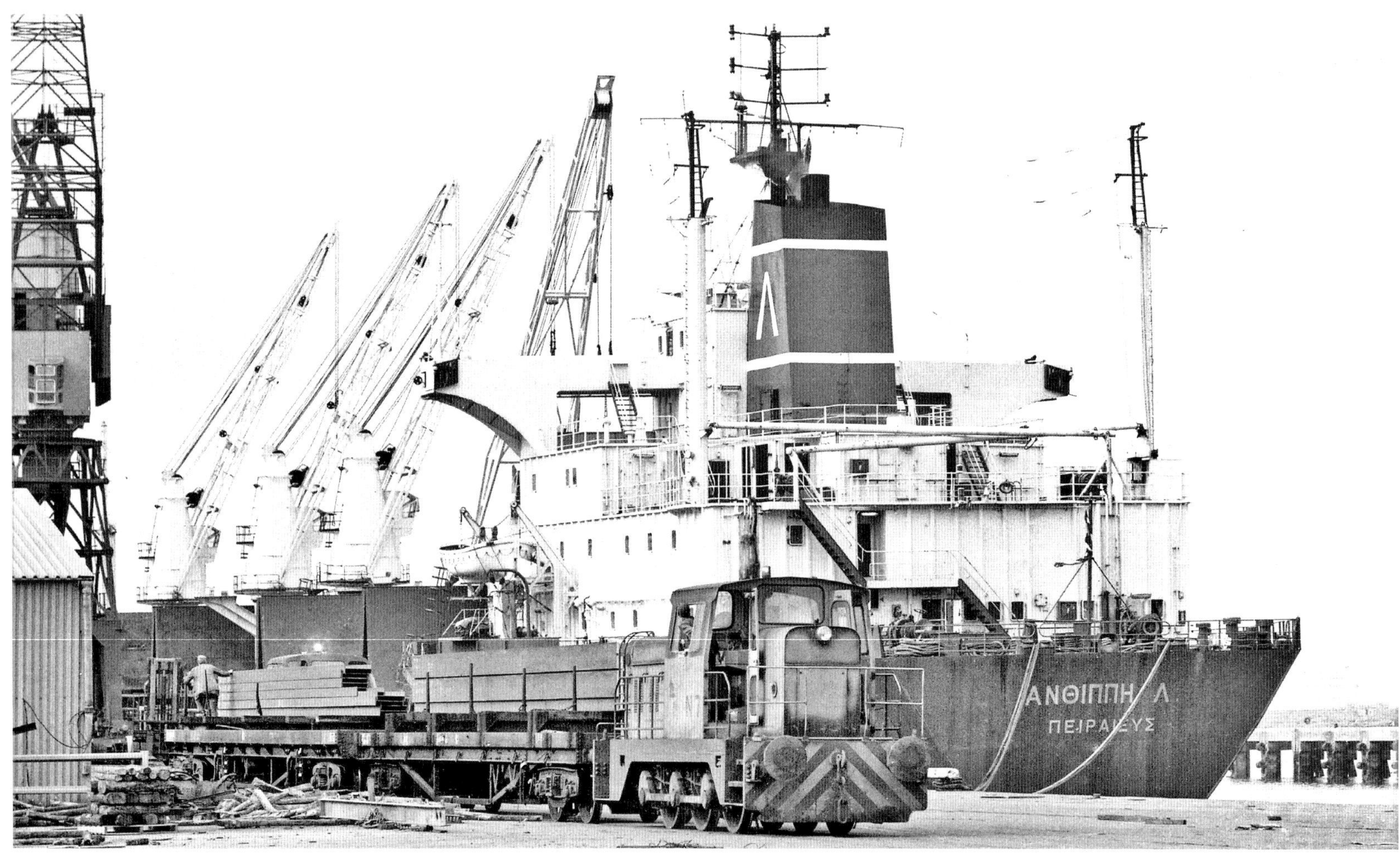

On 25 September 1986, Tees & Hartlepool Port Authority, Grangetown, Sentinel 0-6-0 diesel-hydraulic N7 (W/No. 10095 of 1962) positions a consignment of steel alongside the Piraeus-registered ship *Anthippi L.* (Kevin Lane)

2

ON THE NARROW GAUGE

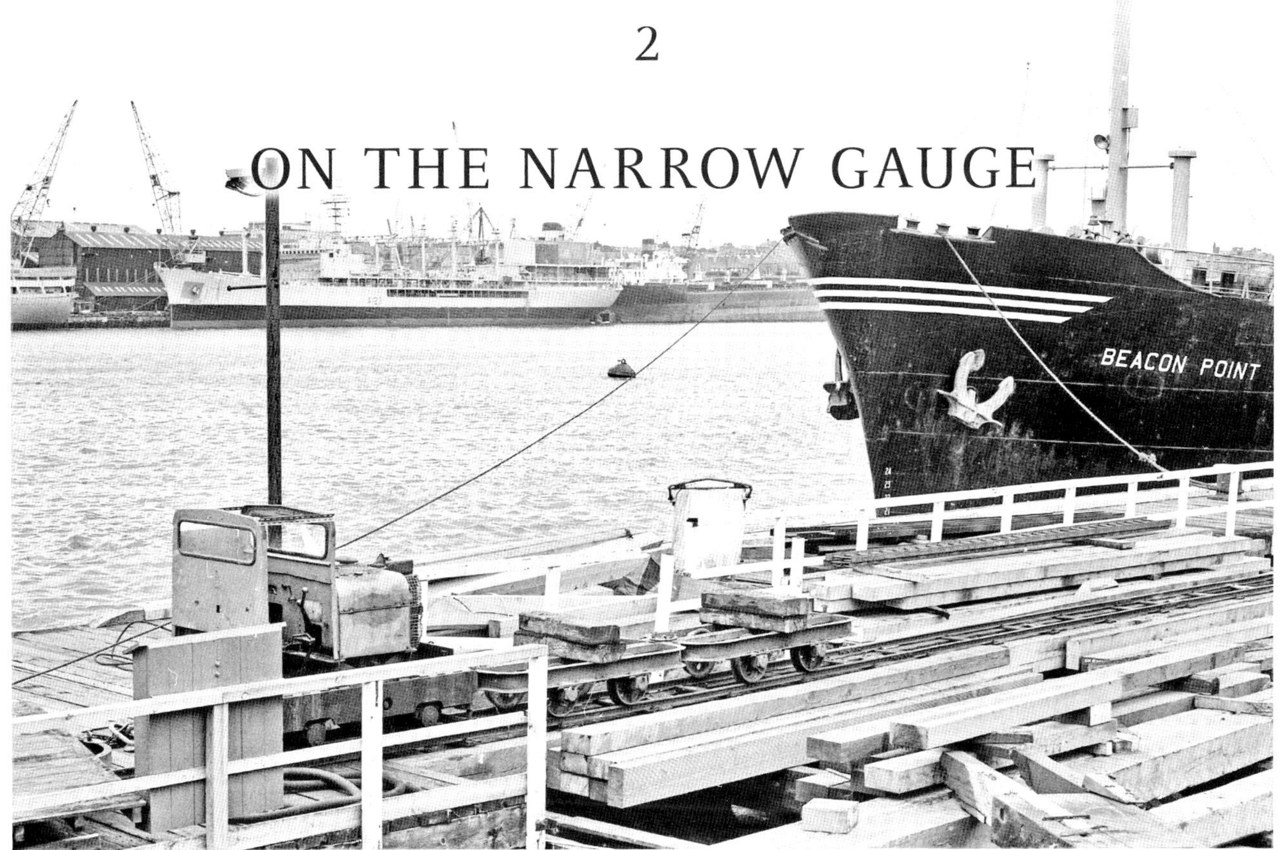

The temporary 2-foot gauge tramway of contractor Jones & Bailey at Harton staiths in September 1981 (*see page 73*), with a Motor Rail four-wheel diesel-mechanical (W/No. 22237 of 1965) coupled to the chassis of two former 'V' skips, forming a rudimentary 'bolster wagon' for conveying the large replacement timber sections into place. In the background is the Royal Navy replenishment tanker A123 RFA *Olna*. During the following year she embarked for the South Atlantic as a member of the second wave of ships deployed to the Falklands for refuelling the aircraft carrier battle group. She was decommissioned at the Port of Gibraltar in 2000 and was eventually broken up in Turkey. The general cargo ship *Beacon Point*, built in 1969, is berthed at the staiths in the foreground. (Kevin Lane)

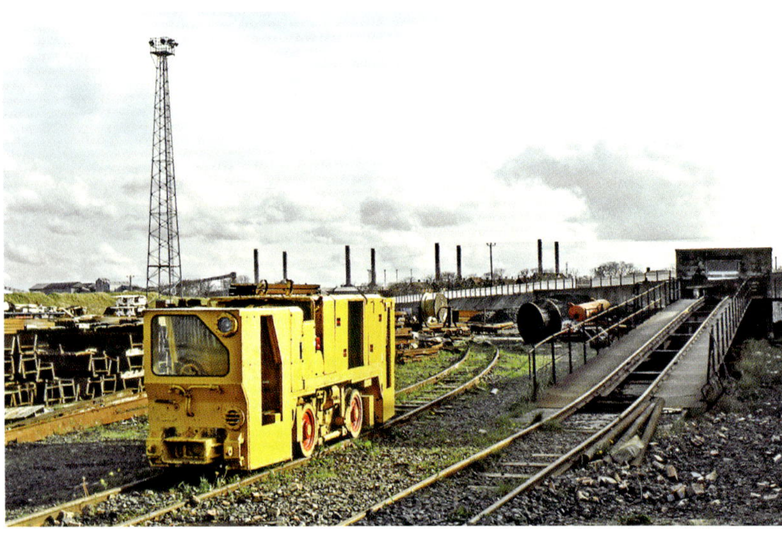

Left: An underground fire at Lynemouth colliery in 1966 resulted in the Bewick drift mine being driven to gain access to the coal face beyond where the fire had taken place. Additionally, Lynemouth and Ellington collieries were linked underground, making it the largest undersea mining complex in the world. Coal from both was then drawn by conveyor through this drift, thus avoiding the congestion at the two shafts and enabling coal to be moved onward by conveyor directly to the washery at Lynemouth, which provided coal for burning at Alcan's Lynemouth aluminium smelter power station. At this time rail traffic ceased between the two collieries, and in 1972 a 3-foot gauge surface system was installed at British Coal Bewick to handle mining materials. On 24 April 1992, Clayton flameproof four-wheel diesel-hydraulic No. 20/110/738 (W/No. B0190 of 1974 – rebuilt W/No. B2293 of 1983) was in use at the drift mine stockyard. The mine was finally sealed in January 2005, when UK Coal took the decision to close Ellington colliery, the last deep mine in the North East. (Author)

Below left: During an evening visit on 24 April 1992, 3-foot gauge Clayton four-wheel battery-electric No. 2 (W/No. B3060 of 1983) was working at Bewick Drift Mine, seen here at the head of a rake of flat wagons. Once a common feature at collieries up and down the country, the drift mine stockyard railway was by this time one of only two such narrow-gauge stockyard systems then remaining in use in the United Kingdom. Happily, the Clayton Equipment Co. Ltd, based at Burton-upon-Trent, continues to build and refurbish battery locos for use in the now limited home market, but increasingly locos are supplied for use overseas, including during 2018, filling orders for customers with narrow gauge mine railways in Austria, Canada and South America. (Author)

Opposite page top left: A 2-foot gauge Hudswell Clarke 0-6-0 diesel-mechanical (W/No. DM842 of 1954) at the NCB North East Area Seaham Training Centre on 18 March 1983. The 100 hp mines loco was a single-ended version, fitted with a jackshaft drive, and had previously worked underground since new at Vane Tempest colliery. The Centre was part of the Seaham colliery site, where certified training for underground loco drivers took place, as well as compulsory refresher courses that were required every three years. To the left can be seen the foot of a gradient, where trainees received mandatory gradient and speed retarder practice. First established in July 1965, the centre was closed in 1991, after which driver training was undertaken at the few remaining collieries. (Roy Burt)

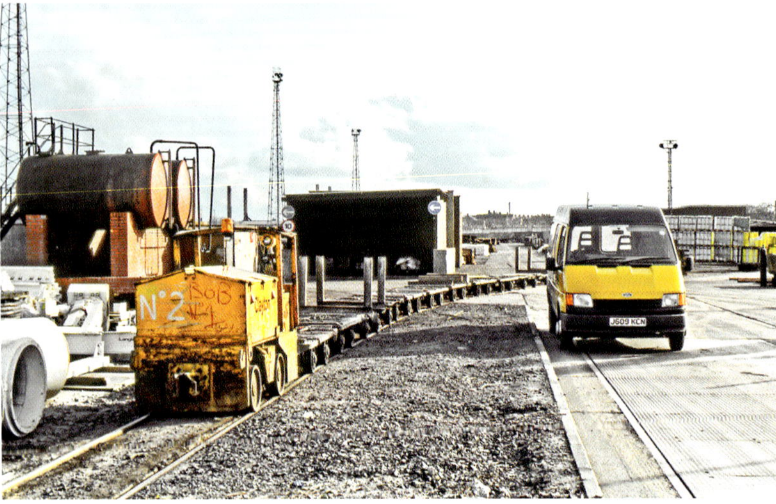

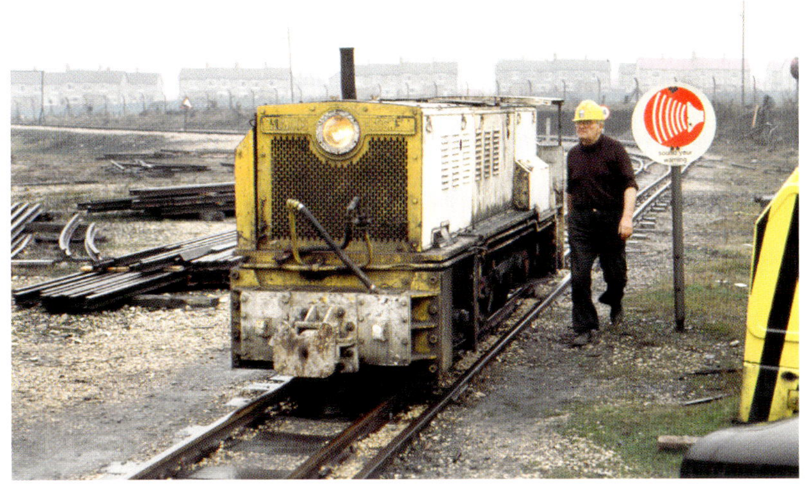

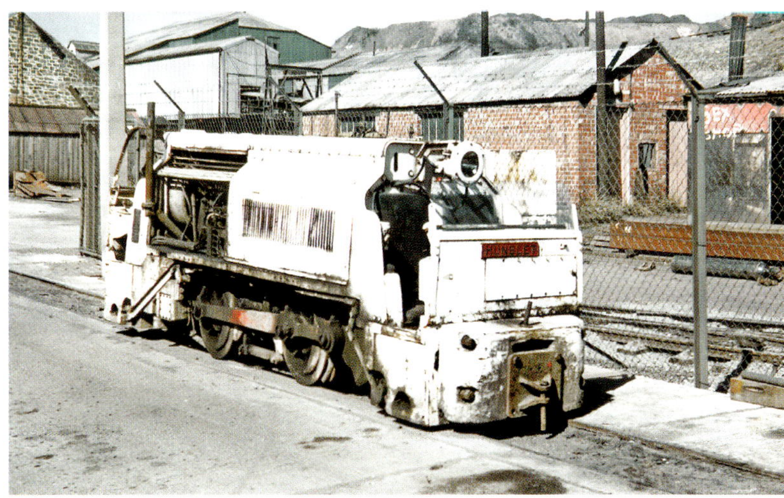

Above right: A Hunslet flameproof Class 66DE 0-4-0 diesel-mechanical (W/No. 6619 of 1966) on the NCB Whittle colliery's 2-foot gauge stockyard surface system on 1 September 1971. Usually employed underground, it was equipped with flame traps and an exhaust 'scrubber' system. All controls are air-operated from either of the two cabs. Spending time at Seaham Training Centre, it is now a member of the Leighton Buzzard Narrow Light Railway fleet. (Author)

Right: Whittle colliery used a 2-foot gauge railway, running alongside part of the standard gauge branch line, to transport men and materials between the drift mine and the main colliery entrance, as well as moving materials about the surface stockyard system. On 1 September 1971, Ruston & Hornsby 48DL-Class four-wheel diesel-mechanical No. 2 (W/No. 268866 of 1949) was working a rake of man-riding cars. From 1978, Whittle was linked underground to nearby Shilbottle colliery, with all coal being drawn at Whittle. Both collieries were renowned for producing some of the best quality steam coal in the country. Shilbottle closed in 1981, and Whittle in 1987, the latter opening again under licence, but eventually going into receivership and closing by 1997. (Author)

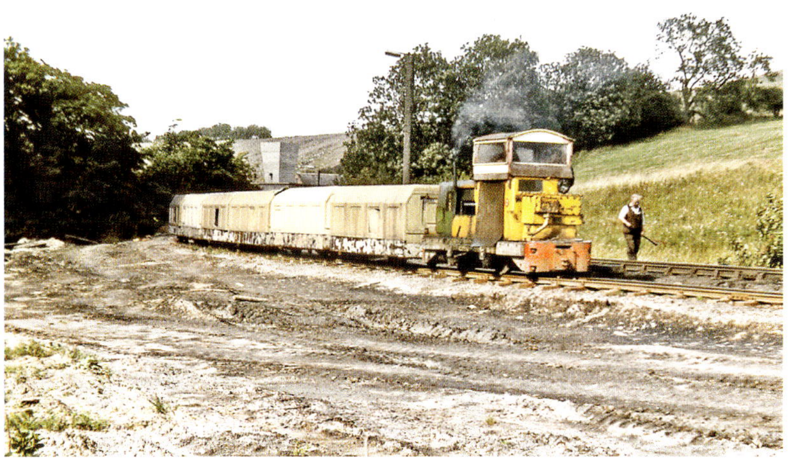

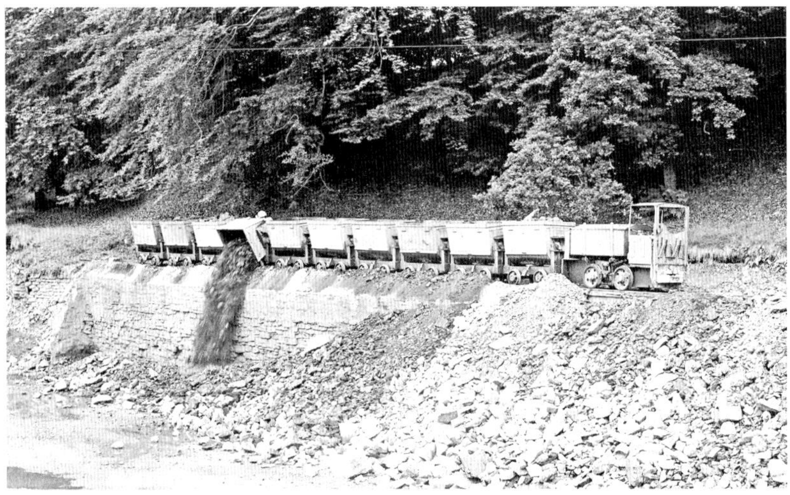

Left: Several small mines in Weardale used narrow-gauge railways, mainly of 2-foot gauge, and employed battery-electric locos in the latter years to convey coal and minerals such as ironstone, lead ore and fluorspar from drifts to stockyards and tipping docks. The Stanhopeburn mine, near Stanhope, had been worked by several owners from around 1846, exploiting ironstone, lead and, in later years, fluorspar. The quality of the lead ore concentrates was found to be poor when the mine was first exploited, but rich fluorspar reserves were discovered in the late nineteenth century. This led to it being exploited by the Weardale Lead Company in the early twentieth century, with it becoming the leading producer in the area. On 16 August 1979, then under the ownership of Swiss Aluminium (UK) Ltd, the Shield Hurst level of the mine was being mined for fluorspar when a 2-foot gauge 1978-built Wingrove & Rogers four-wheel battery-electric loco was found in use at the tipping dock. It was last worked commercially in January 1982, following the collapse of the fluorspar market. (Kevin Lane)

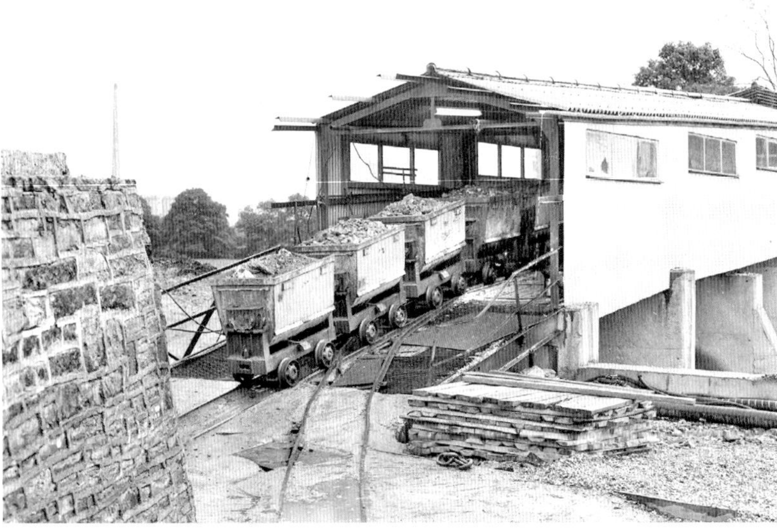

Below left: Cambokeels mine, near Eastgate, was first exploited in 1841 by the Beaumont family, who had control of much of Weardale's lead mining industry in the nineteenth century. The lead mine changed ownership several times during its history, and had ceased lead exploitation on three separate occasions, before being acquired in 1969 by two local entrepreneurs, Maddison and Brown, who exploited it for fluorspar. Between 1971 and 1982 it was worked by Swiss Aluminium Mining (UK) Ltd. In this 16 August 1979 scene, loaded 'U' skips are awaiting discharge at the ore tipping shed, which had twenty-two unloading chutes. The 2-foot gauge track dropped steeply into the adit and the line in the foreground provided access for locos to the maintenance and battery charging shed, which maintained eight Wingrove & Rogers four-wheel battery-electric locos built between 1965 and 1978. In August 1982 the site was taken over by Weardale Minerals Ltd, but mining operations fluctuated thereafter with market demands, and when it was closed in 1989 it was the deepest mine in the area. Within five years of its closure the site had become derelict and the abandoned remains can still be found today, between the north bank of the River Wear and the A689 Bishop Auckland to Alston road. (Kevin Lane)

Opposite page: A brand-new Wingrove & Rogers four-wheel battery-electric loco with a loaded train of tubs outside the Shield Hurst Level adit on the 2-foot gauge Stanhopeburn Mine system of Swiss Aluminium Mining (UK) Ltd on 16 August 1978. The battery charging/loco shed is to the right of the loco. (Kevin Lane)

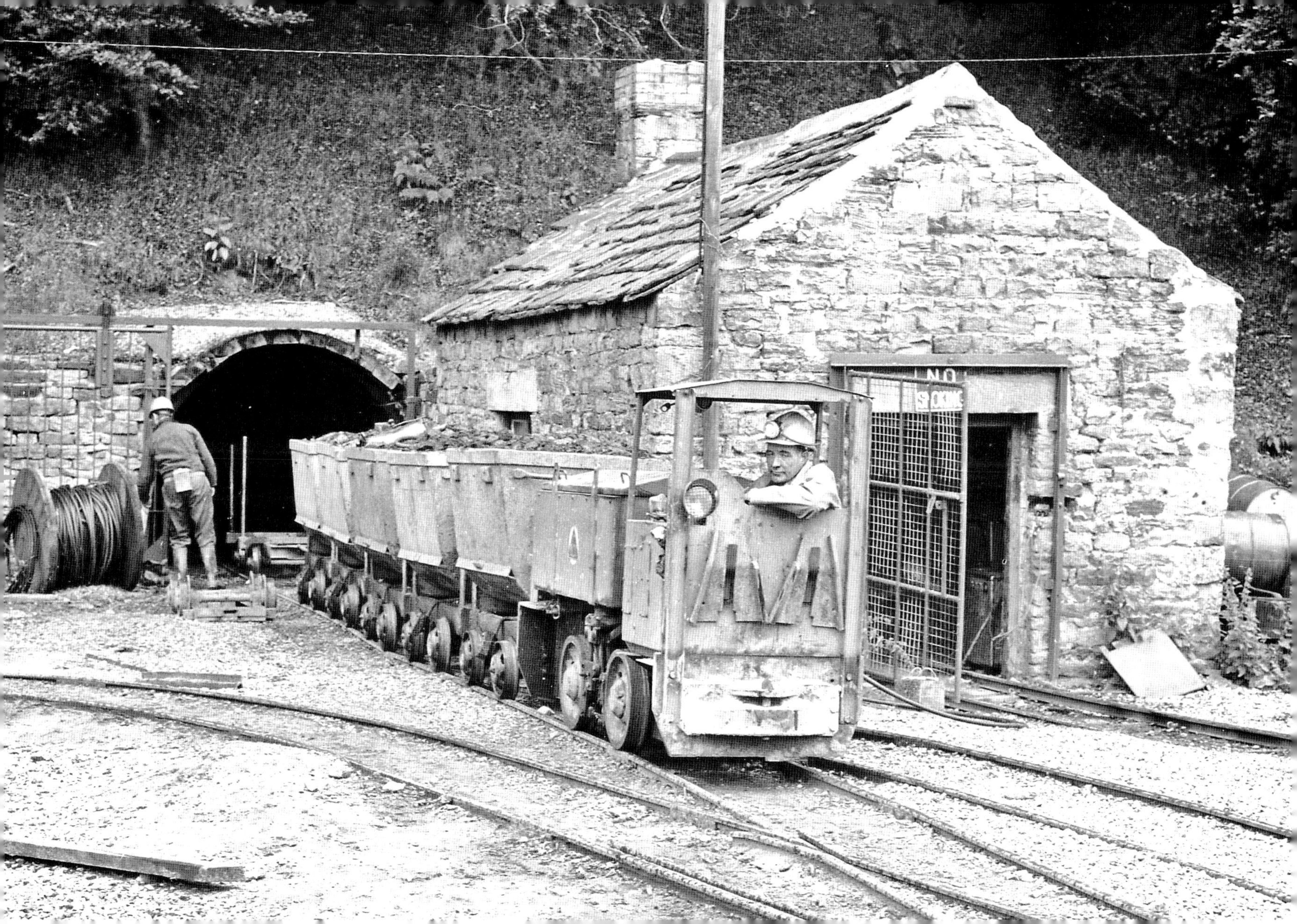

NO
SMOKING

3

COUNTY DURHAM COAL

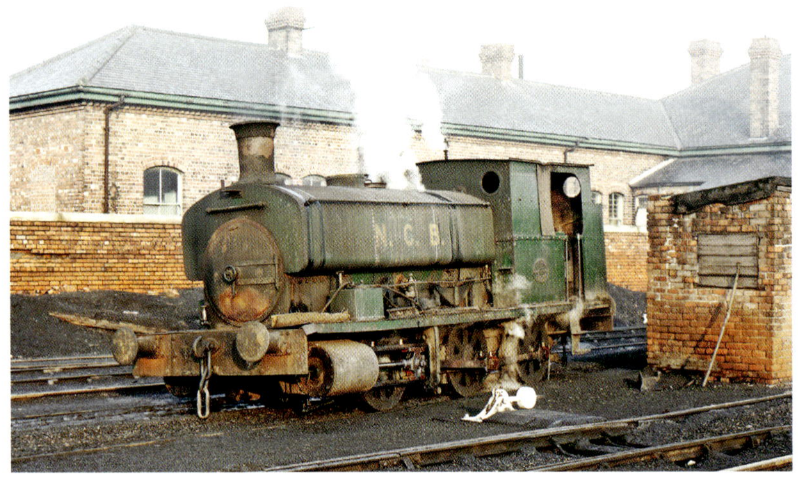

Above left: Shotton colliery, initially known at Shotton Grange colliery, was located 2 miles west of Peterlee and the first coal is believed to have been won there in 1841. Horden Collieries Ltd developed the mine after its acquisition in 1901 and it was shunted by shire horses until after the First World War. In 1904 the company took delivery of its first loco, a 15 x 22-inch outside cylinder Andrew Barclay 0-6-0 saddle tank (W/No. 1015), which was to spend most of its career there, apart from a short-term loan to Horden colliery in the mid-1950s. A coking plant and brickworks were co-located with the colliery, also shunted by the colliery locos, but coke production ceased in 1958 and the brickworks, by then in private ownership, closed in 1959, its two 2-foot 6-inch gauge Hunslet 1950s-built diesel-mechanical locos experiencing an unknown fate. In September 1971, the by then decrepit-looking and work-stained Barclay was eking out its final days in action for the NCB at Shotton. Its restoration to full working order was nearing completion at the Tanfield Railway in 2019. (Author's collection)

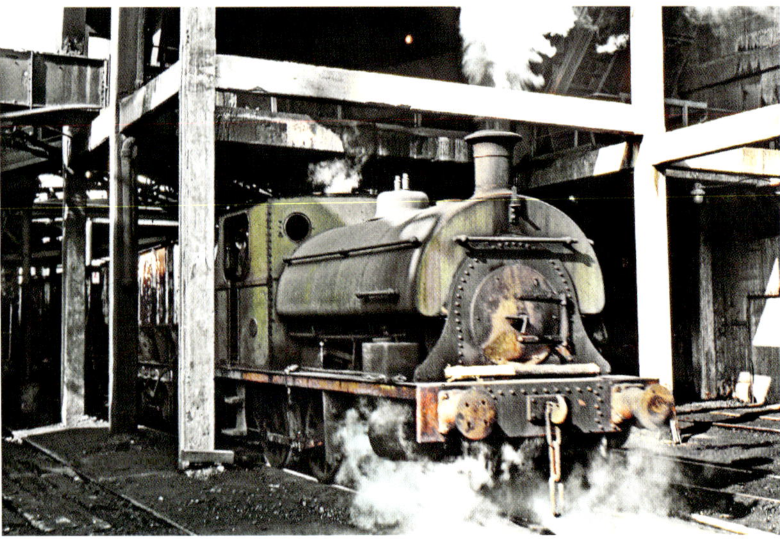

Below left: Shotton colliery was served by a ¾-mile branch with the BR Sunderland–Stockton line. In the mid-1960s, Peckett 0-6-0 saddle tank (W/No. 1310 of 1914) was hard at work, wheezing beneath the colliery screens as it attempted to propel a rake of 21-ton coal hoppers for loading. The B2 Class Peckett, originally named *Horden*, was supplied new from the Bristol manufacturer to Horden Collieries Ltd, but, unlike the Barclay, it had seen much service elsewhere, at Blackhall, Horden, Easington and Thornley collieries. Following the colliery's closure on 1 September 1972, it succumbed to the cutter's torch in November 1972. The closure of the colliery saw around 800 job losses, but this was a far cry from the post-war days when almost 2,000 locals were collectively employed above and below ground. Today there is very little sign of mining ever having taken place, apart from the name of the village, which now offers only limited local employment with the call-centre companies established between Shotton Colliery and Old Shotton. (Author's collection)

Above right: The 3rd Marquess of Londonderry founded Seaham Harbour in 1828, installing railways and inclines to serve the new facility, and in turn encouraging the growth of the population around Seaham. This move heralded the massive upsurge in coal exploitation south of the River Wear and the development of the private railways to effectively transport the product to port. The rail-served wooden staiths at Seaham Harbour's South Dock, completed in 1939, were a remarkable sight to witness until their demolition took place in 1979 (*see page 23*). However, it was to be the North Dock, following its opening in 1831, where initially the loaded chaldron wagons would be lowered down a self-acting incline for discharge alongside the waiting ships. Business expanded rapidly and the Seaham dock operation was soon to become a victim of its own success. An Act of Parliament was sought and passed in 1898, which created the Seaham Harbour Dock Company Ltd. This saw the company take over the harbour and sidings, thus enabling the expansion of the South Dock and the eventual construction of staiths capable of handling much greater volumes. Loaded wagons would be emptied through bottom discharge hatches and down chutes, directly into the collier boats berthed in the dock below. Equally remarkable was the survival of the veteran 1877-built Lewin 0-4-0 saddle tank No. 18 (W/No. 683) into the early 1970s, here seen in steam at Seaham Harbour in the early 1960s. Originally built at Lewin's Poole foundry as a well-tank, during its 100-year service at Seaham it took on the guise of a side tank with an enclosed cab, and then a saddle tank from 1927. Its short wheelbase and small profile ensured its survival, enabling it to work on the low-level lines beneath the staiths and through the narrow connecting tunnels to the North Dock quays and breakwater, carrying materials for maintaining the structure of the breakwater walls, thus ensuring the continued protection of the harbour and the North and South Docks. The Lewin remained active in this role until the early 1970s, after which it was deservedly retired to the Beamish Museum. (Colour Rail)

Below right: Prior to the acquisition of a uniform fleet of diesels in 1967, the Seaham Harbour Dock Company had a penchant for purchasing pre-owned locos. On 3 April 1964, Robert Stephenson & Hawthorns 0-4-0 saddle tank No. 183 (W/No. 7347 of 1947) was still showing some signs of its former steel industry glory, with its lined light green livery. It arrived at Seaham in June 1963, along with three others from Dorman Long's Acklam works, Middlesbrough, and survived until it was cut up at Seaham Harbour in December 1967. (Author's collection)

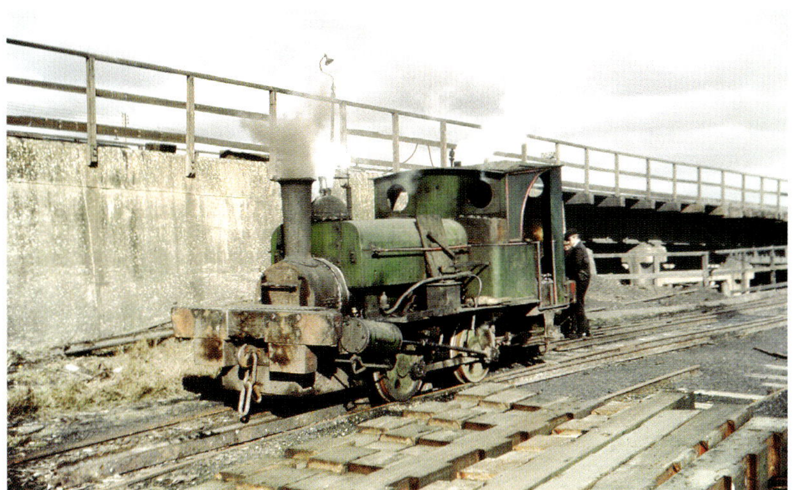

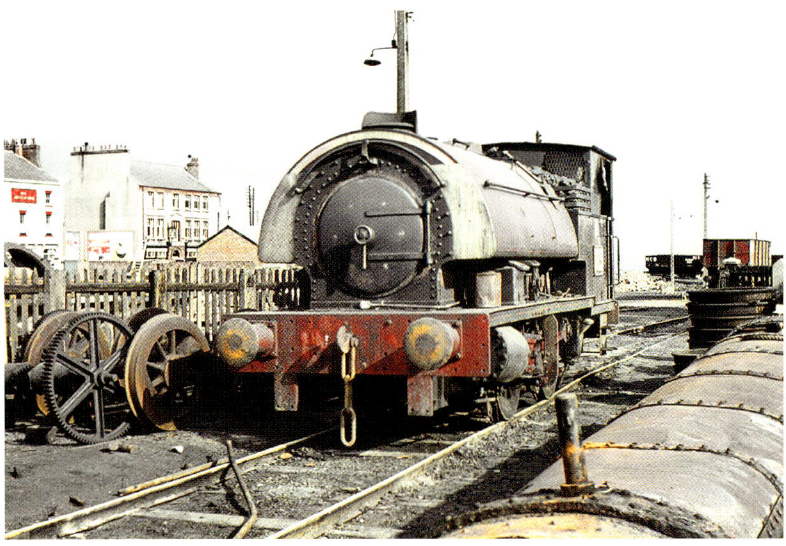

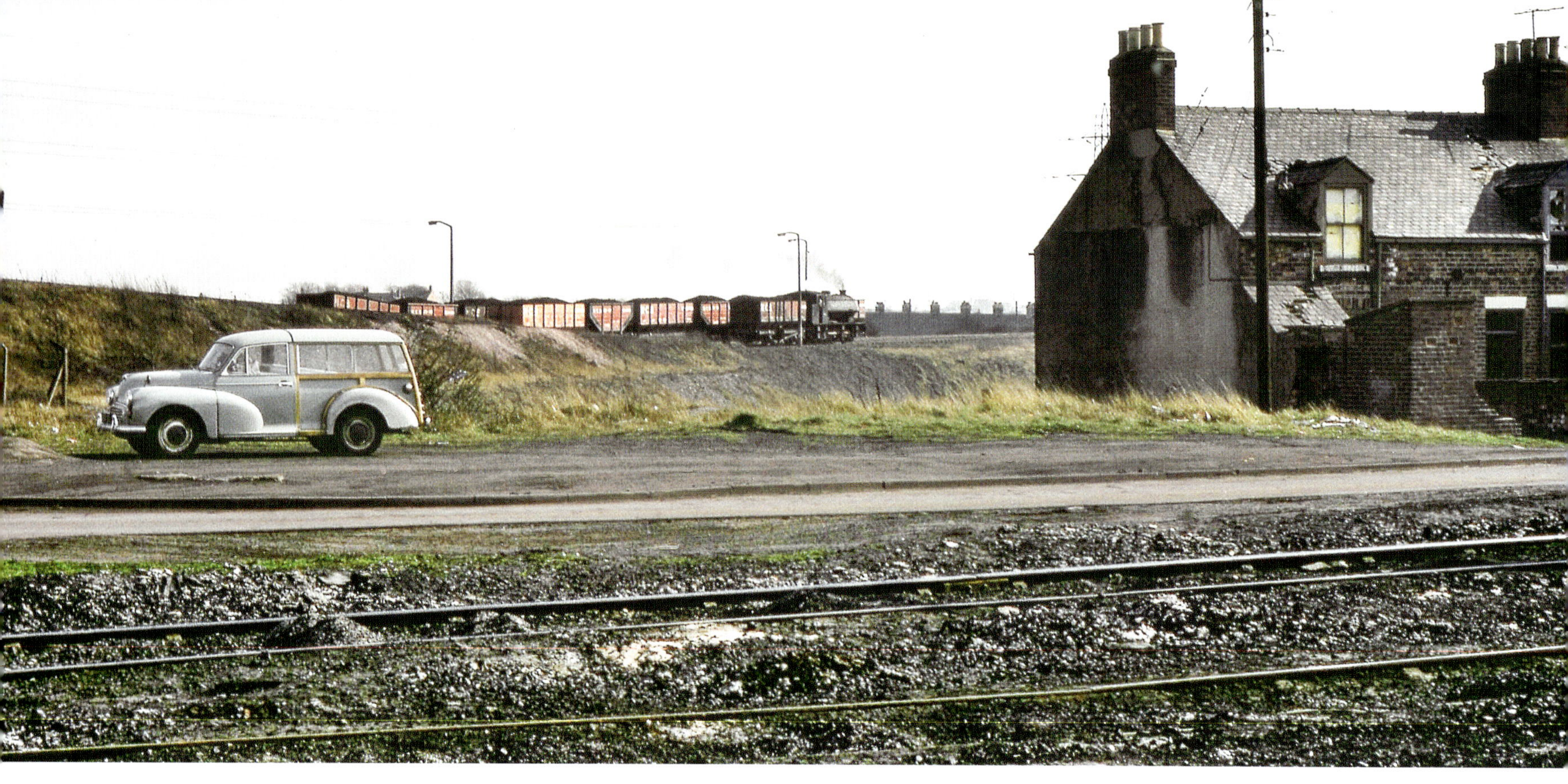

Hunslet Austerity 0-6-0 saddle tank No. 68 (W/No. 3784 of 1953), glimpsed between a Morris Minor 'Traveller' and a row of abandoned miners' dwellings on the South Hetton Railway on 23 March 1973. Remarkably, the South Hetton Railway was to be the home of the last commercially operated steam loco in industry in County Durham, as well as hosting the last commercially worked inclines in the North East. (John Sloane)

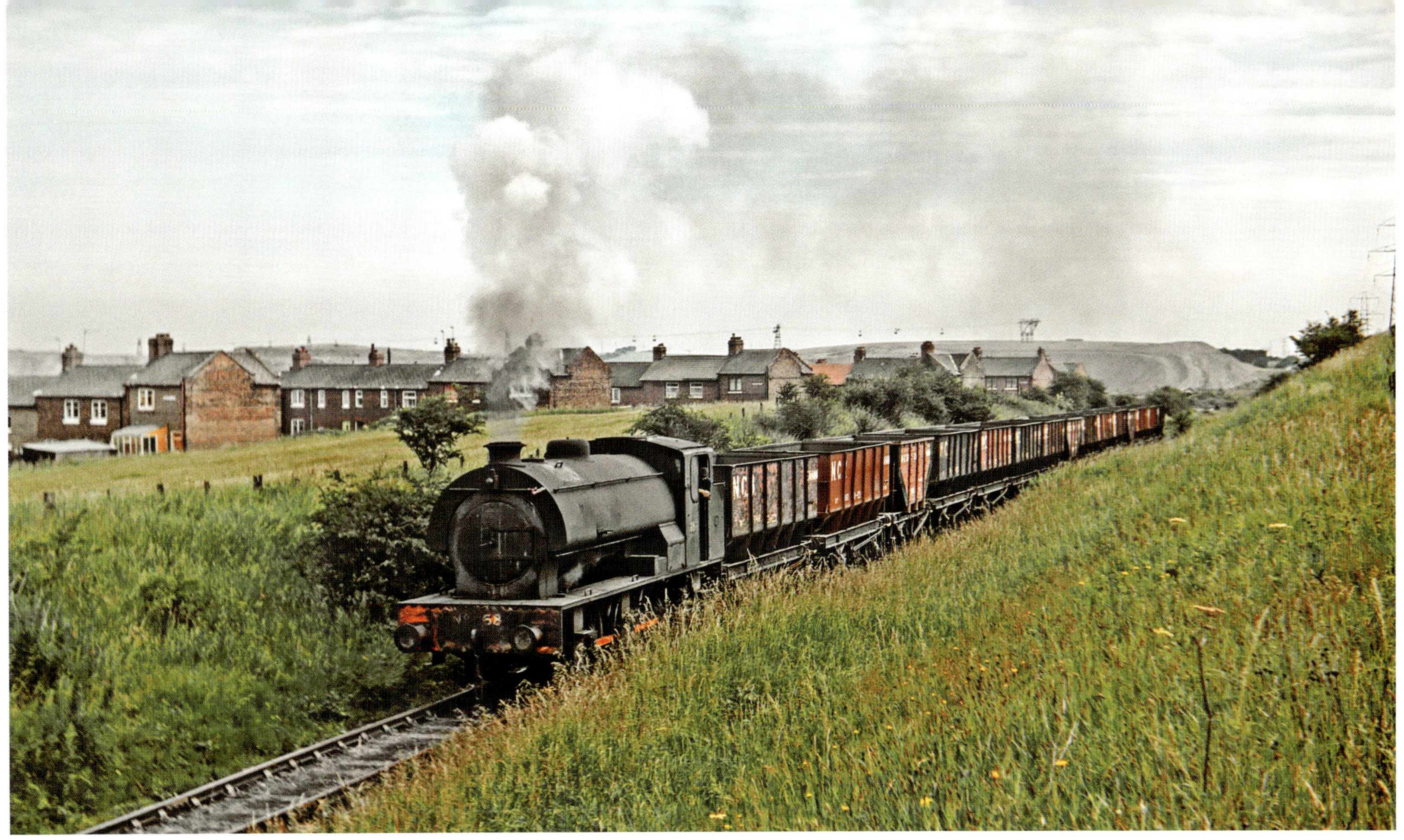

South Hetton was a large, productive colliery, familiar as a destination for many a BR Class J27 and Q6-hauled train of empties via Seaton Bank until 1967. Diesel locos began to replace steam from 1973, and on 9 July 1973 just one steam loco was found in action. Austerity 0-6-0 saddle tank No. 68 approaches the colliery at Hesledon Moor on its return from Hesledon Bank Head with empty internal-user hopper wagons. These will have carried spoil for dumping at sea at Dawdon, being subsequently dragged up the self-acting incline from Seaham (*see page 20*). The South Hetton Austerities were fitted with steam-driven 12 volt generators to enable the use of radios and lights. The drag line in the distance on the Murton colliery tip is another aspect of coalfield scenery that has now disappeared. (Richard Stevens)

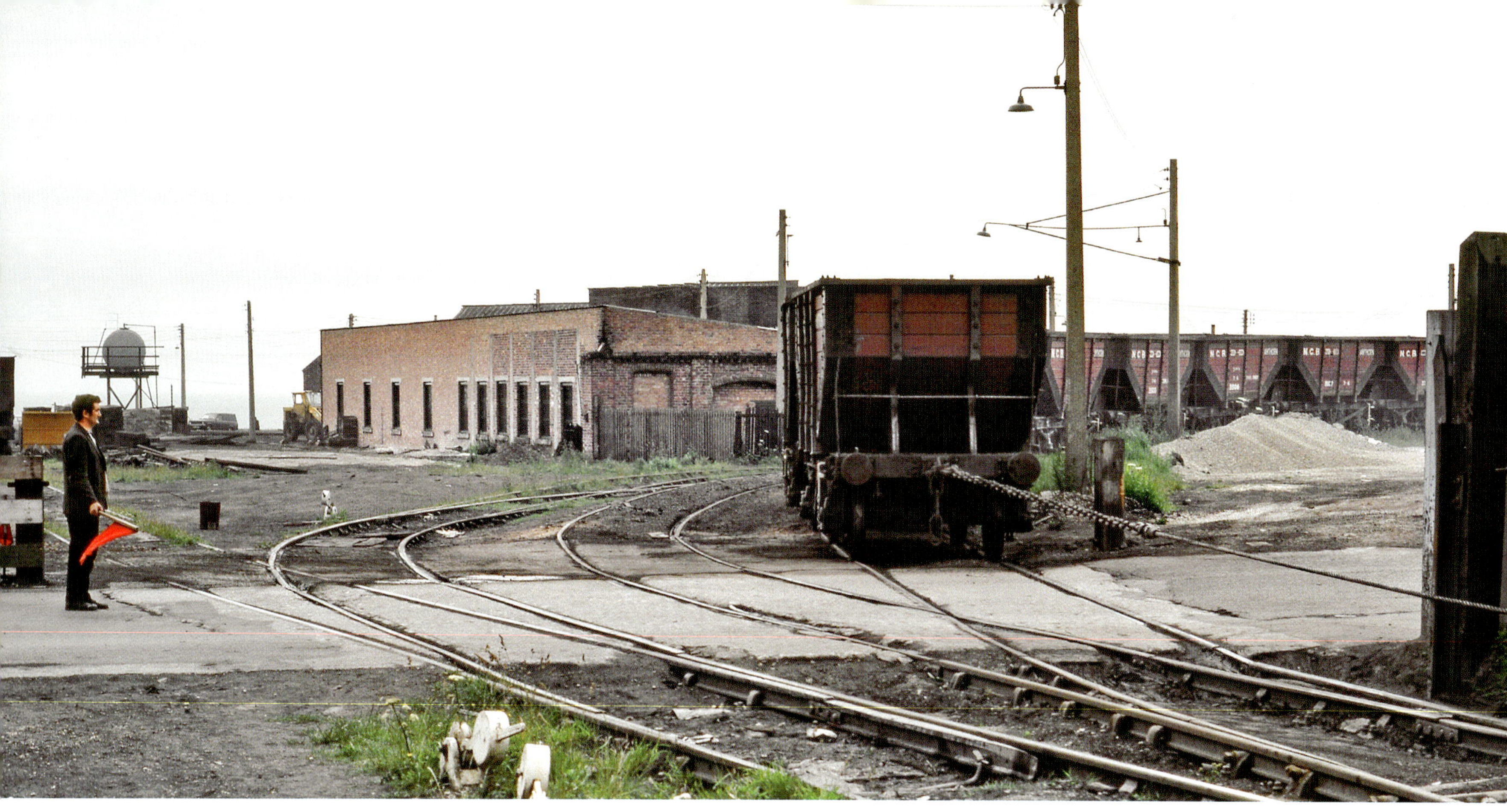

Above: Empty 16-ton internal-user wooden-bodied wagons used for colliery waste, leaving Seaham Harbour by rope on 23 June 1978 via the two Cold Hesledon inclines and destined for Hawthorn Combined Colliery. This incline was abandoned after the 1984–85 miners' strike. The Dock Company's workshop and loco stabling point is seen behind. (John Sloane)

Opposite page: Seaham Harbour Dock Co. Ltd Hawthorn Leslie 0-4-0 saddle tank No. 10 (W/No. 3352 of 1918), and a sister loco in the distance, pollute the sky above the South Dock and staiths as they shunt BR 21-ton coal hopper wagons on 9 July 1966. Another purchase from the Acklam works of Dorman Long in June 1963, its service at Seaham proved to be short-lived, and it had less than a year's service remaining when photographed, eventually being scrapped by March 1967. (Author's collection)

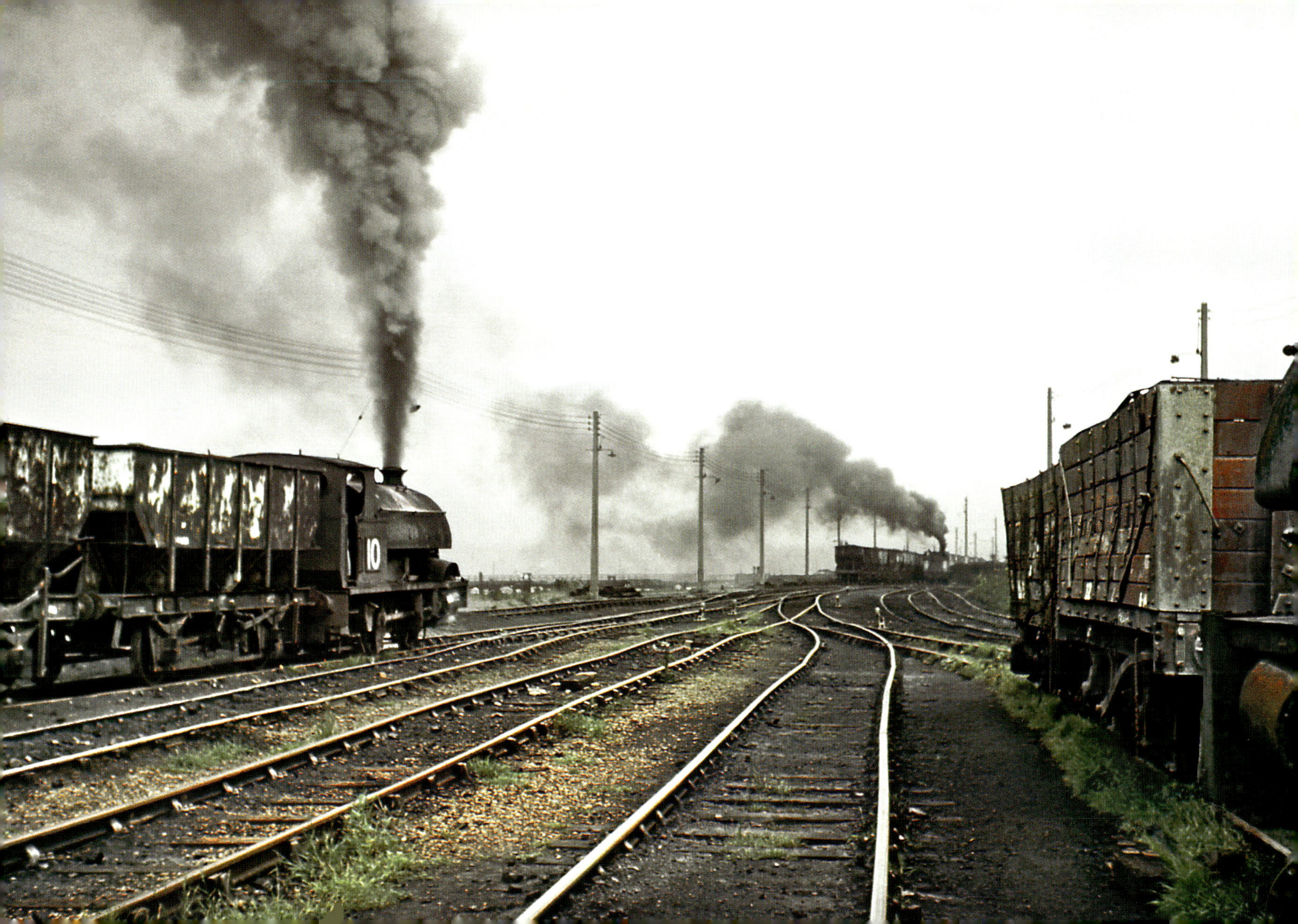
10

Dieselisation at Seaham took place in 1967, with the delivery of five English Electric six-coupled 305 hp diesel-hydraulics from the Vulcan Works. On 23 June 1978, D3 (W/No. D1193 of 1967) stands with an internal five-plank and a flat wagon while engaged in preparatory work prior to demolition of the staiths. Dawdon colliery, perched high on the clifftop, can be seen behind. (John Sloane)

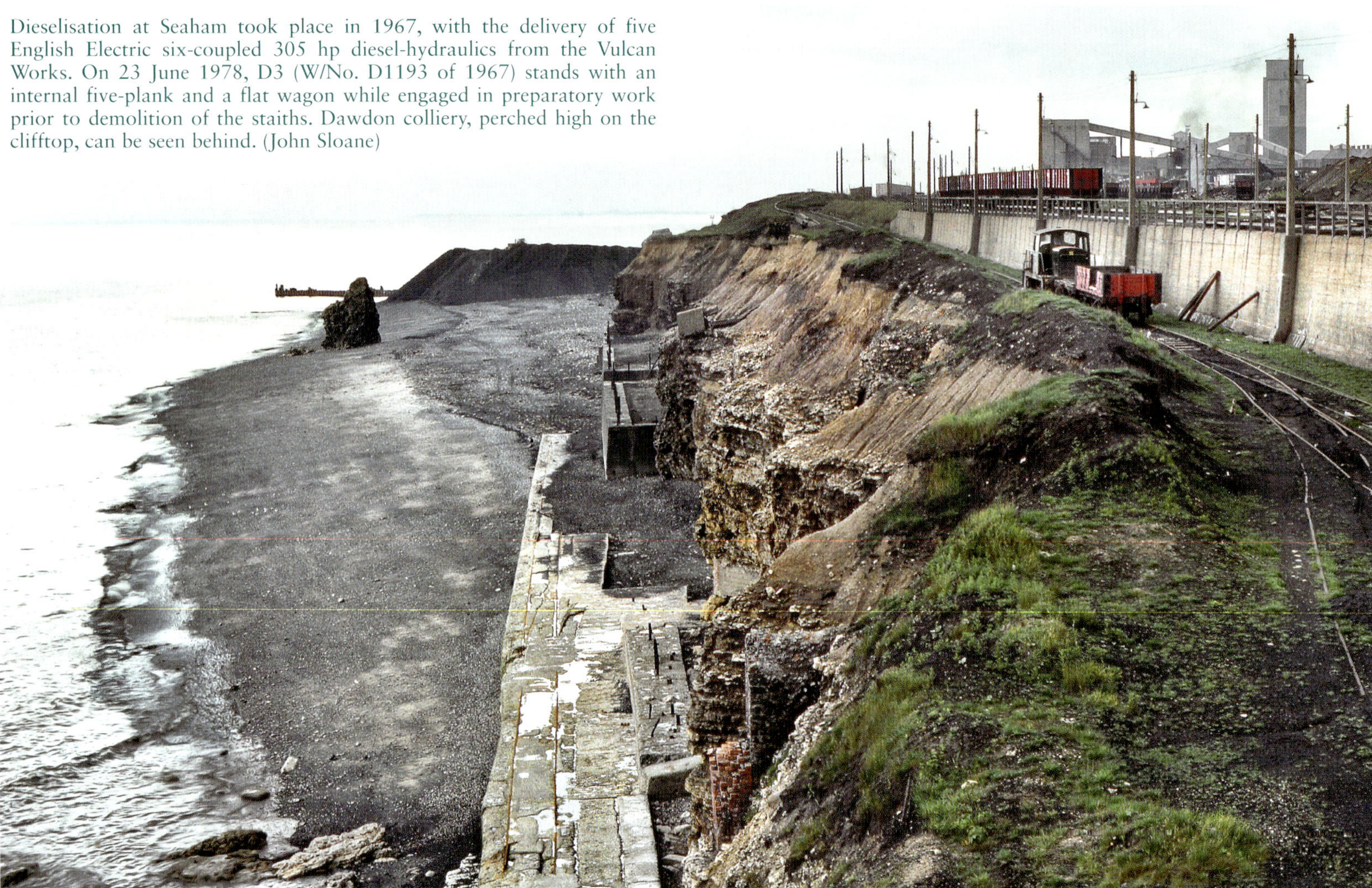

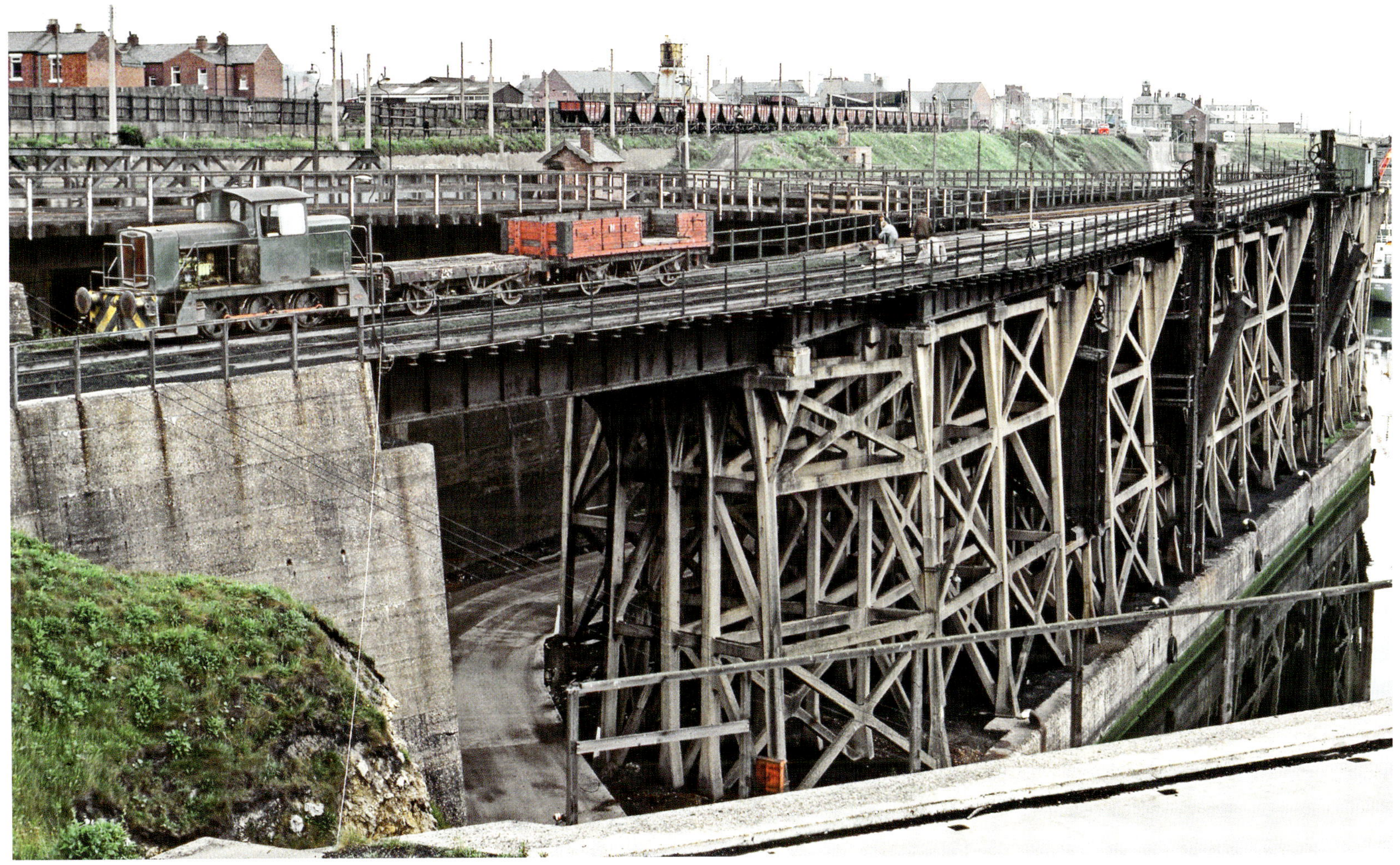

Another view of English Electric D3 on 23 June 1978 with its short works train, as labourers clear the lines of coal shortly before the demolition of the remarkable but by then obsolete rail-served staiths. In the foreground is New Berth and behind is Castlereagh Berth. The last two diesel locos left Seaham for scrap in 1994. (John Sloane)

Right: Hunslet 0-4-0 saddle tank *Dick* (W/No. 628 of 1895) at Seaham Harbour in the early 1960s. Noteworthy are the full-length wooden block buffers for working both conventional and the 4-ton capacity chaldron 'black' wagons once synonymous with Seaham, some of the latter visible behind. The 'L' on the wagon's side is a reminder of the days around Seaham of Londonderry Railway ownership. This veteran Hunslet, originally involved in the construction works of Seaham South Dock between 1905 and 1907, was scrapped in December 1963. (Tony Brown)

Below: Seaham Harbour Dock Co. Ltd's Robert Stephenson inside-cylinder 0-6-0 saddle tank *Mars* (W/No. 2238 of 1875) was formerly North Eastern Railway No. 1661 and was acquired in 1907. It is seen in action at Seaham in the early 1960s, but was sadly cut up in July 1963, along with sister loco *Milo*, formerly North Eastern Railway No. 1662. (Tony Brown)

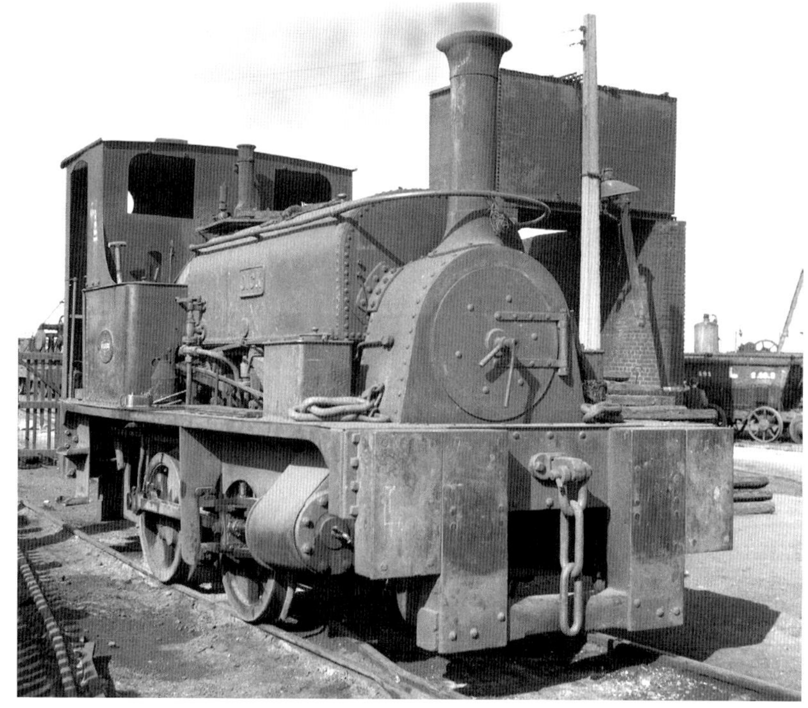

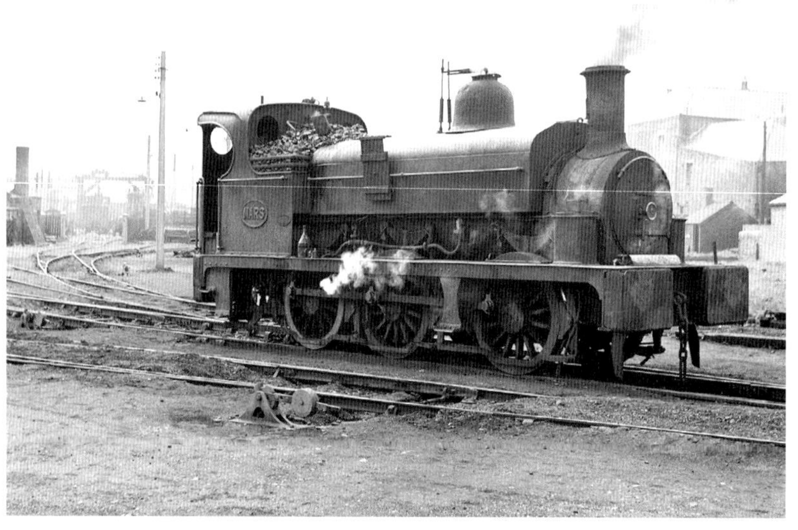

Opposite page: Four-coupled saddle tank No. 173 (W/No. 3919 of 1937) was another of Seaham's four Hawthorn Leslies, with their squat chimneys and white warning panels front and rear. Purchased in June 1963, it is to be hoped that they were acquired from Dorman Long at a 'knock-down' price, for they had only a very limited working life at Seaham, after many years of arduous steelworks tasks. They were all consigned for scrap between November 1966 and December 1967, allegedly being unpopular with the crews and considered to be poor performers on the sharp gradients at Seaham. In its final year, No. 173 was found hard at work, having collected a rake of mixed internal wagons of washery waste from South Hetton and Hawthorn collieries at the foot of the Cold Hesledon incline, with the waste destined for disposal in the sea at Dawdon. (Jon Marsh)

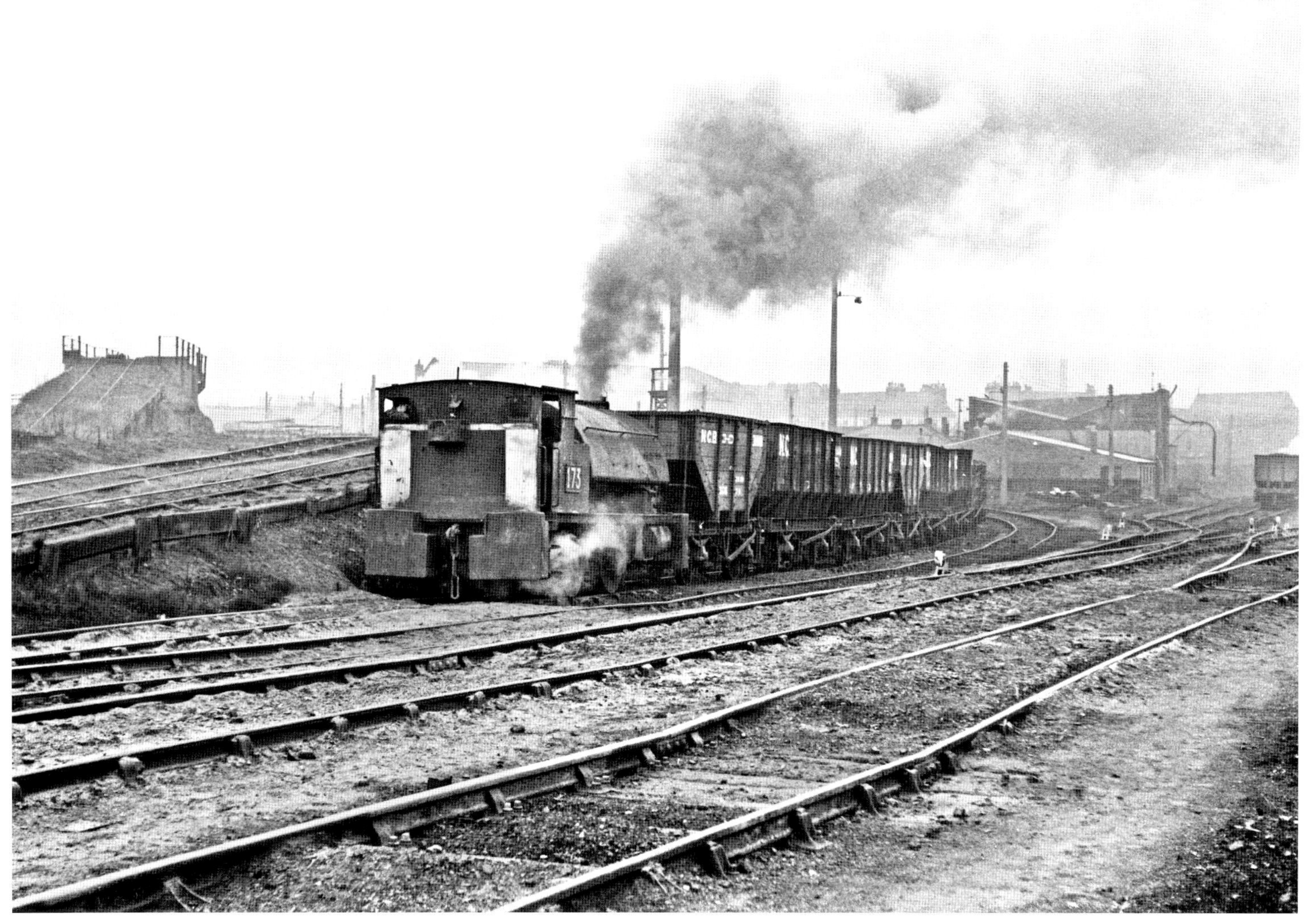

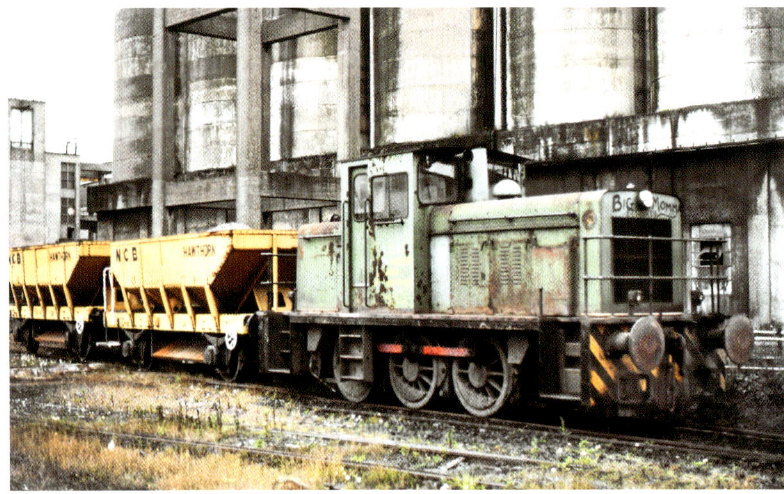

Above left: The Hawthorn Combined Mine first drew coal in September 1959 and from January 1960 coal was subsequently brought to the surface there from the collieries at Elemore, Eppleton and Murton. This, and the adjoining coking plant, which had opened slightly earlier, were fully colour-light signalled and were worked by locos from South Hetton loco shed of South Hetton Railways until March 1987, when this shed was closed after a new stabling point had been installed at Hawthorn Combined Mine. Most of the coal and coke was despatched through the BR exchange sidings at South Hetton, with internal trains of stone and washery waste being sent the 4 miles via the two self-acting Cold Hesledon inclines (Stony Cut and Swine Lodge) to Dawdon for disposal at sea via conveyor (*see previous page*), and from 1985 to Tuthill Quarry due to the closure of the Hesledon inclines. This Andrew Barclay 400 hp 0-6-0 diesel-hydraulic (W/No. 594 of 1974), originally supplied new to Dawdon colliery, stands at Hawthorn Combined Mine, probably in the late 1970s, with two hopper wagons of track ballast. Hawthorn coke works ceased production around 1985 and the Combined Mine was closed in November 1991. (Author's collection)

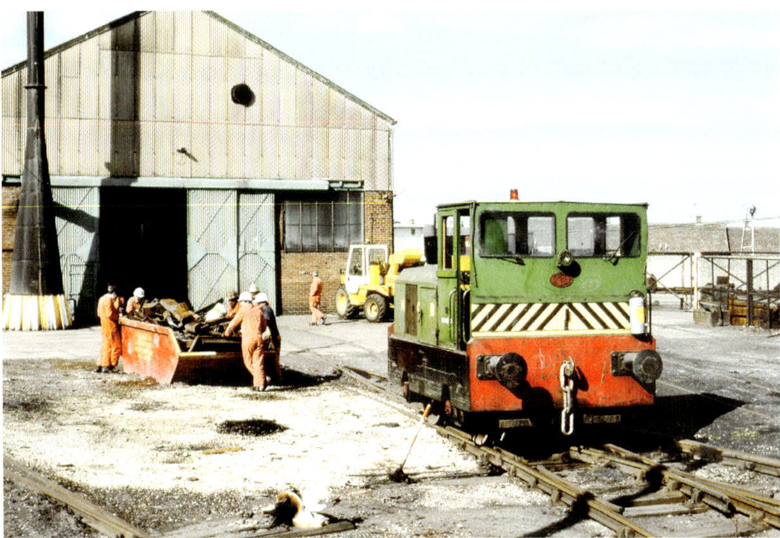

Below left: The Seaham Wagon Works at Dawdon was originally established by the Londonderry Railways and, as well as repairing its own wagons and the NCB's after Vesting Day in 1947, it also repaired those of the Seaham Harbour Dock Company. It was served by sidings off the west side of the BR Seaham–Hartlepool line, half a mile south of Seaham station, and the NCB had running rights over the BR lines from Seaham. This diminutive 85 hp Motor Rail four-wheel diesel-mechanical, No. 05200/100 (W/No. 5766 of 1963), was the works shunter on 17 September 1986 (*also see page 109*). The works, administered by the NCB's Engineering Department, was to close on 20 March 1987, and was quickly demolished. (Roy Burt)

Opposite page: Further south from Seaham, some 4 miles, and fringing the BR Seaham–Hartlepool line was Easington colliery, which had opened in 1910. It was originally intended to be connected to Seaham Harbour by a branch from the Londonderry Railway, but this never came about. During its final decade of production, on 17 September 1986, Andrew Barclay 0-6-0 diesel-hydraulic locos were the order of the day for shunting, and an anonymous 400 hp Barclay is seen positioning internal 16-ton NCB steel-bodied hopper wagons for tipping. The mine was closed on 7 May 1993, with the loss of 1,400 jobs. (Roy Burt)

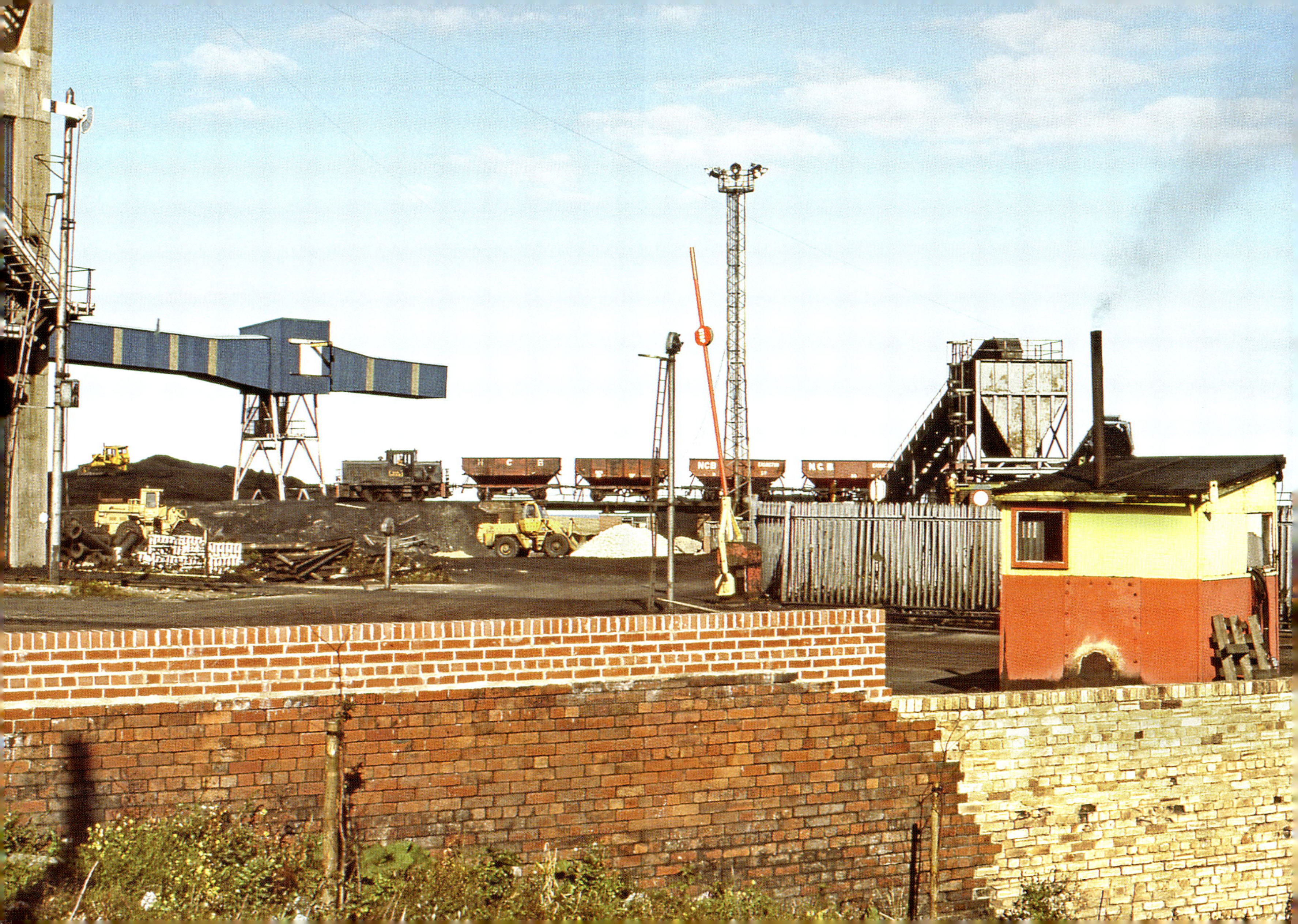

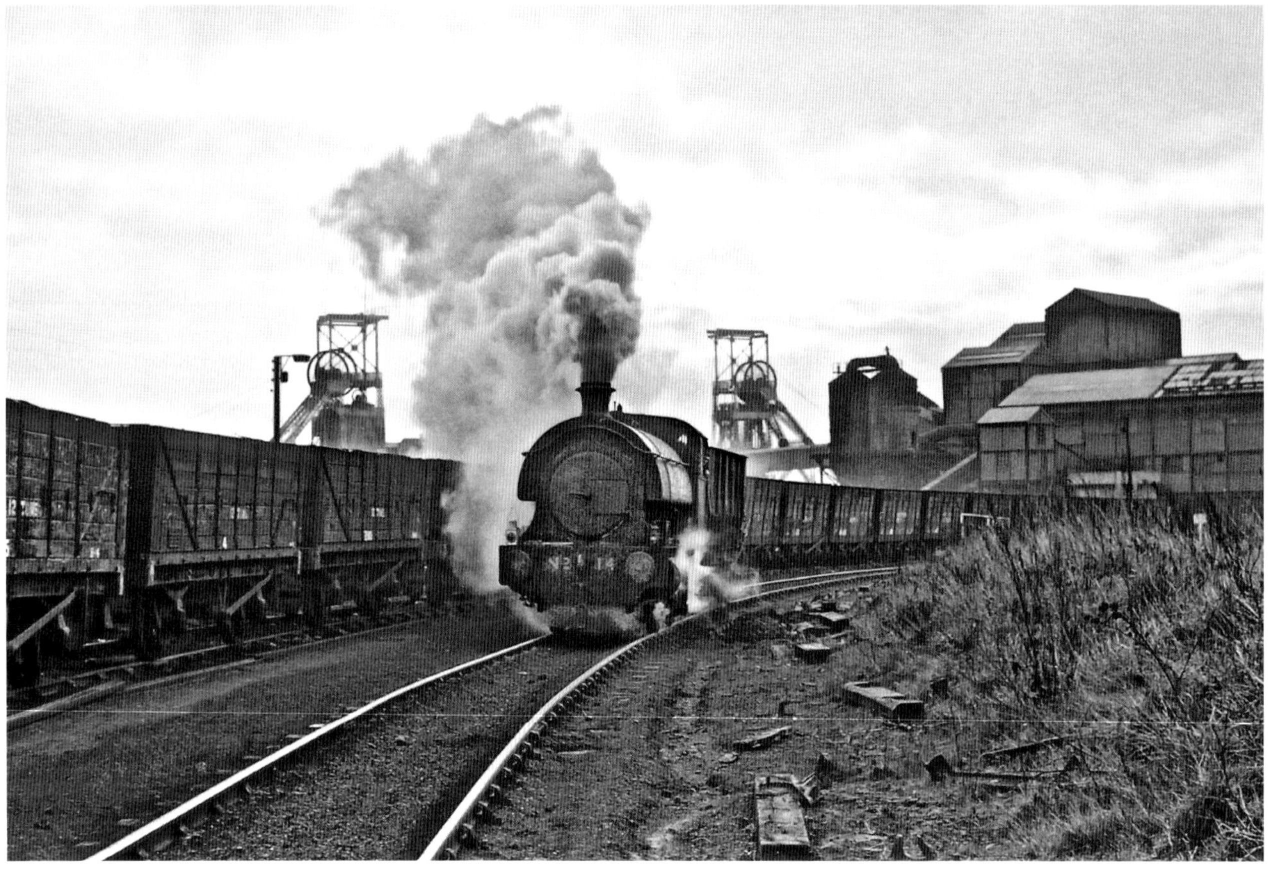

Perched high on the clifftop to the north of Seaham Harbour, and exploiting seams beneath the North Sea, Vane Tempest colliery was opened in 1929. Named after Lord Vane Tempest, the Marquess of Londonderry's eldest son, the ancestors of the Marquess had significantly influenced the development of parts of the Durham coalfield over many years previously. Vane Tempest was served by a half-mile branch from the BR Sunderland–Hartlepool line and was merged with nearby Seaham colliery from February 1982, where its output was then wound, until the official closure of British Coal's Vane Tempest/Seaham combine in May 1993. During happier times, in late 1966, Hawthorn Leslie 0-4-0 saddle tank No. 14 (W/No. 3056 of 1914) was captured moving a single BR 21-ton steel hopper wagon past a long rake of NCB wooden-bodied internal-user wagons. (Tony Brown)

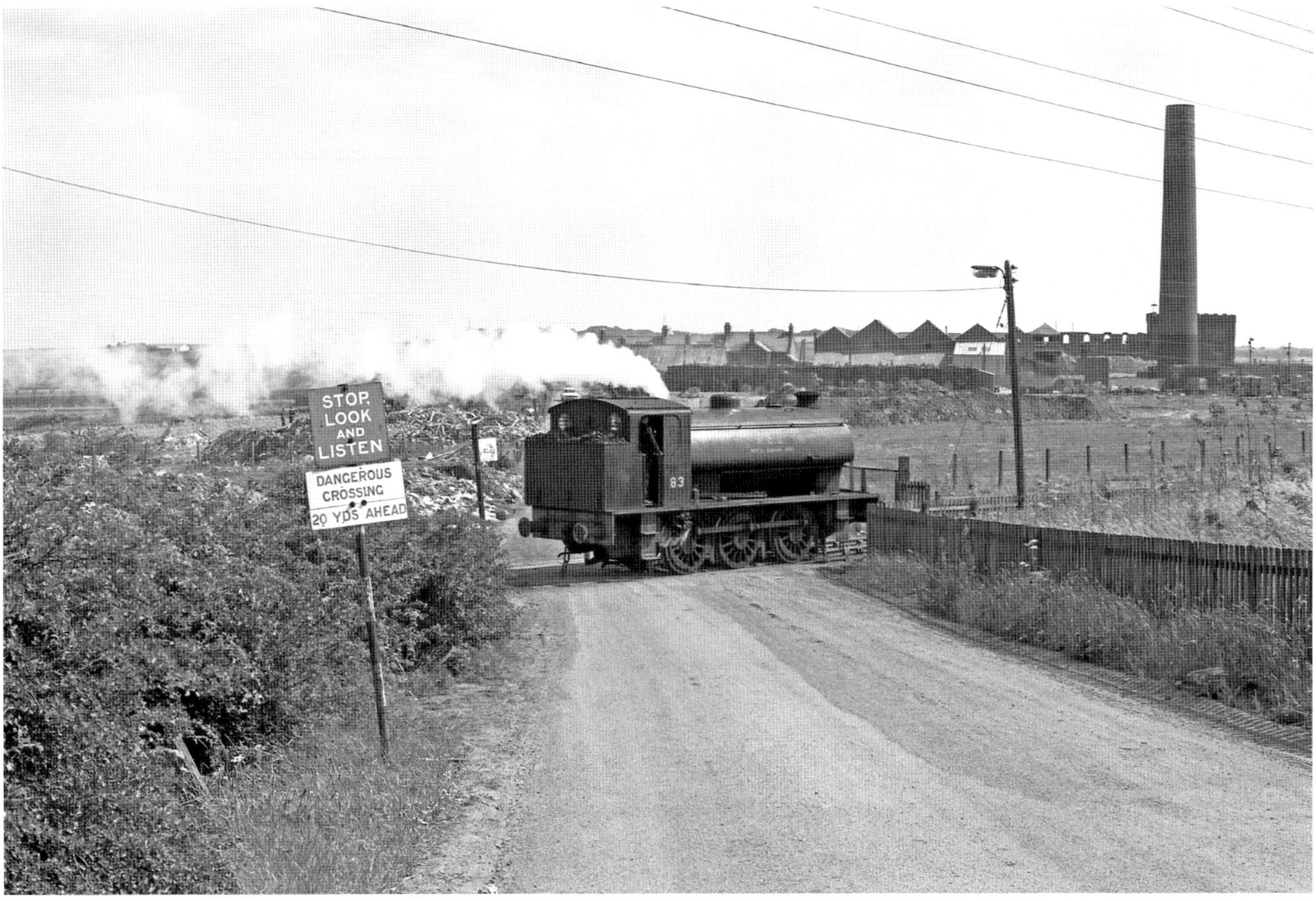

Morrison Busty colliery, near Annfield Plain, was opened in 1927 and had a connection with main line exchange sidings at Oxhill via a spur off the Consett line. On 9 July 1973, shortly before the colliery's closure in the October of that year, Austerity 0-6-0 saddle tank No. 83 (Hunslet W/No. 3688 of 1949), one of two at the colliery at that time, returns light engine from the exchange sidings to the colliery, crossing a minor road leading to the brickworks at Langley View. Both Austerities were scrapped in July 1974. (Richard Stevens)

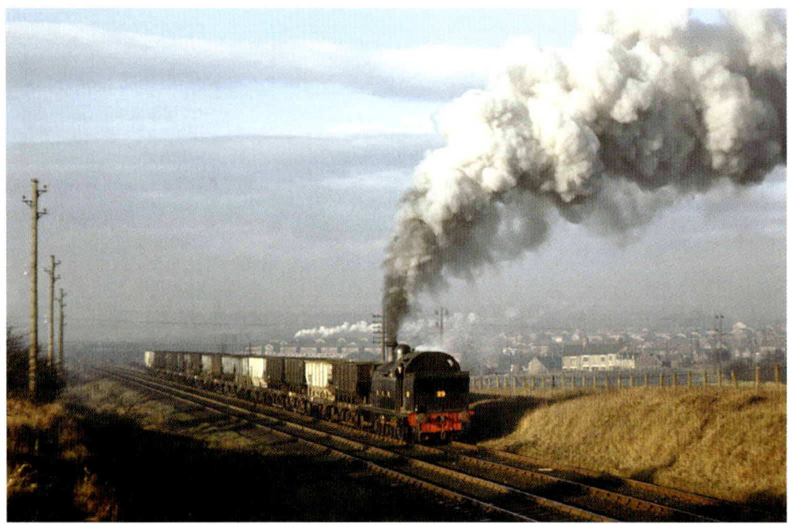

The Lambton Railway was the largest of the private railways in County Durham and its history can be traced back over three centuries. In 1911 the Lambton and Hetton collieries and their railway systems merged, followed in 1924 by the Joicey collieries. The incorporated mines of the Lambton, Hetton & Joicey Collieries Ltd (LH&JC) formed the largest coal company in the North East, but their mines were located several miles inland from the River Wear staiths. The LH&JC had no direct independent rail connection to the Sunderland staiths, but enjoyed running rights over the Leamside Line. The company's distinctive 0-6-2 'Lambton Tanks', first introduced to the Lambton Railway in 1904, were used exclusively on main line work, some surviving until the demise of steam at Philadelphia. Using their running rights, in addition to working coal to Lambton staiths via Penshaw, the destination of most Lambton coal, the 'Lambton Tanks' also worked through to Sunderland South Dock via Millfield and Fawcett Street Junction, until the staiths were closed during 1967. Various four and six-coupled saddle tank types were used for other duties, including the ubiquitous Austerities, their rounded cab tops synonymous with the railway. All Lambton Railway locos were maintained at the engine works at Philadelphia, where the fitting and wagon shops and loco sheds were also located, as well as an elevated coal gantry with its two coaling chutes. Following the end of BR steam in the area in 1967, the railway around Philadelphia became something of a Mecca for railfans, with up to five steam locos being found in use daily. But the end for steam traction came all too soon, in February 1969, when former BR Class 11 0-6-0 diesel-electrics and Class 14 0-6-0 diesel-hydraulics took over all diagrams. Although the Class 14 Paxmans were to subsequently move on to Northumberland in the mid-1970s following NCB fleet rationalisation, the Class 11s were to remain and dominate the Philadelphia scene for the following decade and a half, witnessing the contraction of mining in the area until Herrington, the last colliery serving the railway, went over to road transport and closed shortly thereafter, in 1985. The remaining section of the railway, between Lambton coke works and BR at Penshaw, was to close in January 1986, followed by the famous Lambton Engine Works in December 1989. Early on a frosty morning in February 1969, and with another train below in the valley, Kitson 0-6-2 tank No. 29 (W/No. 4263 of 1904) climbs up the grade towards Philadelphia with a rake of BR 21-ton hopper wagons from the BR exchange sidings at Penshaw (*left*), and (*below*) the same train approaches Philadelphia Junction Bank Top. (John Marsh).

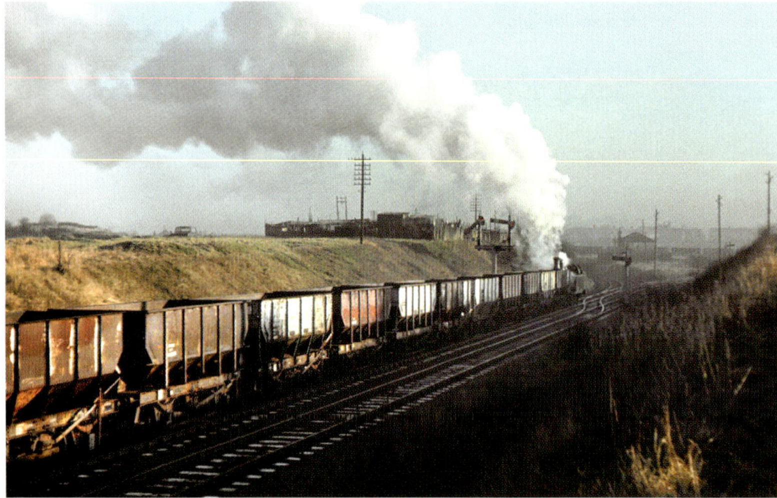

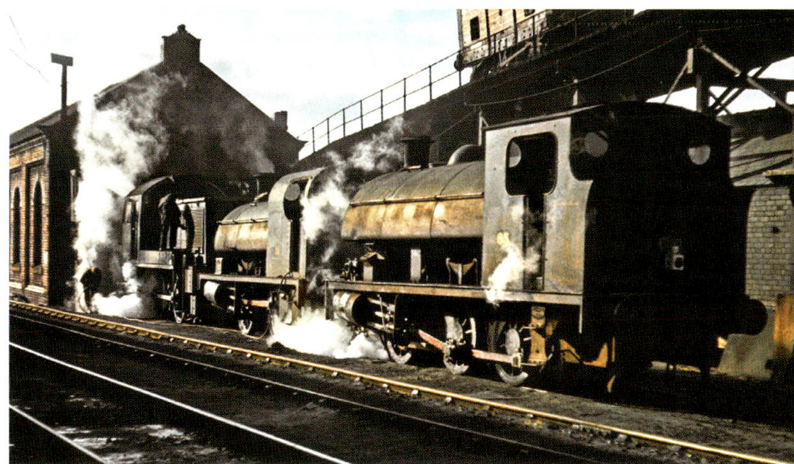

Above: In the late afternoon sunlight in February 1969, Robert Stephenson & Hawthorns 0-6-0 saddle tank No. 63 (W/No. 7600 of 1949) and Hudswell Clarke 0-4-0 saddle tank No. 11 (W/No. 1412 of 1920) simmer outside Philadelphia running shed. An ex-BR Class 14 is receiving a steam clean, having just been delivered from BR – a portent of the new order. (Jon Marsh)

Right: Robert Stephenson 0-6-2 tank No. 5 (W/No. 3377 of 1909) at Philadelphia shed in February 1969. Withdrawn from traffic on 15 February 1969, it was privately purchased and was found a home on the North Yorkshire Moors Railway, under the care of the North Eastern Locomotive Preservation Group. (Jack Patience)

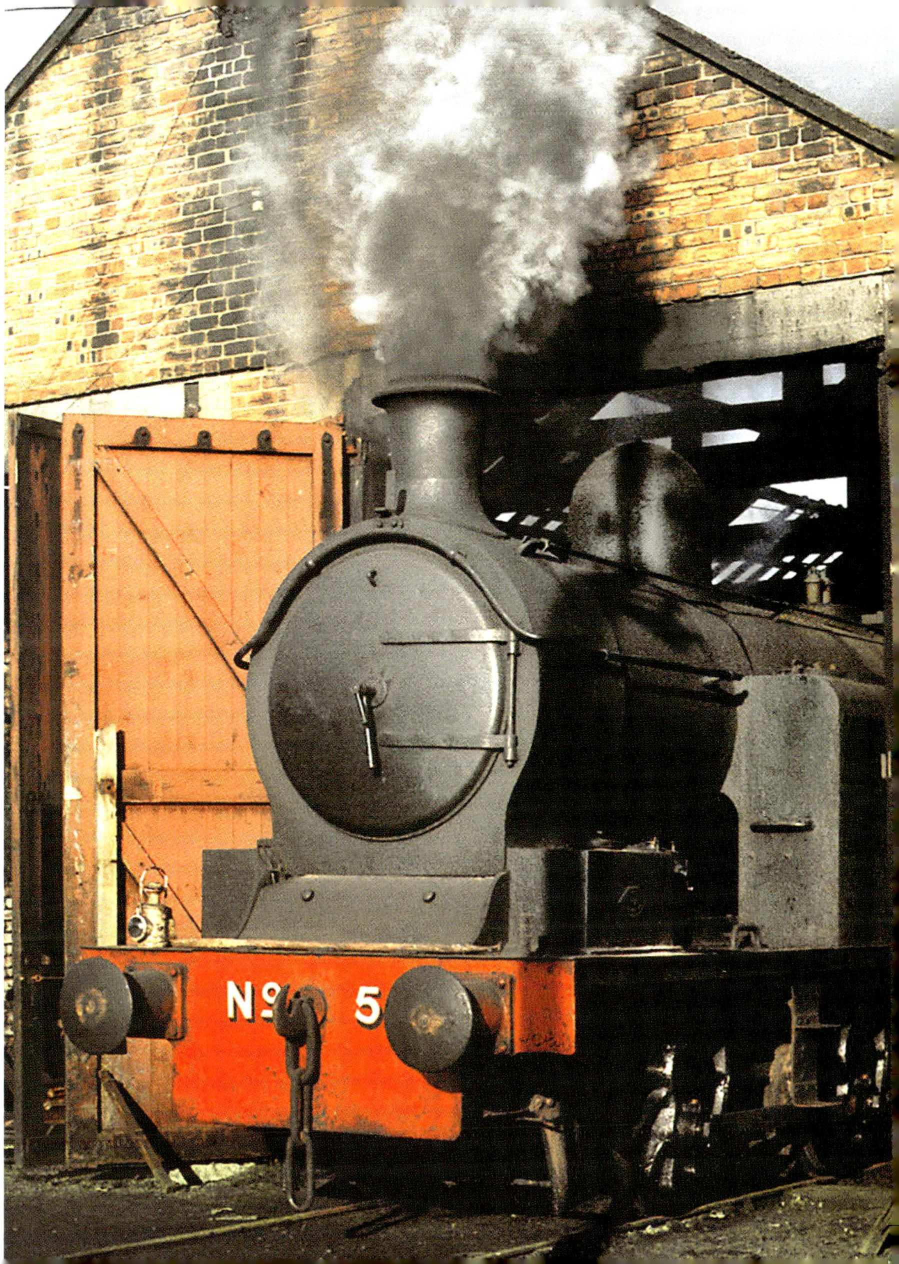

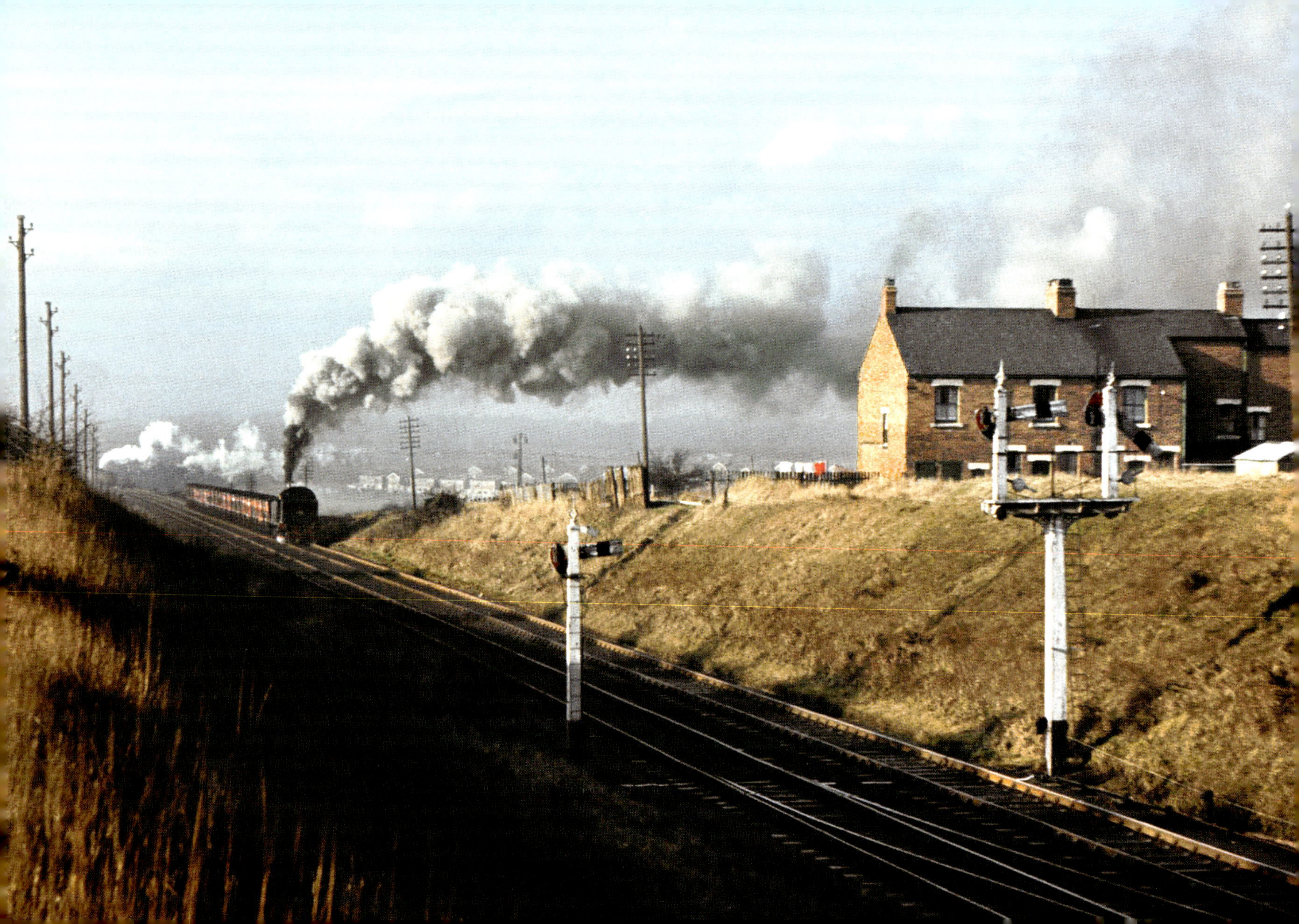

Opposite page: In February 1969, Kitson 0-6-2 tank No. 29 approaches West View as it makes an assault of the steep climb up from Burnmoor (also referred to locally as Bournmoor) to Philadelphia Junction Bank Top with a rake of wooden-bodied internal-user wagons. In the foreground are the signals operated from Junction Bank Top signal box. The lower quadrant Signal No. 15 is pulled off, suggesting that the empties are destined for Herrington colliery, via Philadelphia. This signal box (*visible in the photo at the foot of page 30*) and associated signalling was completed in summer 1922 and was a rare installation in Britain as it controlled all three sides of a triangle. It was most certainly the only such box in the country on an industrial railway. The thirty-lever Lambton & Hetton Collieries Ltd Cabin, also known locally as Houghton Junction, Philadelphia Junction, or just 'The Triangle', controlled lines to and from Sunderland, Penshaw and Burnmoor, to Herrington colliery via Philadelphia, and to Houghton colliery. By the time of this visit, the Lambton and Sunderland South Dock staiths had closed, bringing an end to the NCB through working over BR metals via Penshaw, suggesting that this train of empties could have originated from the Burnmoor coke works. In this view another train is seen on the descent of Junction Bank with a loaded train, while in the distance another loco is to be seen moving along in the region of Burnmoor crossing, heading towards the Lambton coke works and washery complex. (Jon Marsh)

Above right: A pair of 'Lambton Tanks' repose outside the four-road loco shed at Philadelphia in February 1969. The variation of the designs of the 1904-built Kitson 0-6-2 tank No. 29, and the later 1909-built Robert Stephenson 0-6-2 tank No. 5 are noteworthy, particularly the side tanks and cab arrangements. No. 29 was the first 0-6-2 tank to be employed on the system and even received a full overhaul at the Lambton Engine Works in 1968, which, as it turned out, was just a matter of months before the quite sudden demise of steam at Philadelphia. (Jon Marsh)

Below right: A mid-1960s scene of Hudswell Clarke 0-4-0 saddle tank No. 11 (W/No. 1412 of 1920 rebuilt 1948) moving on to the shed at Philadelphia. It was purchased new by Lambton & Hetton Collieries Ltd and, apart from a couple of short-term loans elsewhere, it remained loyal to Philadelphia until the end of steam. The single-road shed to the right of the loco was used to house the 1918-built Dick Kerr four-wheel battery-electric loco No. 51, which was exclusively employed on shunting the Philadelphia power station sidings until its closure in 1936. (Colour Rail)

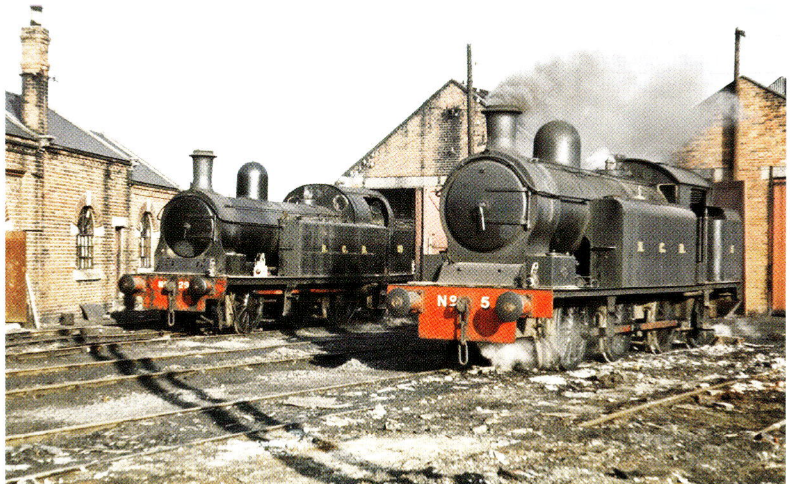

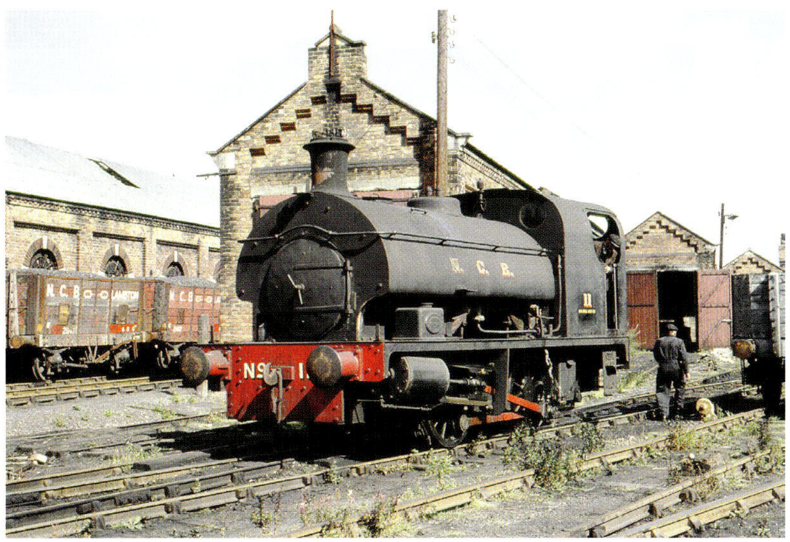

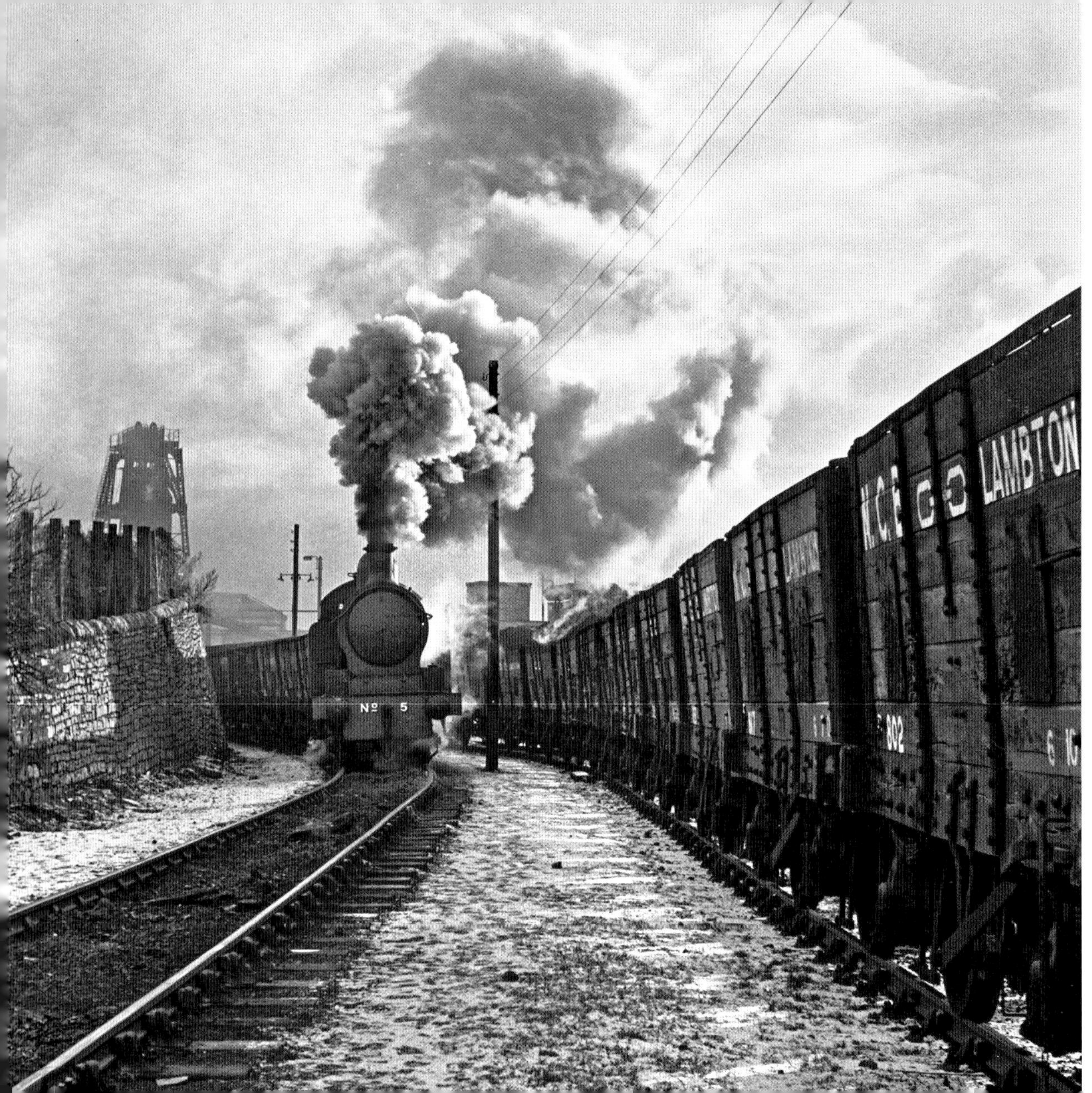

Left: Not rigidly observing the 1956 Clean Air Act, Robert Stephenson 0-6-2 tank No. 5 works hard away from Houghton colliery yard in February 1969. The productive colliery at Houghton-le-Spring first wound coal around 1827 and was located at the end of a 1-mile branch line from Philadelphia Junction Bank Top triangle. NCB rail traffic ceased in 1975 in favour of road transport. Prior to that, traffic was mainly in the hands of ex-BR Class 11 locos. The colliery finally closed in October 1981. (Jon Marsh)

Opposite page top left: Hudswell Clarke 0-4-0 saddle tank No. 11 and an Austerity 0-6-0 saddle tank on Junction Bank in February 1969. The permissive working on the same running line was presumably due to congestion around the junction at Burnmoor where the lines diverged (right) for Penshaw and (left) for Lambton 'D' washery and coke works. At this point the wagon brakes, pinned before descending the bank, were released prior to proceeding either into the coke works with internal wagons or to the exchange sidings at Penshaw with loaded BR hopper wagons. (Jon Marsh)

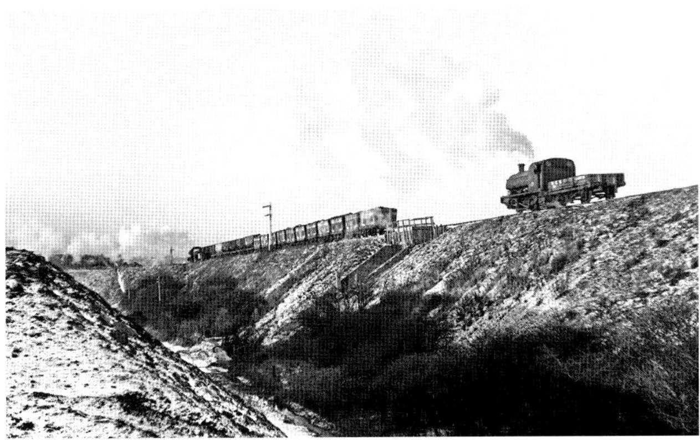

Right: Another scene, during the same visit to the Lambton Railway in February 1969, of Hudswell Clarke No. 11 shunting the extensive Lambton Engine Works and Wagon Shops yard at Philadelphia. The workshops replaced those originally located opposite the Philadelphia running shed. In the 1920–30s, new and larger facilities were installed further north-east along the Herrington colliery branch and thereafter the works built the 12-ton wooden hopper wagons used on the Lambton Railway, and then 15, 16 and 20-ton steel wagons from the mid-1950s. As well as shunting around Philadelphia, four-coupled saddle tanks from Philadelphia shed were out-stationed at Harraton colliery (until May 1965), Houghton and Herrington collieries, Lambton staiths and Silksworth colliery for handling the coal traffic to the staiths on the River Wear. The Silksworth to Sunderland line was originally part of the Hetton Railway, but installation of the Hawthorn Combined Mine (*see page 26*) enabled the six inclines on the railway to be closed in September 1959, leaving only traffic from Silksworth to the River Wear staiths, worked by the Lambton Railway locos from the staiths' loco shed (*as featured on page 44*) until closure of the staiths in 1967. (Jon Marsh)

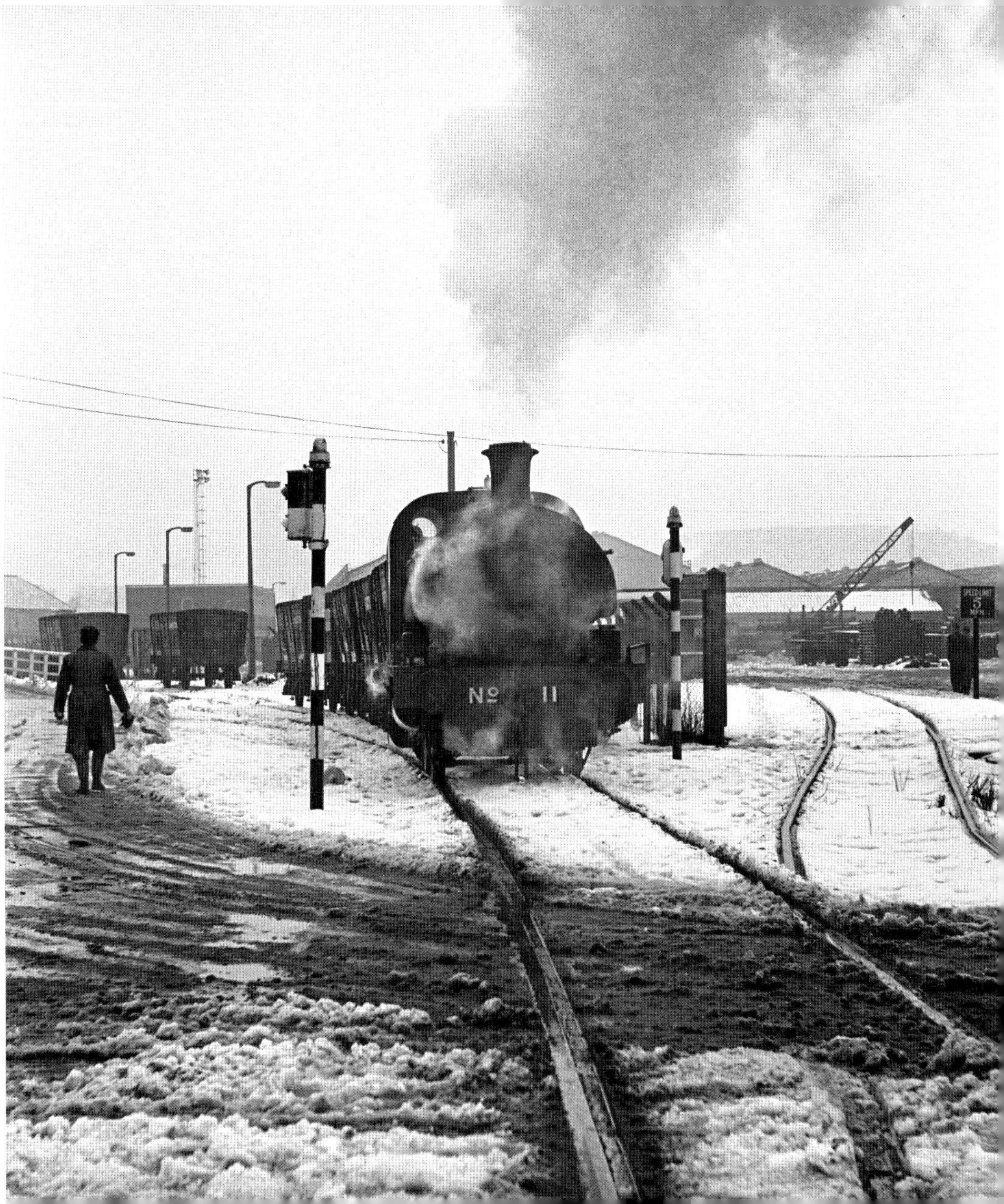

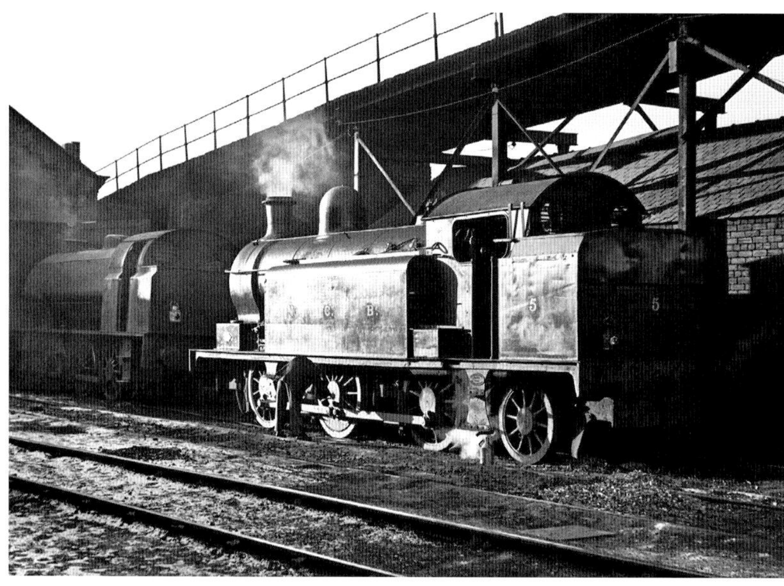

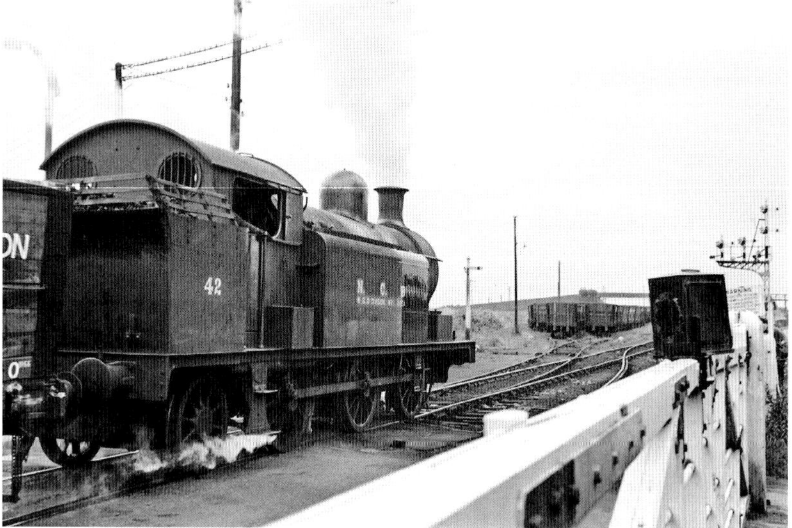

Left: 'Lambton Tank' No. 5 and Austerity 0-6-0 saddle tank No. 59 (Vulcan Foundry W/No. 5300 of 1945) outside the running shed at Philadelphia in February 1969. This two-road shed was built in 1917 and became the main operational running shed, with its adjoining coaling gantry. The original wagon shops, on the opposite side of the two-track Herrington to Bank Top running line, was converted into a four-road loco shed in the 1930s, providing additional accommodation for the expanding fleet of locos at that time. The Philadelphia shed-based Lambton-style round cab-top Austerities, Nos 7, 58 and 59, were to be found further duties working from the NCB's Derwenthaugh shed upon dieselisation of the Philadelphia system in 1969 (*see pages 60–71*). (Jon Marsh)

Right: Robert Stephenson 0-6-2 tank No. 42 (W/No. 3801 of 1920) was another of the 'Lambton Tanks' that worked until the end of steam at Philadelphia and is seen passing the Philadelphia level crossing gates, heading towards the triangle at Philadelphia Junction Bank Top with coal from Herrington colliery destined for Lambton 'D' washery, which supplied the adjoining coking plant. This photo was taken some time after June 1965, when the Lambton Railway came under the NCB No. 1 (North-East Durham) Area, as per the lettering on the loco's side tank. The closure of Lambton 'D' and Lumley collieries, in 1965 and 1966 respectively, significantly reduced the tonnage of coal carried over the railway to Lambton staiths. No. 42 was to work the last train of empties away from the staiths on 6 January 1967, after which they were closed. There was to be no more running over BR metals and the only work available for the 'Lambton Tanks' until their withdrawal from NCB service on 15 February 1969 was coal between Herrington and Houghton collieries for Lambton 'D' washery and working to and from the Penshaw BR exchange sidings. (Author's collection)

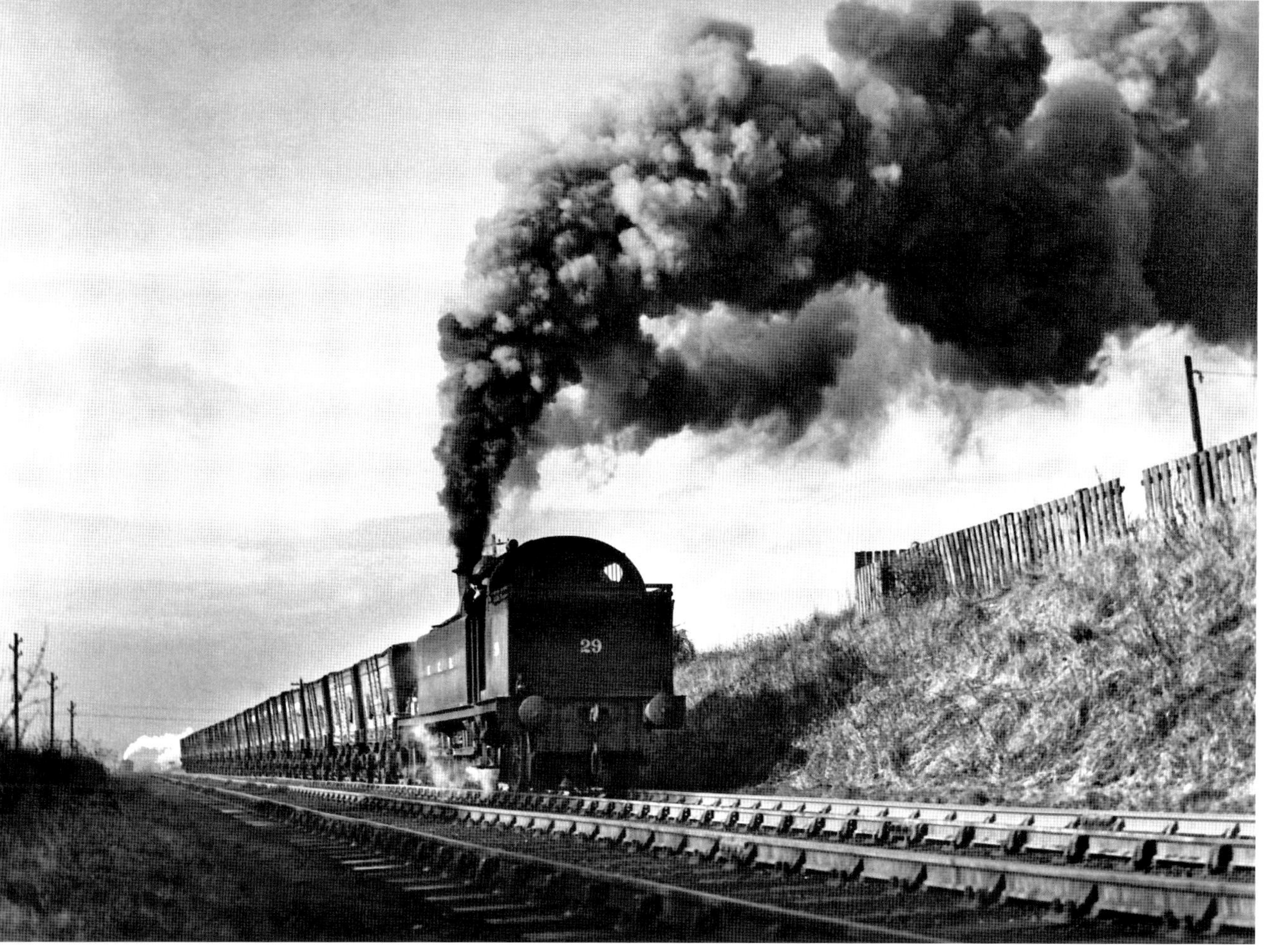

In February 1969, 'Lambton Tank' No. 29 with empty internal-user wagons blackens the sky at West View cottages, on the sharp climb up the Junction Bank incline. (Jack Patience)

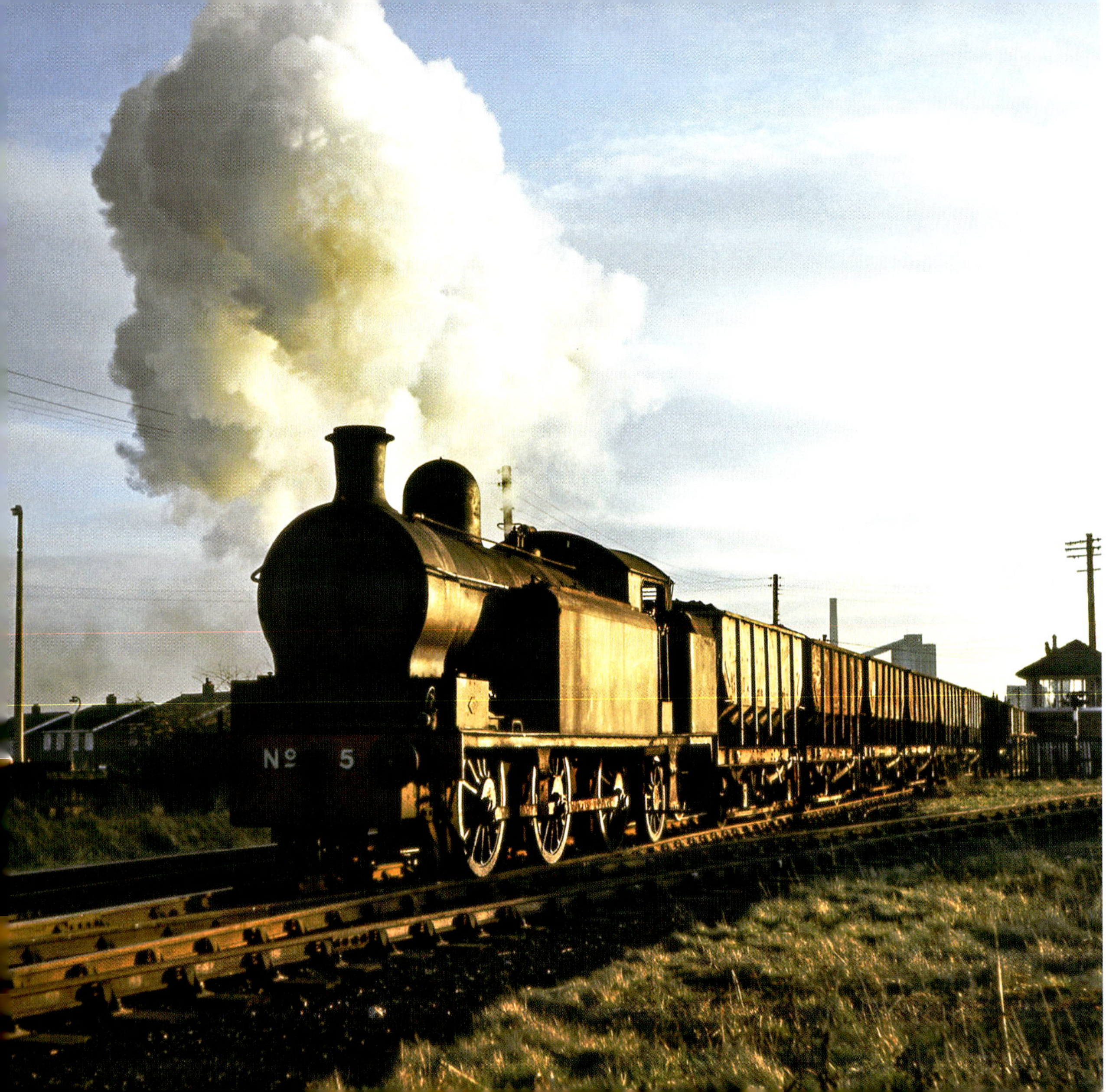

Left: With loaded BR 21-ton hoppers for the BR exchange sidings at Penshaw in February 1969, Robert Stephenson 0-6-2 tank No. 5 heads away from Lambton 'D' coke works and across the Burnmoor level crossing and past the twenty-eight-lever signal box. This was the very last section of the former Lambton Railway to be used and was closed, along with the coke works, in January 1986. (Jack Patience)

Opposite page: In February 1969, Kitson 0-6-2 tank No. 29 makes a fine sight heading a loaded train past the Philadelphia running sheds, approaching the Shop Row level crossing and signal box by the A182 road. The Dorothea shaft headstocks of Newbottle colliery stand behind the two-road running shed. The colliery, which closed in 1956, supplied the adjoining power station. This generated electricity for the Lambton Railway complex at Philadelphia and the Sunderland District Electric Tramways, as well as concerns elsewhere. (Jack Patience)

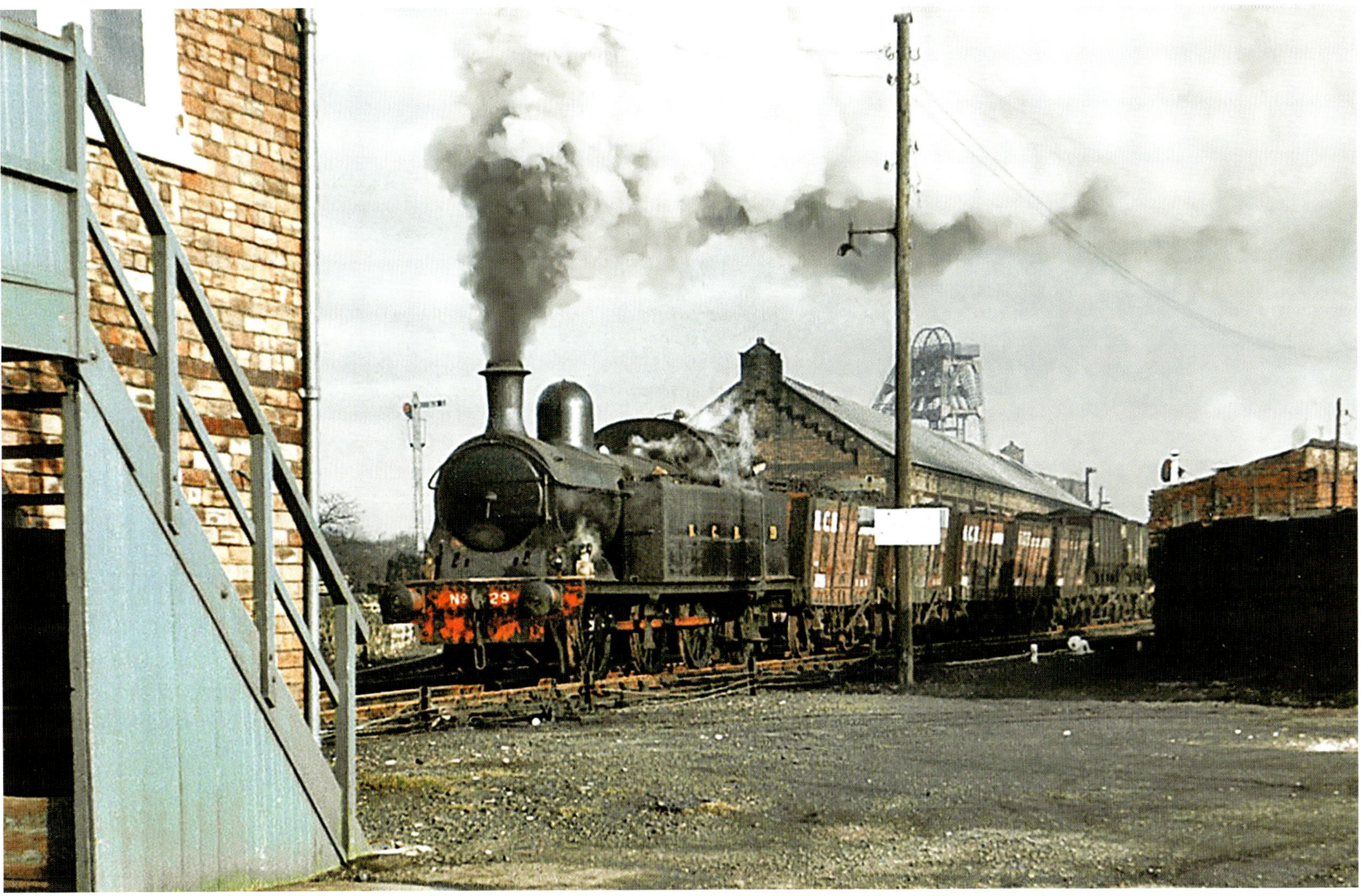

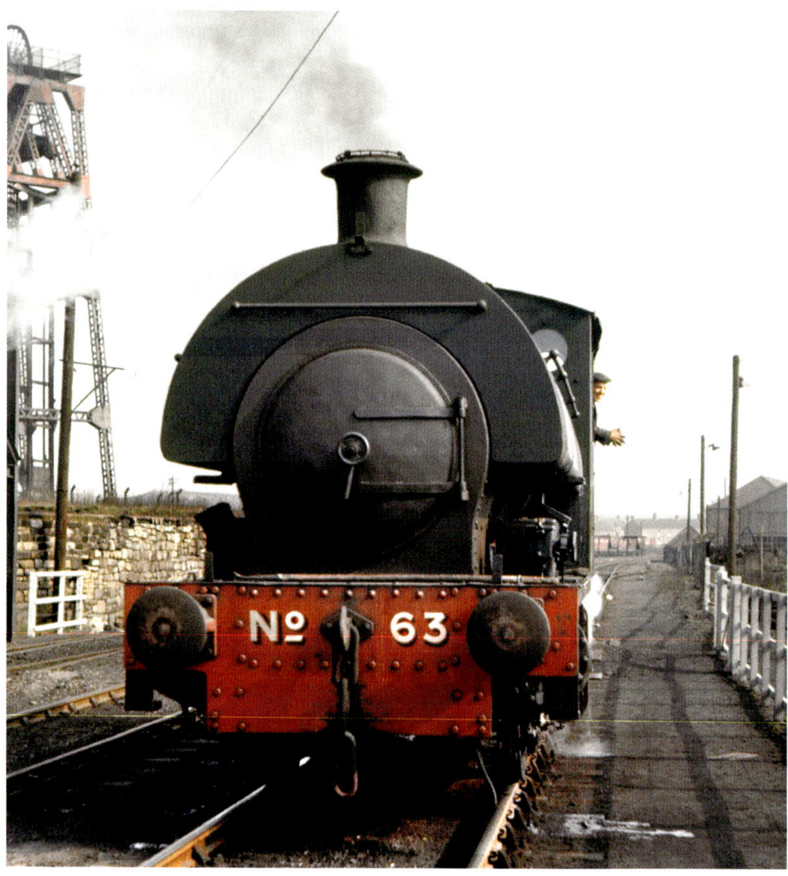

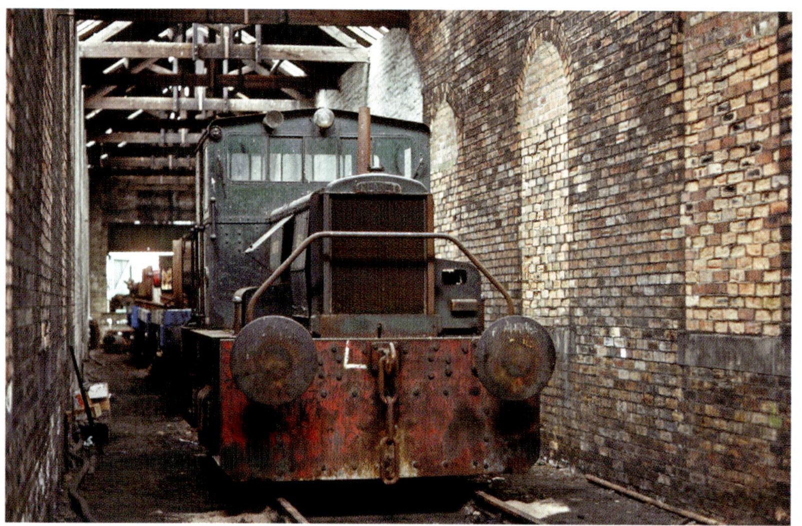

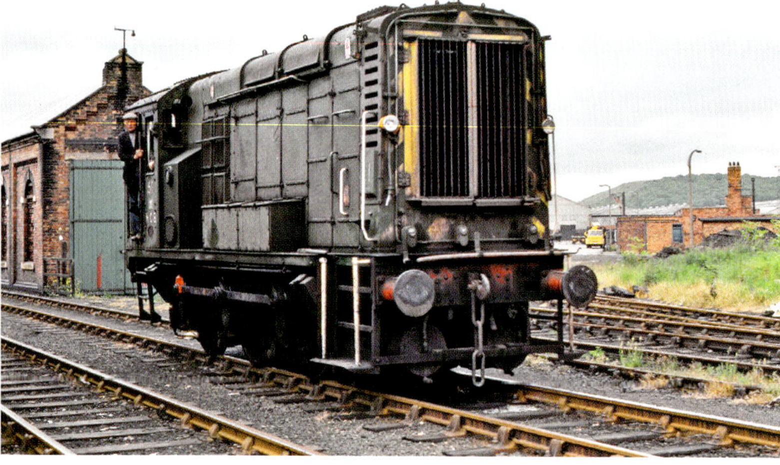

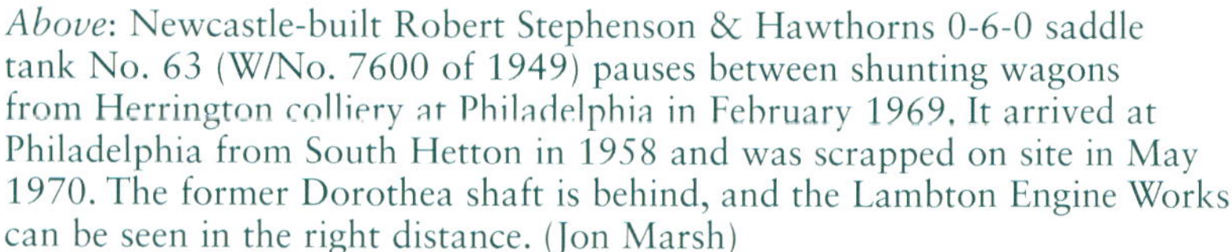

Above: Newcastle-built Robert Stephenson & Hawthorns 0-6-0 saddle tank No. 63 (W/No. 7600 of 1949) pauses between shunting wagons from Herrington colliery at Philadelphia in February 1969. It arrived at Philadelphia from South Hetton in 1958 and was scrapped on site in May 1970. The former Dorothea shaft is behind, and the Lambton Engine Works can be seen in the right distance. (Jon Marsh)

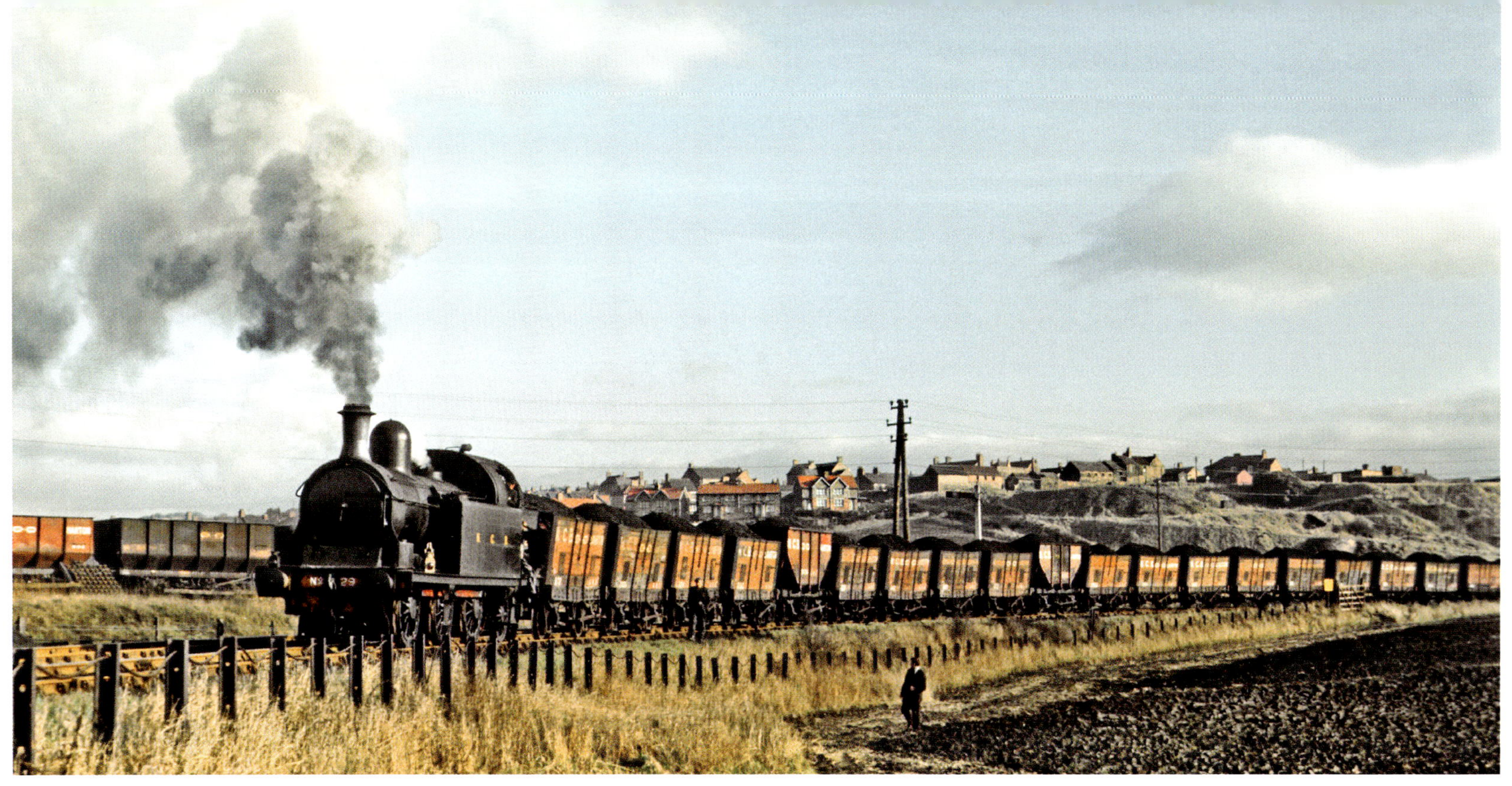

Above: In February 1969, Kitson 0-6-2 tank No. 29 negotiates the curve on the triangle at the top of Junction Bank with a loaded train from Houghton colliery, destined for Burnmoor. The fireman clambers back on to the footplate of No. 29, having just pinned down the wagon brakes to assist braking during the descent of the steep bank. (Jack Patience)

Opposite page above right: Frank Hibberd Planet four-wheel diesel-mechanical No. 101 (W/No. 3922 of 1959) at Philadelphia on 23 June 1978. Moved from Dudley colliery, Northumberland, in April 1977, it was not used at Philadelphia, and passed into preservation at the Bowes Railway, Springwell, two years later. (John Sloane)

Opposite page below right: BR Derby works-built 350 hp 0-6-0 diesel-electric No. 511 at Philadelphia shed on 23 June 1978. It entered BR service in 1952 as No. 12133. Following BR withdrawal, the NCB purchased it from BR at Immingham in May 1969 and it served the railway until closure of Philadelphia shed in 1985. (John Sloane)

N.   C.   B.
No 1 AREA   DURHAM
45

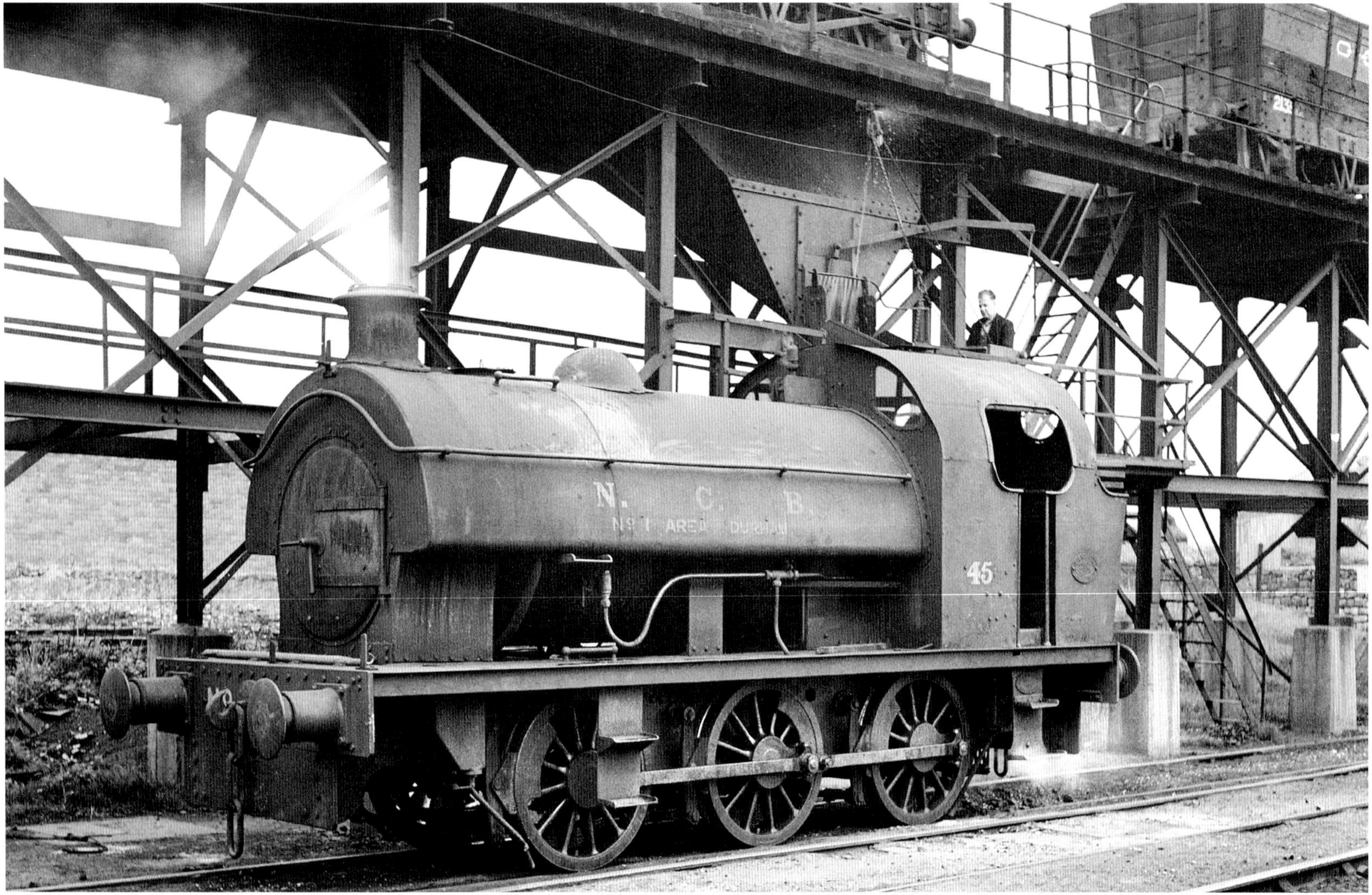

Opposite page: Former LH&J Railway Hawthorn Leslie 0-6-0 saddle tank No. 45 (W/No. 2932 of 1912) alongside the Philadelphia running shed's coaling gantry in 1967, two years before the demise of steam traction on the Lambton Railway. The 15 x 22-inch inside cylinder loco, originally supplied to Silksworth colliery, was cut up on site in December 1970. (Tony Brown)

Right: Close to the end of steam working on the Lambton Railway in 1969, 'Lambton Tank' No. 5 stands in the four-road loco shed at Philadelphia, the former wagon shops until the 1930s. (Author's collection)

Below: Robert Stephenson 0-6-2 tank No. 10 (W/No. 3378 of 1909) inside the four-road shed, shortly before being scrapped, in January 1969. (Author's collection)

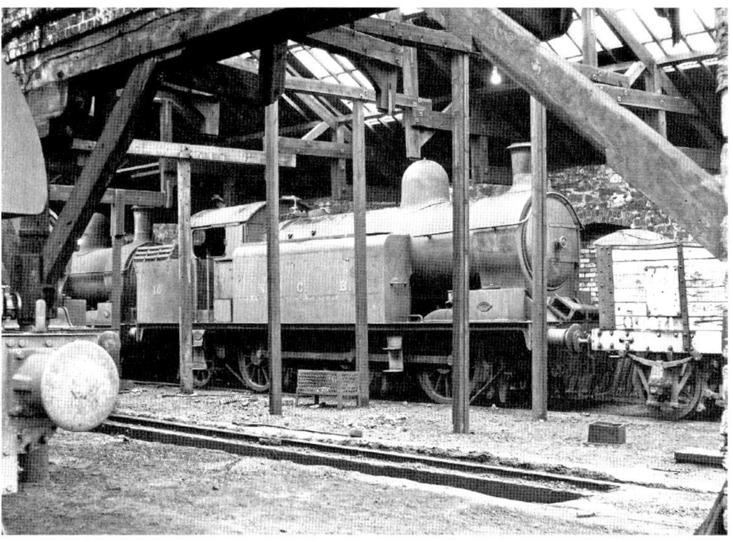

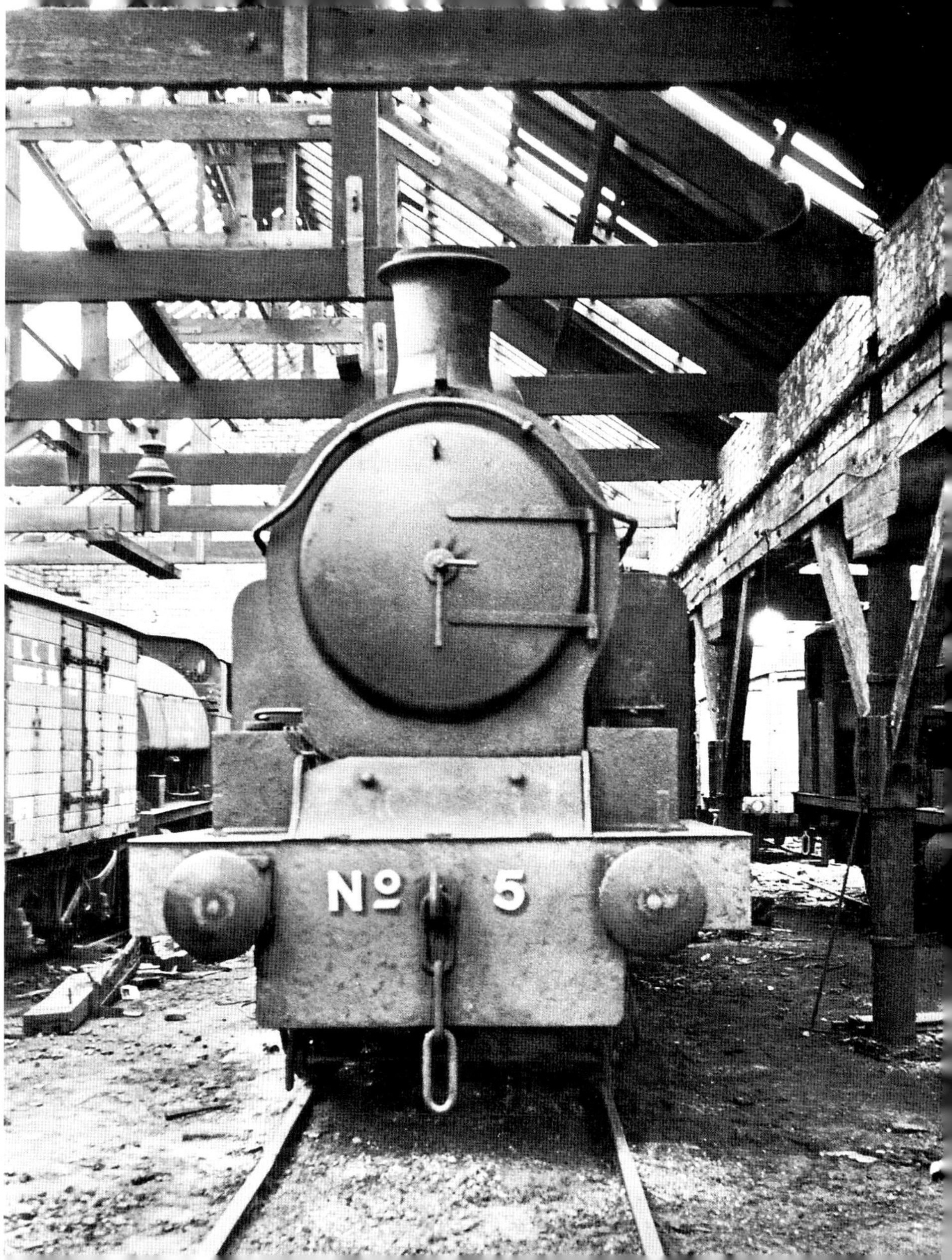

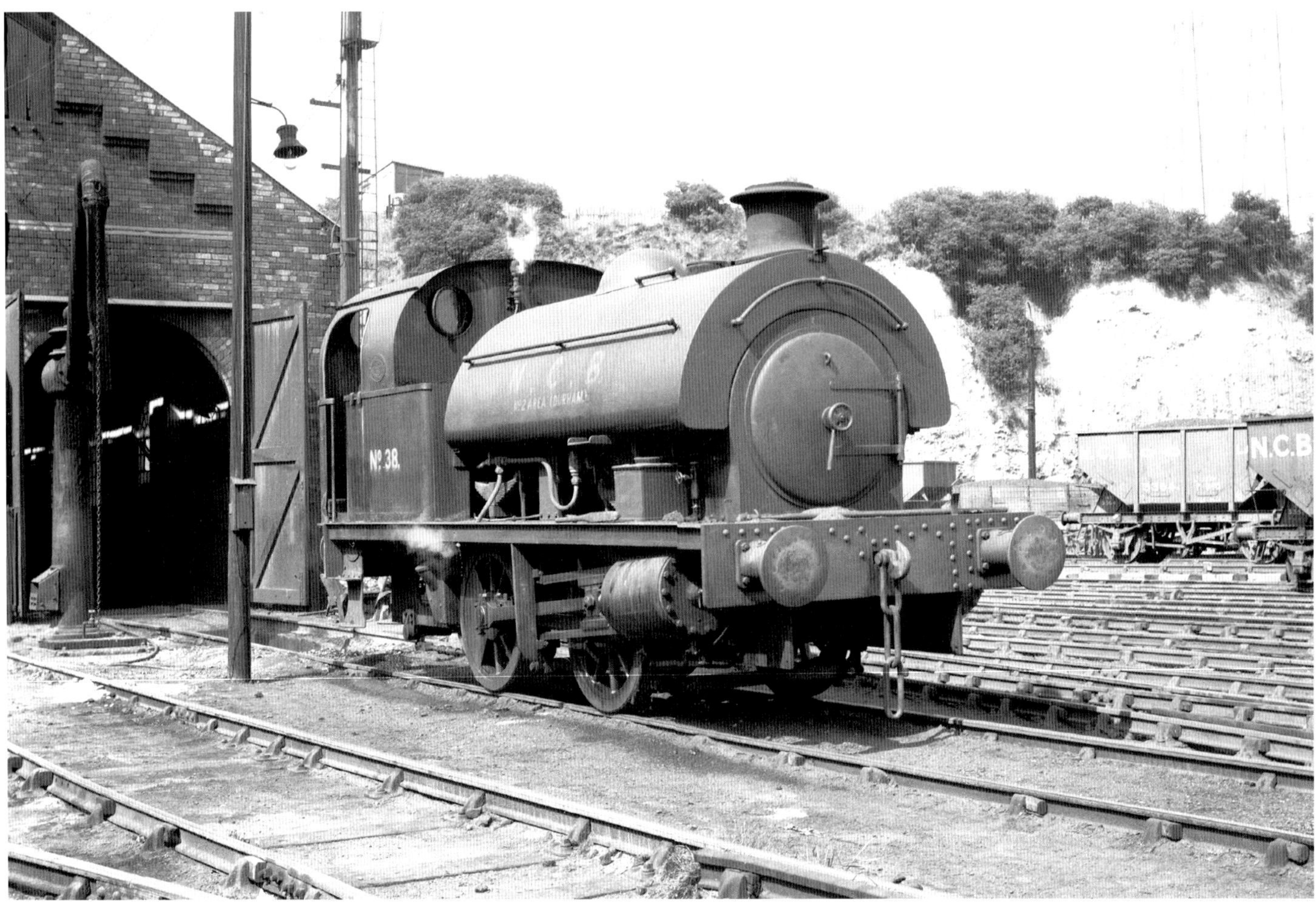

Robert Stephenson & Hawthorns 0-4-0 saddle tank No. 38 (W/No. 7756 of 1953) outside the Lambton staiths loco shed at Sunderland in the early 1960s. Several four-coupled tank locos were maintained at the two-road Lambton Railway shed until the staiths were closed in January 1967. In the 1950s, five locos were required to be in steam daily – three four-coupled locos for staiths duties and two six-coupled locos for Hetton duties. (Author's collection)

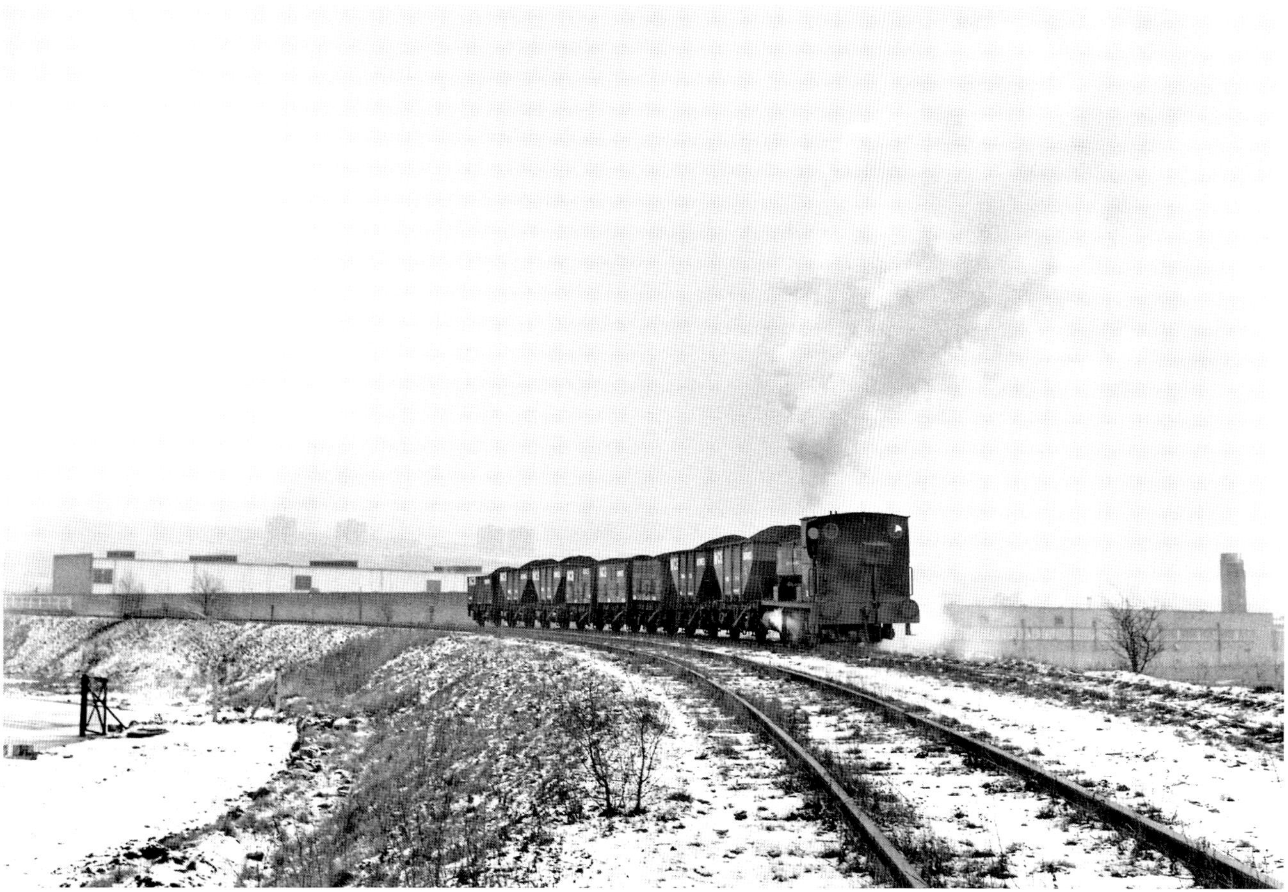

The Bowes Railway originally stretched from Jarrow staiths some 15 miles inland and comprised six rope-operated inclines totalling almost 6 miles, with some loco-worked sections between them. On 5 March 1971, Andrew Barclay 0-4-0 saddle tank No. 32 (W/No. 1659 of 1920) of the Bowes Railway's Starrs loco shed at Wrekenton was propelling loaded wagons from Ravensworth Park drift mine alongside the Team Valley Trading Estate, south of Gateshead, to Allerdene Bank Foot sidings at the foot of the incline. Locos worked this section, as well as between Wrekenton and Springwell, and at Ravensworth Ann colliery. (Author's collection)

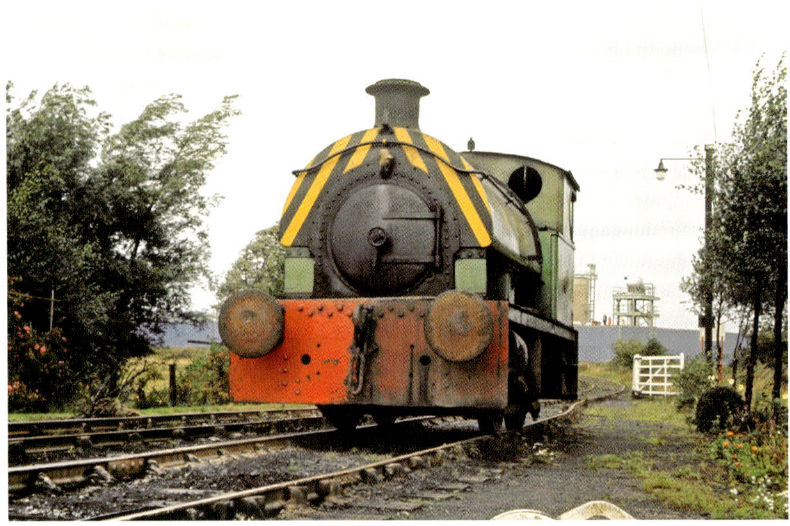

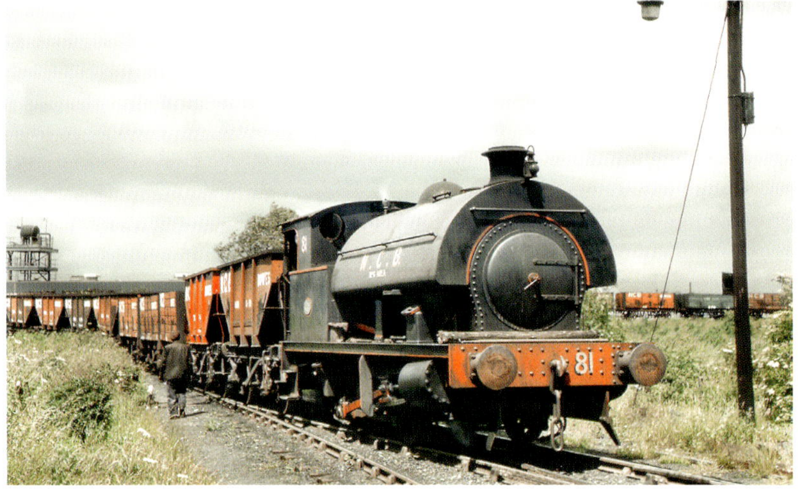

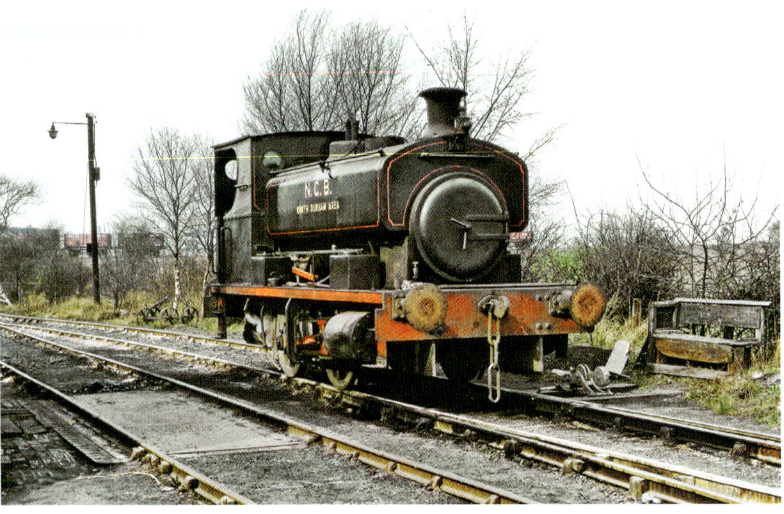

Above left: In April 1968, former Consett Iron Company Hawthorn Leslie 0-4-0 saddle tank No. 52 (W/No. 3474 of 1920) was at Allerdene. It was transferred to Springwell workshops during the following month and scrapped in the December of that year. (Jon Marsh)

Above: Robert Stephenson & Hawthorns 0-4-0 saddle tank No. 81 (W/No. 7604 of 1949) pauses between shunting Shop Pit sidings and the Allerdene incline at Lamesley in July 1970. The incorporation of the Bowes and Pelaw Main Railways in 1959 saw this section and its two stationary electric engine-worked inclines, at Allerdene Shop Pit and Ravensworth Ann, come under the Bowes Railway, connected to that railway at Blackham's Hill. The Pelaw Main Railway once linked several inland mines with staiths on the River Tyne near Hebburn. (Author's collection)

Below left: Andrew Barclay 0-4-0 saddle tank No. 32 (W/No. 1659 of 1920) at the foot of Allerdene Bank on the Bowes Railway on 23 March 1973 – a couple of weeks before this section of railway was closed – when Ravensworth Ann and Kibblesworth colliery on the Bowes Railway were linked underground, thereby bringing steam to an end on the Bowes Railway. (John Sloane)

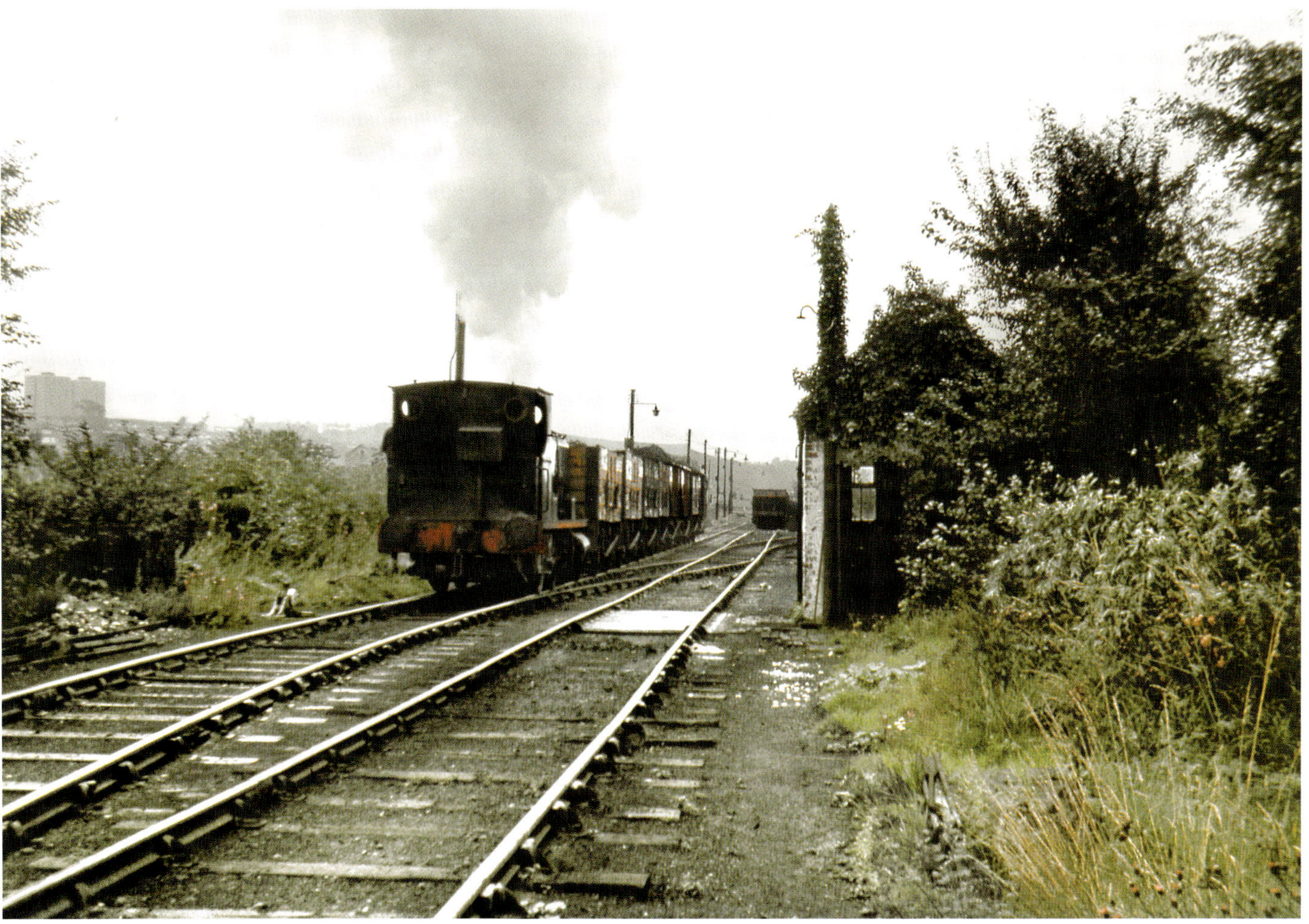

On a wet 25 August 1971, alongside the weighbridge building, Andrew Barclay 0-4-0 saddle tank No. 32 positions loaded internal-user Bowes Railway wagons from Ravensworth Park to the foot of the Allerdene incline. (Author)

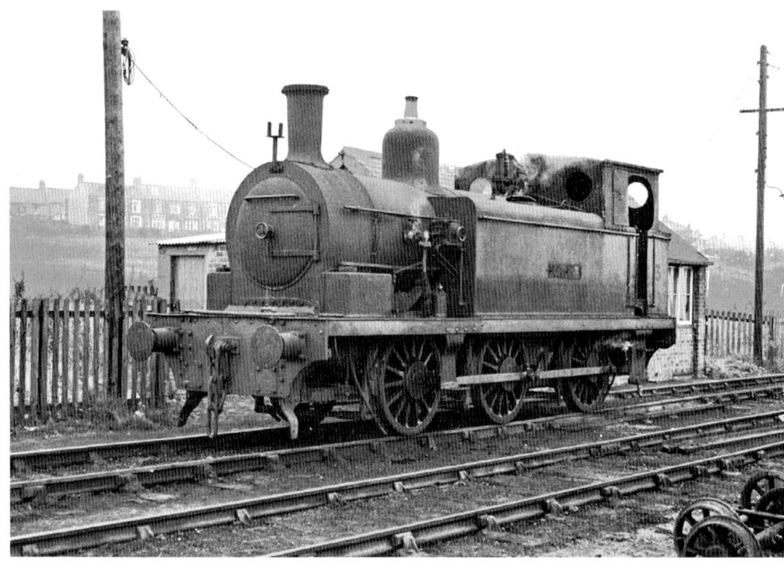

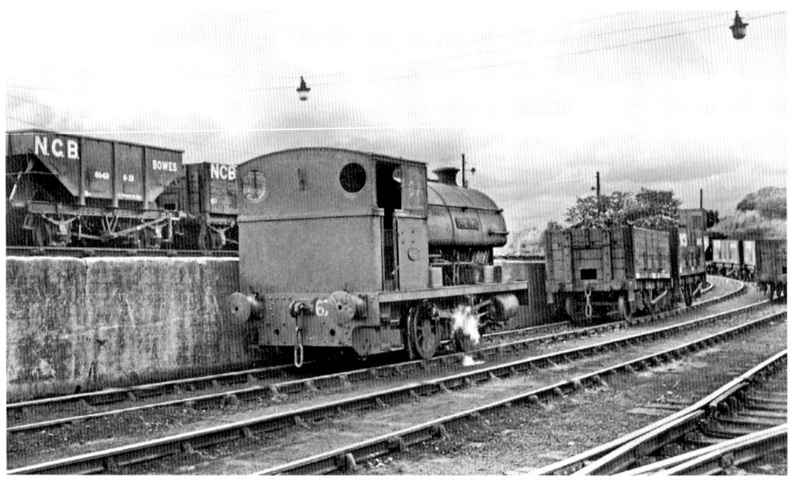

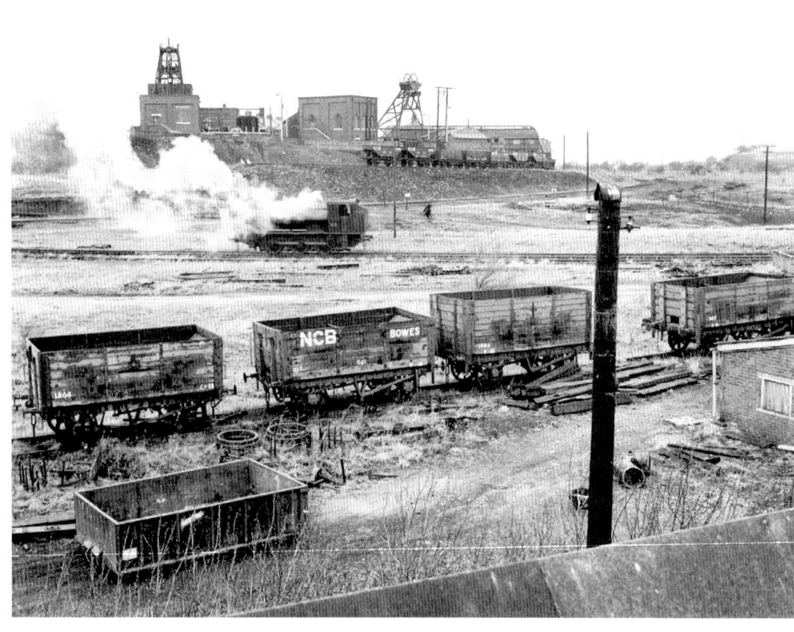

Above left: Robert Stephenson 0-6-0 tank *Twizell* (W/No. 2730 of 1891), originally of the Lambton, Hetton & Joicey Collieries Ltd at Morrison Busty colliery in the late 1960s. (Jon Marsh)

Left: Bowes Railway Peckett 0-4-0 saddle tank No. 67 *NCB-Pelaw* (W/No. 2093 of 1947) resting between shunting duties at Ravensworth Ann colliery in May 1966. (Author's collection)

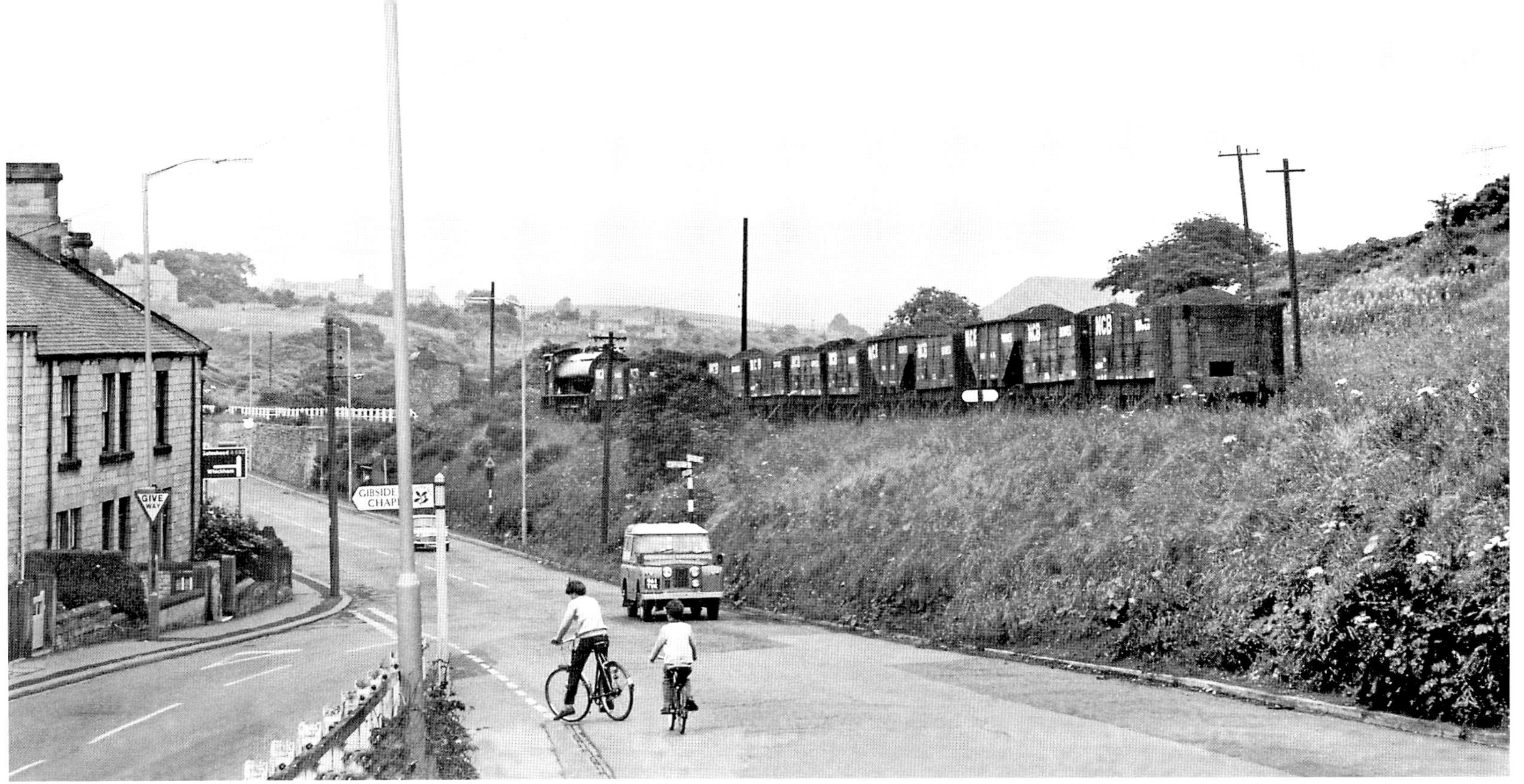

Above: In summer 1968, Marley Hill shed's Vulcan Foundry Austerity 0-6-0 saddle tank No. 28 (W/No. 5298 of 1945) drifts down the Bowes Railway's Hobson Bank, at Burnopfield village, with a loaded train from Burnopfield colliery. This bank, originally a rope-worked incline until 1900, had a ruling gradient of 1 in 35, with a short section of 1 in 20 near Burnopfield colliery. The maximum permitted load was eighteen empties up the grade and twenty loaded wagons down. (Author's collection)

Opposite page above right: A general view of Marley Hill colliery: Austerity 0-6-0 saddle tank No. 83 (W/No. 3688 of 1949) shuffles through the yard, its exhaust whipped away on the cold north-easterly wind. The colliery had sidings adjoining the Bowes Railway, but in 1952 it was linked underground to Clockburn drift mine (*see page 60*), to which most of its output was then despatched. The small remaining volume, hitherto sent via the Bowes Railway, ceased in July 1971 and Marley Hill colliery finally closed on 3 March 1982. The present day Tanfield Railway running shed and workshop incorporates the buildings in the foreground of this photograph. Nature has taken over the former colliery site with, at first glance today, very little sign of it having ever existed. (Author's collection)

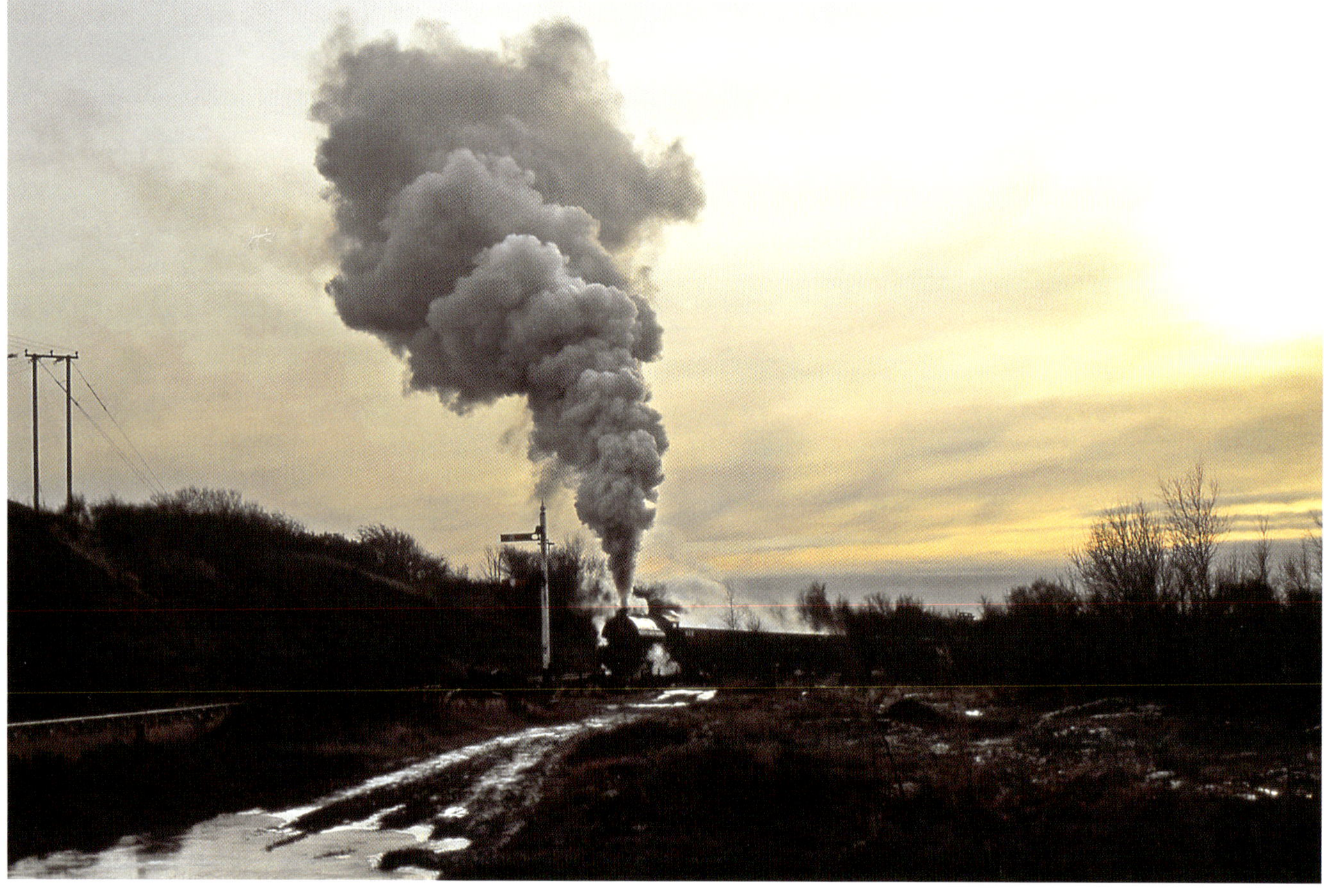

With a rake of NCB internal-user coal hoppers, Tanfield Railway's Robert Stephenson & Hawthorns 0-6-0 saddle tank No. 38 (W/No. 7763 of 1954) claws its way out of Marley Hill sidings on a freezing January afternoon in 1998. The former Marley Hill colliery site, to the right of this view, has experienced rapid tree growth over the two decades since this was taken. The Newcastle-built saddle tank was one of several identical locos that were used at Northumberland collieries, No. 38 being employed initially on the Ashington system (*see page 85*) and latterly finding use at Shilbottle and Whittle collieries, following dieselisation at Ashington. (Author)

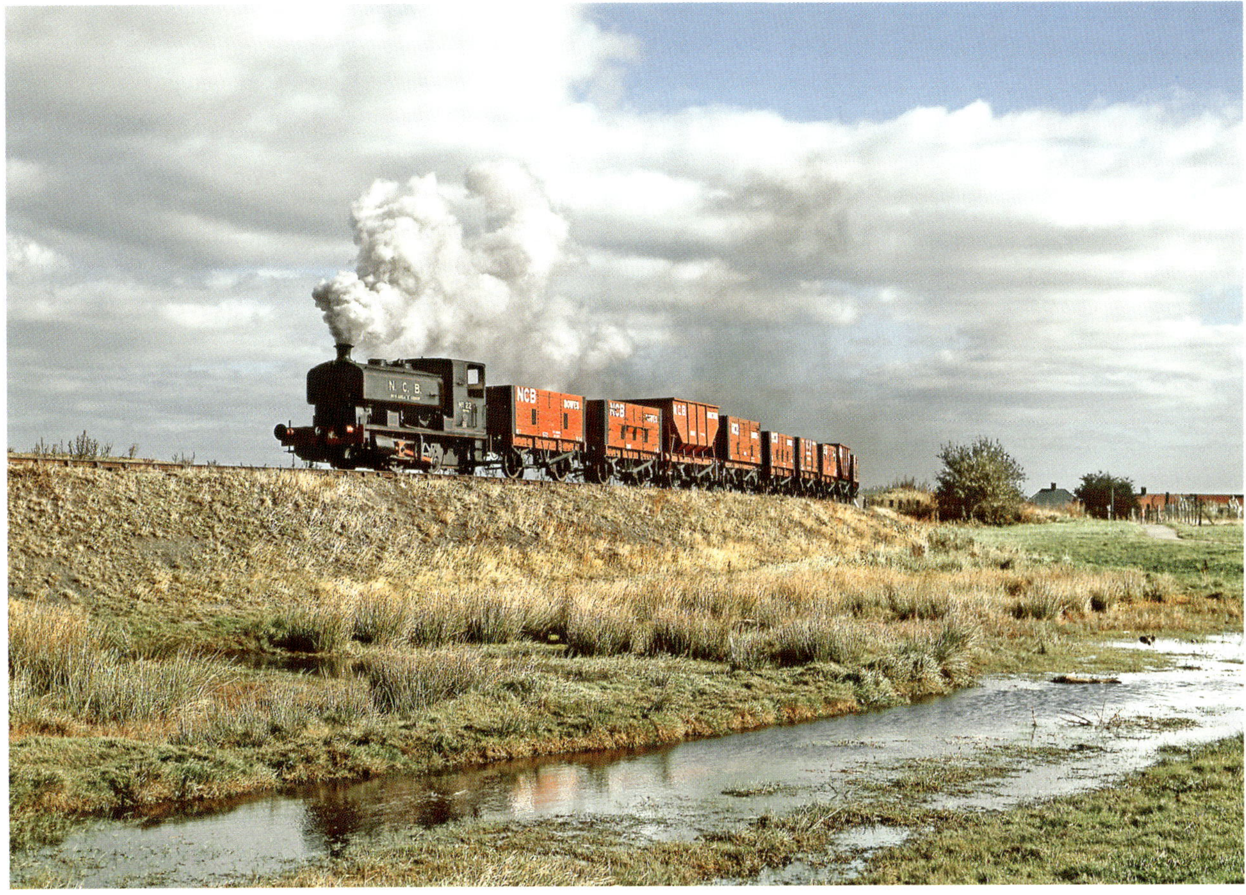

The Tanfield and nearby Bowes Railway in Gateshead offer splendid industrial railway authenticity – that is, as far as it is now possible to recreate – decades after the demise of the coal mining industry in County Durham. On 31 August 1998, former Bowes Railway Andrew Barclay 0-4-0 saddle tank No. 22 (W/No. 2274 of 1949) negotiates the Pelaw Curve, near the Blackham's Hill incline, working a demonstration coal train. The 14 x 22-inch cylinder Barclay was ordered for the East Tanfield colliery, but was delivered new to Springwell Bank Foot loco shed. It subsequently worked at East Tanfield, Tanfield Lea and Marley Hill collieries, finally being employed from October 1970 until the mid-1970s at the St Anthony's tar distillation plant at Walker, north of the Tyne. (Author)

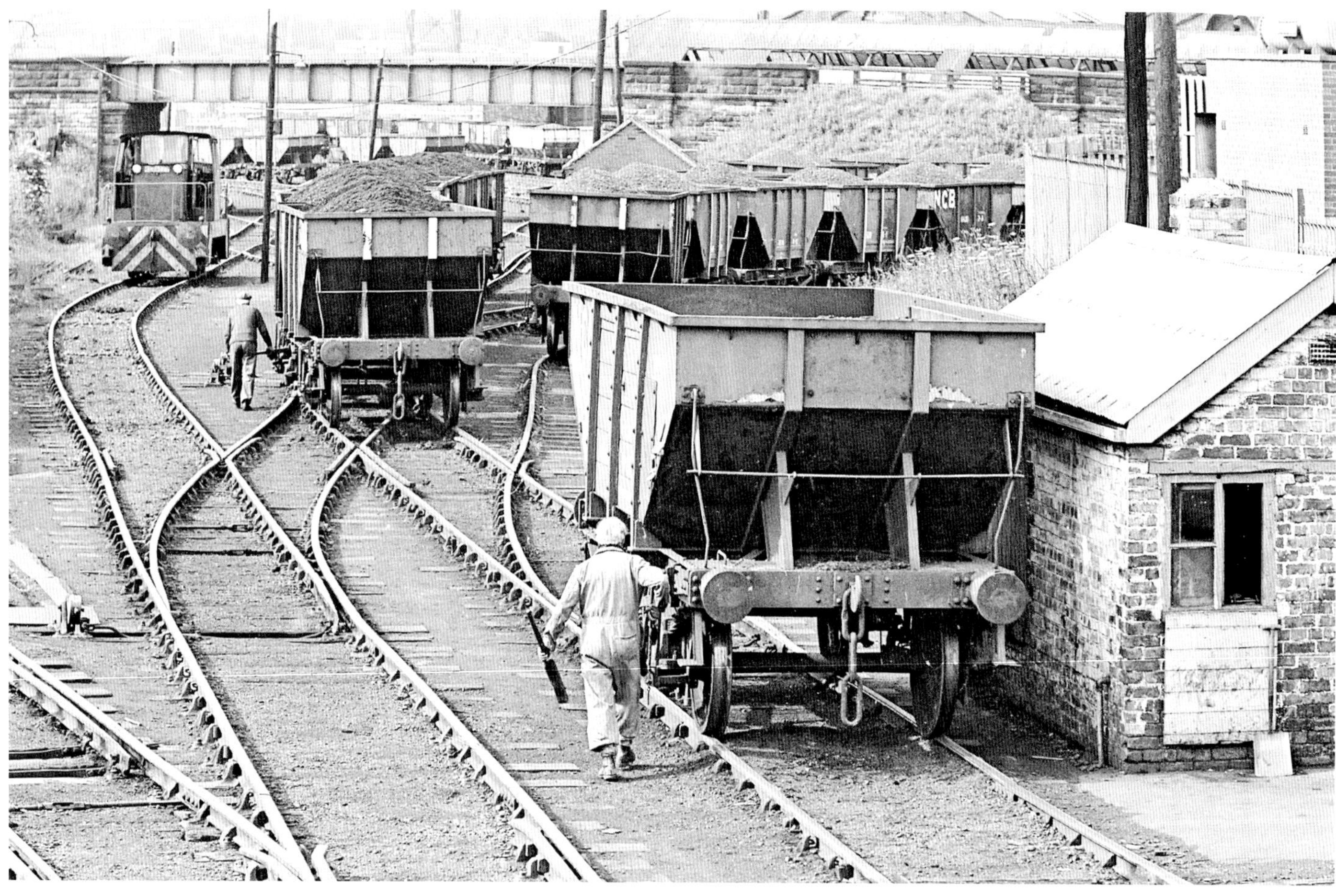

On 3 July 1978, a typical latter-day scene on the surviving section of the former Bowes Railway, by then re-named Monkton Railways, with loaded NCB internal-user hopper wagons being hand-guided by gravity down to the Port of Tyne Authority's Jarrow staiths. Hunslet 311 hp 0-6-0 diesel-hydraulic No. 504 (W/No. 6615 of 1965) of Springwell Bank Foot loco shed waits on an adjacent line. By this time, coal ultimately destined for the Monkton plants or Jarrow staiths was either delivered to Wardley or Pontop Junction at Jarrow by BR. Jarrow staiths closed in December 1985. (Kevin Lane)

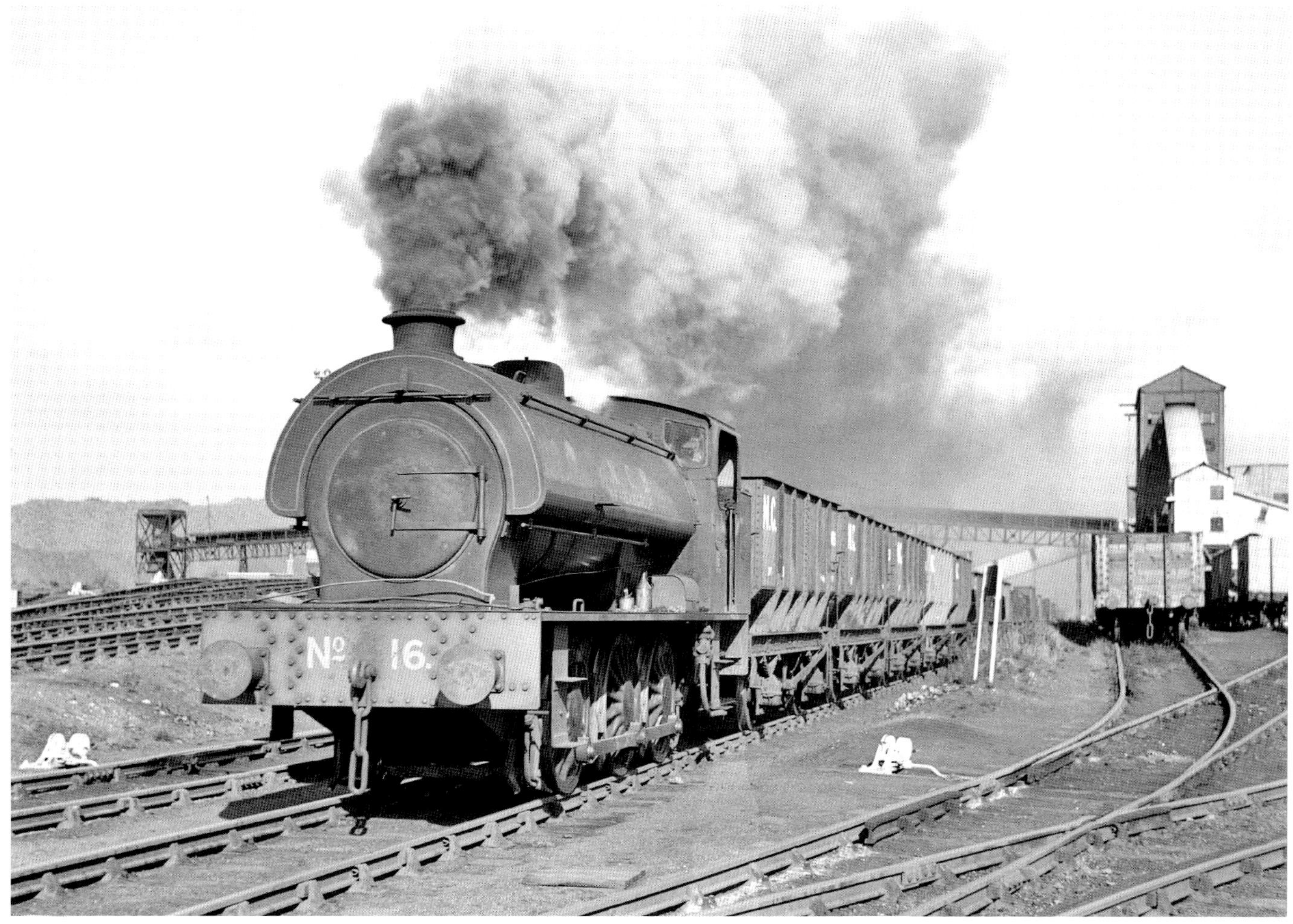

A fine study of an Austerity hard at work: Springwell Bank Foot loco shed's Vulcan Foundry-built 0-6-0 saddle tank No. 16 (W/No. 5288 of 1945) on the Bowes Railway system at Monkton coal preparation plant on 6 October 1958. It was transferred to Derwenthaugh in June 1965. (Brian Webb – IRS collection)

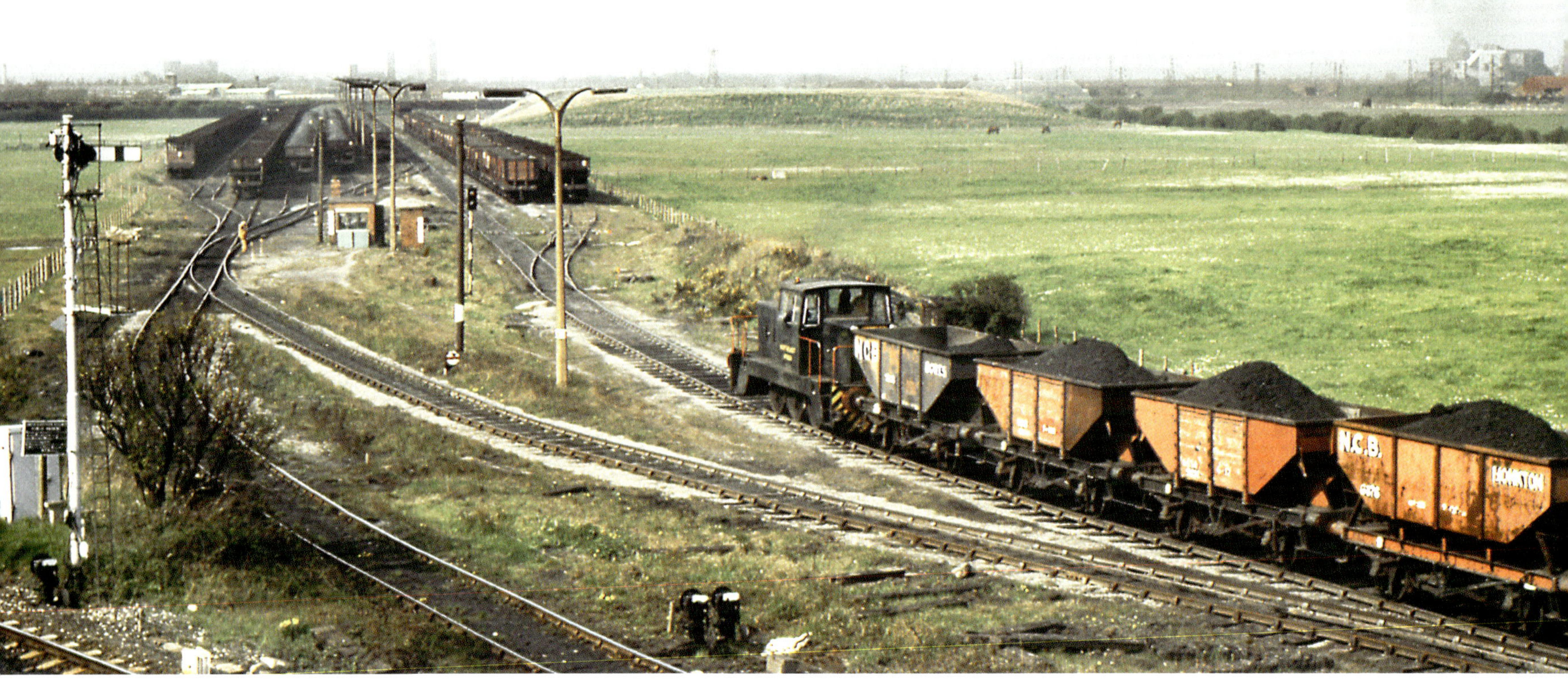

Above: A late 1970s scene at Wardley exchange sidings of Hunslet 0-6-0 diesel-hydraulic No. 504 of Monkton Railways hauling a loaded train of 21-ton internal steel hopper wagons, destined for either the Monkton coke works, seen smoking away to the right in the distance, or the adjacent coal preparation plant. By this time, after the NCB had renamed the remaining section of the Bowes Railway 'Monkton Railways', the wording 'Monkton' was in the process of being painted on the wagons following repair; one example is evident in this loaded rake. The NCB Monkton Railways operation – where coal was brought in by BR to either Wardley or Pontop Junction at Jarrow for transfer by NCB to the Monkton coal preparation and coking plants – ran between October 1974 and December 1985. (Author's collection)

Opposite page: You can almost smell the sulphurous aroma in this scene of the Monkton Coking Plant on 19 November 1990, but in fact this picture was taken just days after the plant had ceased full production. Standing idle are former BR Class 03 No. 03099, a Hunslet 0-6-0 diesel-hydraulic (W/No. 7305 of 1973) and the coking plant's four-wheel overhead wire electric coke oven loco built by Thomas Hill Vanguard (W/No. 313V of 1985). It was to be the last National Smokeless Fuels working plant in the region, ending a long history of coke manufacture in the North East. During the following month the plant was mothballed, with permanent closure coming about in March 1992, followed by demolition and site clearance in 1993. (Author)

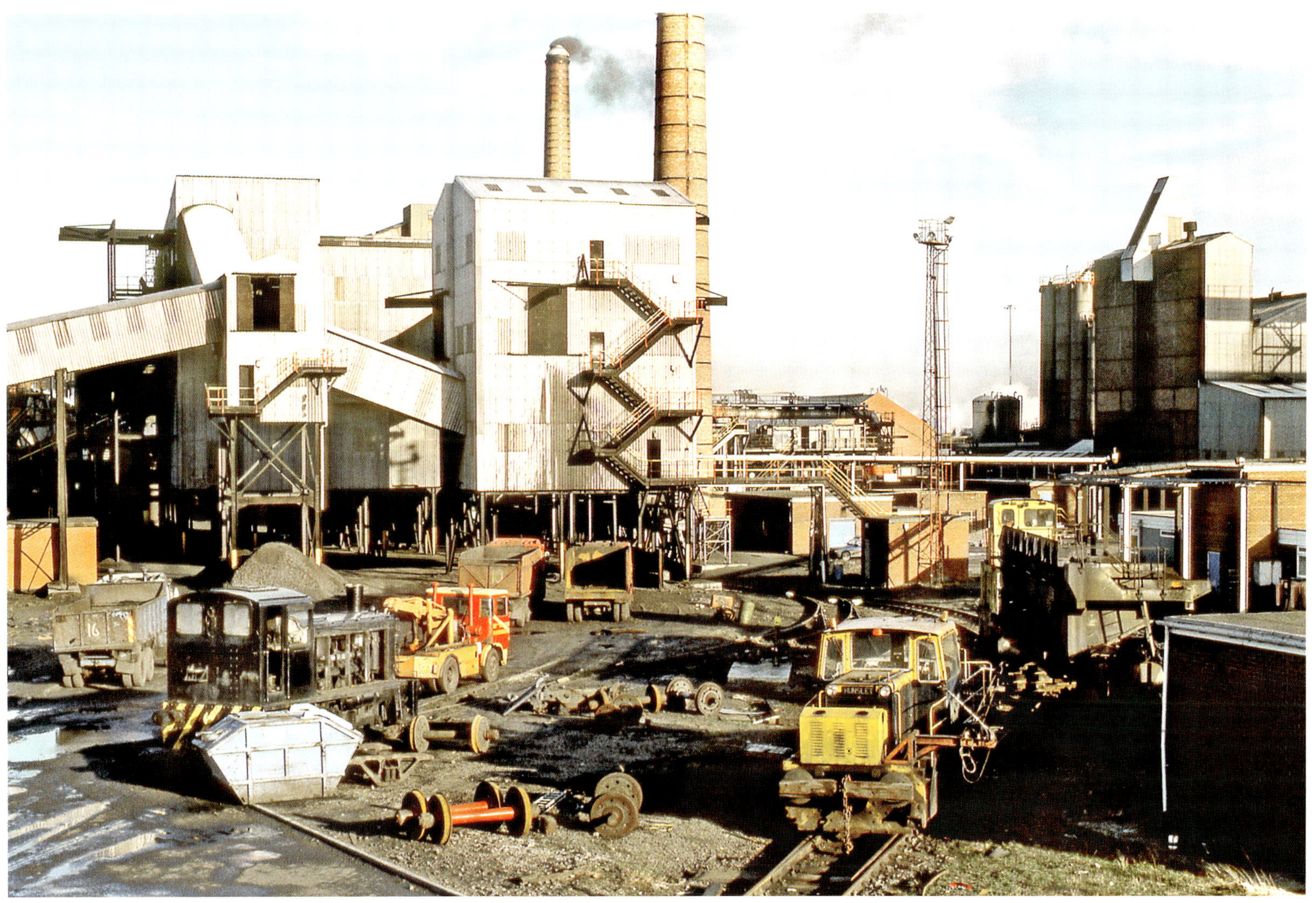

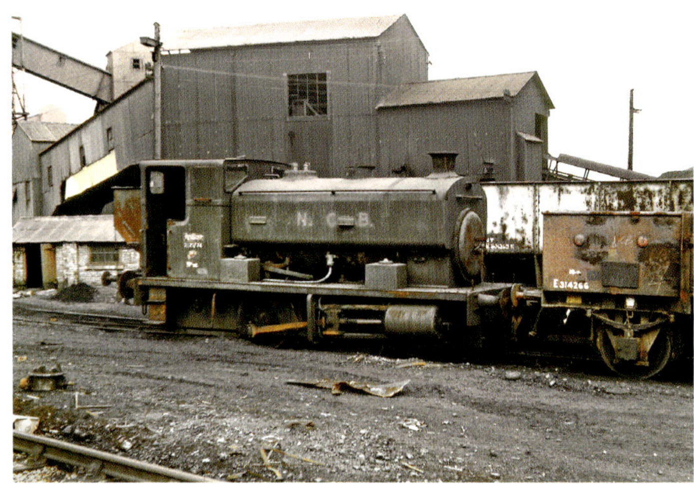

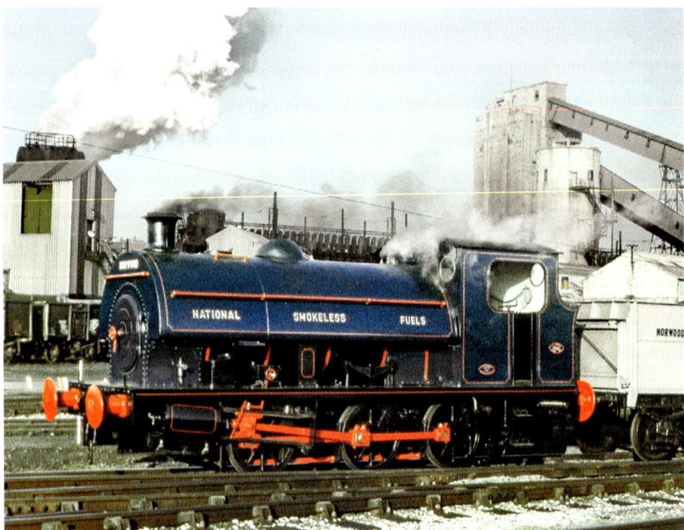

Above left: Dunston's Norwood coking plant opened in 1913. The battery of sixty-six coke ovens, installed by the NCB in 1947, produced up to 340,000 tons of coke per annum, in addition to town gas, crude benzole, sulphate of ammonia and tar byproducts. On 24 August 1971, Andrew Barclay 0-4-0 saddle tank No. 92 (W/No. 2317 of 1950) was out of use at the NCB Coal Products Division's (NCB-CPD) plant, shunting duties having been dieselised from the late 1960s. It was cut up on site during the following week. (*Also see page 121*). (Author)

Below left: On 7 October 1978, a more fortunate Robert Stephenson & Hawthorns Newcastle-built 0-4-0 saddle tank (W/No. 7412 of 1948) was in use at a public event at Norwood, by then under the ownership of NCB-CPD's subsidiary, National Smokeless Fuels Ltd (NSF). It had been retained on standby, but the ovens were finally extinguished in 1980. Following demolition, the site was transformed into the 1990 National Garden Festival and has since been redeveloped into residential housing. (Author's collection)

Opposite page top left: Transferred from Broomhill Disposal Point (DP), Northumberland, in August 1951, work-stained William Bagnall Austerity saddle tank No. 75167 (W/No. 2755 of 1944) adds to the general pollution of the Dunston area as it goes about its shunting work at Swalwell DP in February 1968. (Author's collection)

Opposite page top right: Swalwell DP, constructed on the site of the former Swalwell Garesfield colliery at Dunston, was on the opposite side of the River Derwent from Derwenthaugh shed and exchange yard. It was opened by the Ministry of Fuel & Power in 1945 to handle opencast coal from County Durham and south Northumberland. The NCB Opencast Executive ran the operation from April 1952, sub-contracting in February 1954 to Mechanical Navvies Ltd, and from July 1968 to Johnson's (Chopwell) Ltd. By 6 September 1971, Austerity No. 75167 was immaculately presented, compared to three years earlier. (John Sloane)

Opposite page below left: On 25 March 1986, grubby 'large logo' Class 56 No. 56127 has arrived via the Redheugh Branch sidings and is waiting to collect MGR wagons from Swalwell DP, as a Hunslet 0-6-0 diesel-hydraulic (W/No. 7410 of 1976) is busy making up the load for despatch. (Author)

Opposite page below right: On 25 March 1986, former BR Class 11 No. 12074 stands as a spare loco at Swalwell DP. Introduced into BR service from Derby Works in September 1950, and withdrawn from Chester shed during January 1972, the loco served in industrial service in the North East, along with sister loco No. 12088, before being privately purchased in 1989. Subsequently acquired by dealer Harry Needle, it was broken up at European Metals Recycling, Kingsbury, in July 2002. (Author)

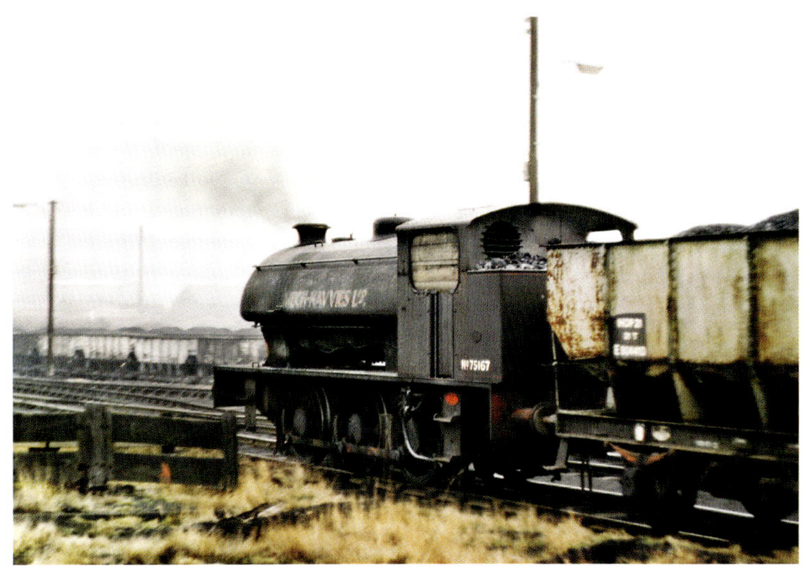

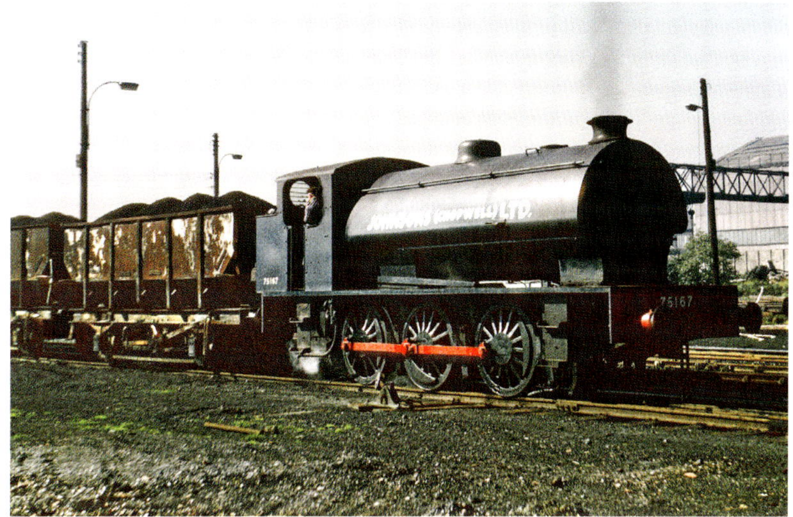

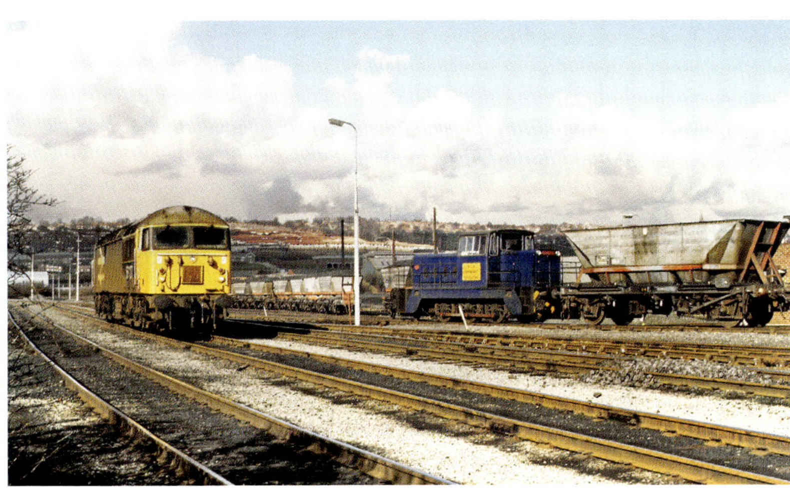

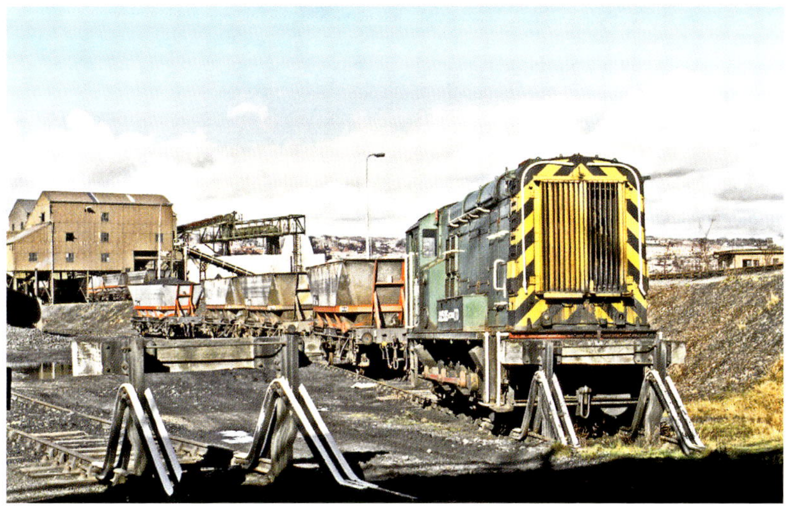

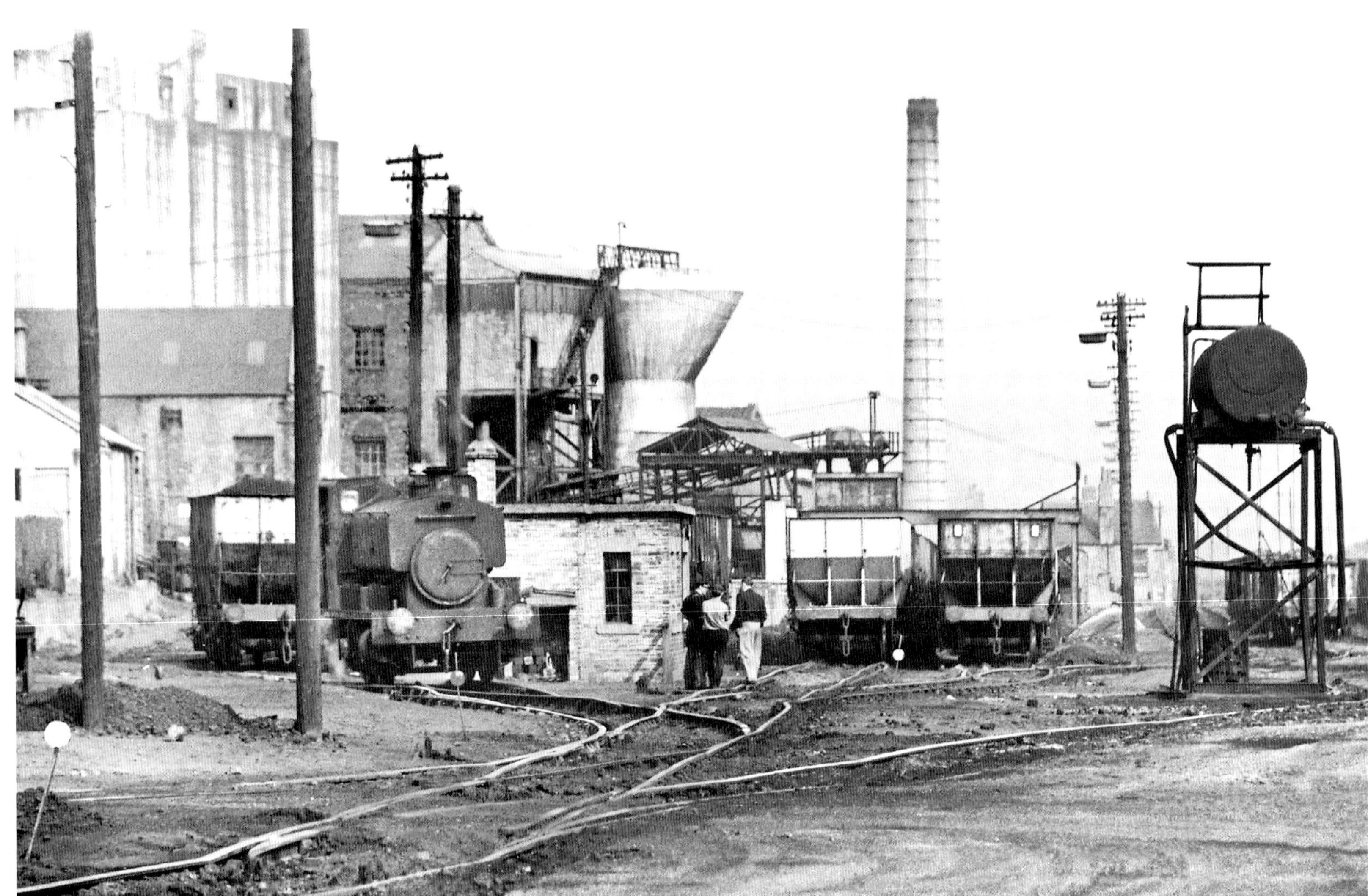

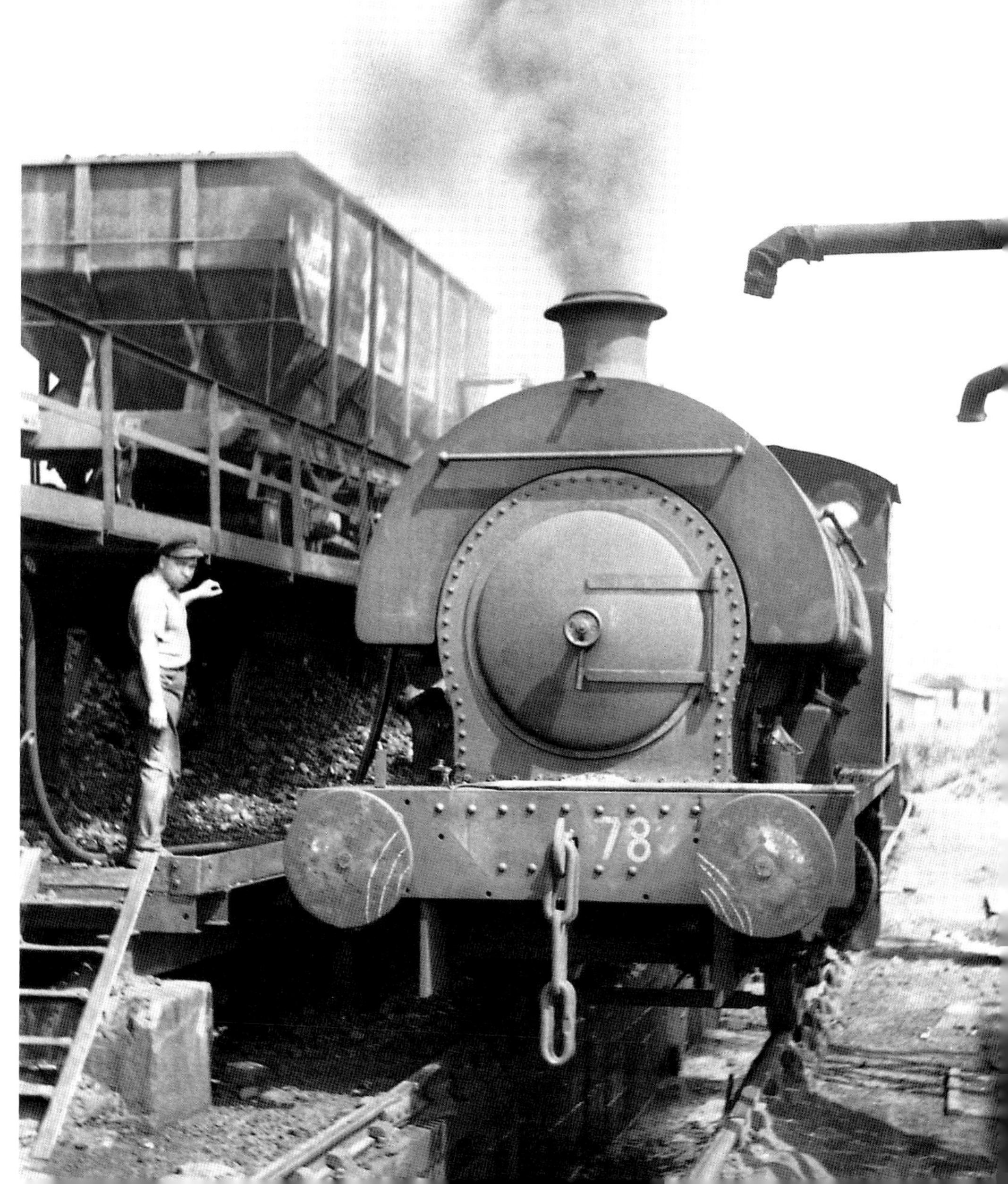

Opposite page: A quiet interlude at the Norwood Coking Plant in summer 1968, with Andrew Barclay 0-4-0 saddle tank No. 92 in steam, but at rest between its shunting duties, which were to be taken over later that year by a new Hunslet four-coupled diesel-hydraulic. However, it did survive in a standby capacity, before eventually succumbing to the scrap man in September 1971. The plant was originally linked at the northern end with the BR Tanfield branch, and at the southern end with the Pelaw Main Railway line to Dunston, but both sections were abandoned in 1962 and 1963 respectively after a new BR rail connection had been installed to the north of the plant, interfacing with the Low Fell to Blaydon freight-only line. Of interest is that a 10-mile-long gas pipeline was built in 1952, inter-connecting both Norwood and Derwenthaugh coke works, and then on to Consett, providing gas for use in steel production at the Consett Ironworks. Coke production finally ceased at Norwood in May 1980. (Author's collection)

Right: Robert Stephenson & Hawthorns 0-4-0 saddle tank No. 78 (W/No. 7538 of 1948) taking on water alongside the coaling gantry at Derwenthaugh loco shed in the late 1960s. It had been transferred from Addison colliery, Ryton, in January 1961, and was to work for a further decade from Derwenthaugh loco shed, finally being scrapped in March 1971. One of the diagrams for the four-coupled locos at Derwenthaugh was to shunt the tar tanks at the coke works. (Author's collection)

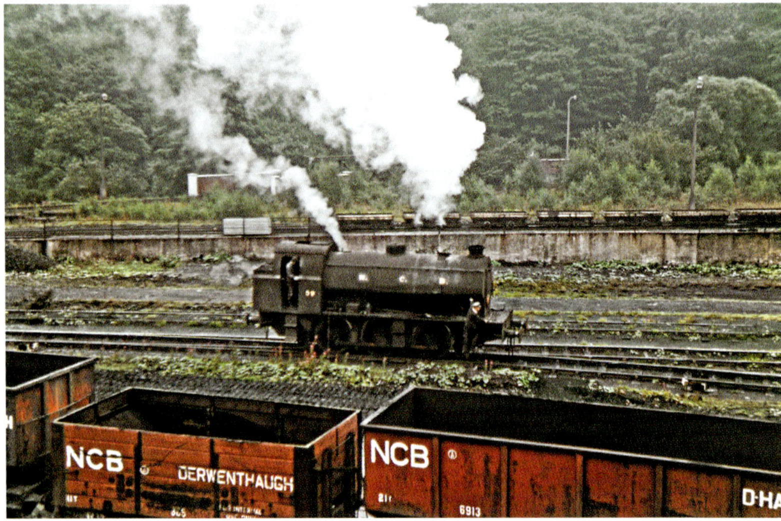

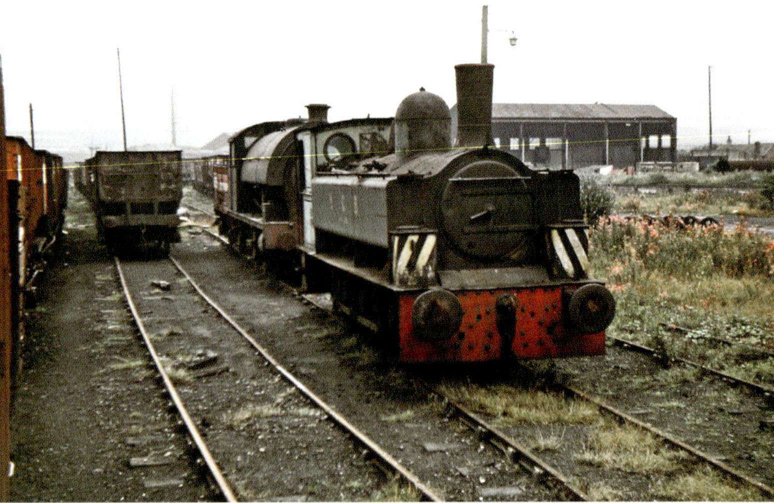

Above left: Just over the hill, north-west of Marley Hill colliery on the site of the former Raine's Foundry, which closed in 1918, was the Clockburn drift mine, connected to Marley Hill by an underground 3-foot 6-inch gauge railway employing a fleet of six Hudswell Clarke 100 hp mines locos – some of the mine tubs can be seen beyond the concrete wall. On a drizzly 24 August 1971, Austerity 0-6-0 saddle tank No. 59 (Vulcan Foundry W/No. 5300 of 1945) shuffles through the yard from Derwenthaugh to collect some loaded internal-user wagons from the Clockburn drift mine yard. Loaded with Marley Hill quality coking coal, they would be destined for the large coking plant complex at Derwenthaugh. The cut-back cab of the Austerity indicates its former Lambton Railway origin, having been transferred from Philadelphia to Derwenthaugh in March 1969. (Author)

Below left: Kitson 0-6-0 pannier tank No. 41 (W/No. 2509 of 1883 rebuilt by Hudswell Clarke in 1900) and Robert Stephenson & Hawthorns 0-6-0 saddle tank No. 6 (W/No. 7603 of 1949) were dumped out of use at Derwenthaugh loco shed on 24 August 1971. The long-boiler pannier tank, formerly Consett Ironworks *A No. 5*, was the last Consett loco to remain in service at Derwenthaugh, finally being taken out of traffic during 1968. Derwenthaugh loco shed, near Dunston-upon-Tyne, provided locos for shunting the Winlaton Mill standard gauge sidings and they also worked traffic between Winlaton Mill, Derwenthaugh coke ovens, the staiths on the River Tyne (until 1960) and the BR yard alongside Derwenthaugh loco shed. (Author)

Opposite page: Derwenthaugh coking plant was opened in 1929 by the Consett Iron Co. Ltd. Around this time the signal boxes and semaphore signalling were introduced to avoid conflict of traffic between the coke works and the frequent coal traffic on the Chopwell & Garesfield Railway, as well as traffic on the line to and from Consett Ironworks. With the abandonment of all lines south-west of Winlaton Mill by January 1967, only the 2½ miles between Winlaton Mill and Derwenthaugh remained. Derwenthaugh shed continued to prepare five working steam locos on weekdays well into 1968, but dieselisation of the system came about in 1972. The closure of Marley Hill colliery and Clockburn drift mine in March 1983 was a blow to the coking plant, then in the hands of NSF Ltd, but its death knell was to be the miners' strike of 1984–85, after which it was forced to close, in December 1985. One year before being cut up, former Bowes Railway Vulcan Foundry Austerity 0-6-0 saddle tank No. 27 (W/No. 5288 of 1945) leaves a smoke screen across the road between Dunston and Winlaton Mill on 27 April 1970 as it engages in shunting the Derwenthaugh coking plant, located alongside the River Derwent. (Author's collection)

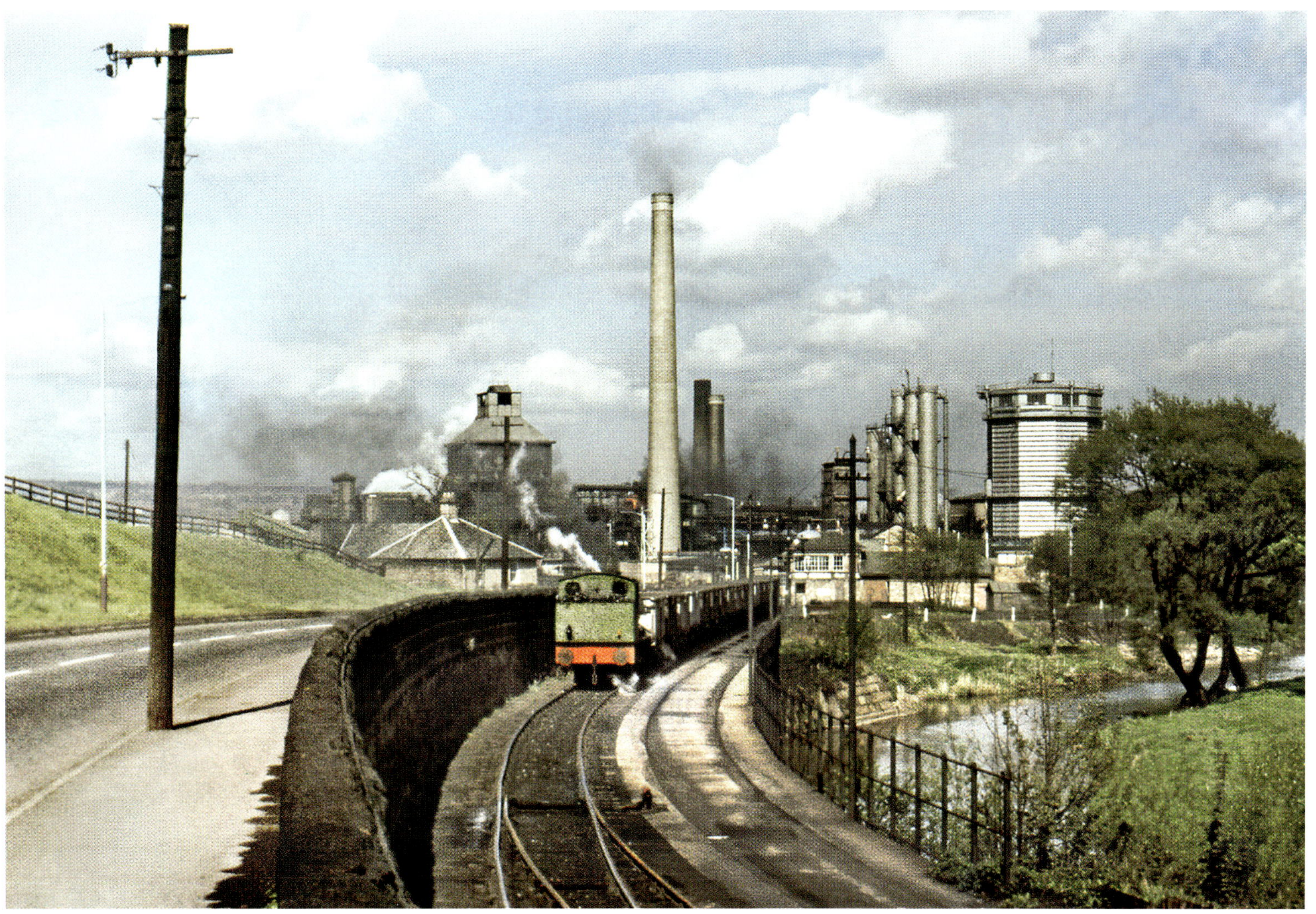

Right: The view through the engineman's bothy window at Derwenthaugh loco shed in late summer 1969, with the driver rinsing his mug after a tea break and looking out on Hunslet Austerity 0-6-0 saddle tank No. 7 (W/No. 3820 of 1954), his loco for that day's shift, which was diagrammed to shunt Derwenthaugh yard and the BR exchange sidings. Six-coupled NCB Hunslet diesels took over from steam in 1972 and some were hired to the coking plant, by then operated by NSF Ltd. Derwenthaugh loco shed and wagon shops were finally closed in November 1983. By that time, over a decade after steam traction had ended, hired-in BR Class 08 diesel locos from Gateshead depot were working the incoming BR coal traffic to the coke works, with coal traffic from Marley Hill colliery/Clockburn drift mine having ceased eight months earlier. (Tony Brown)

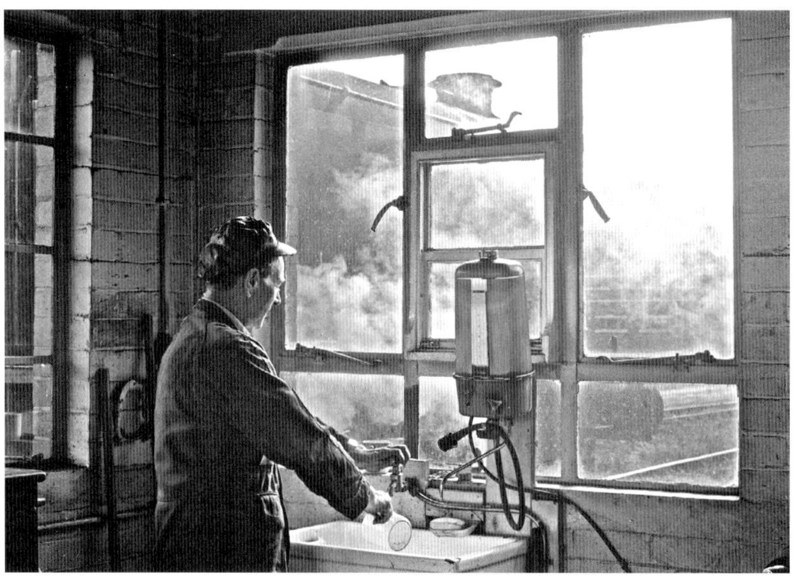

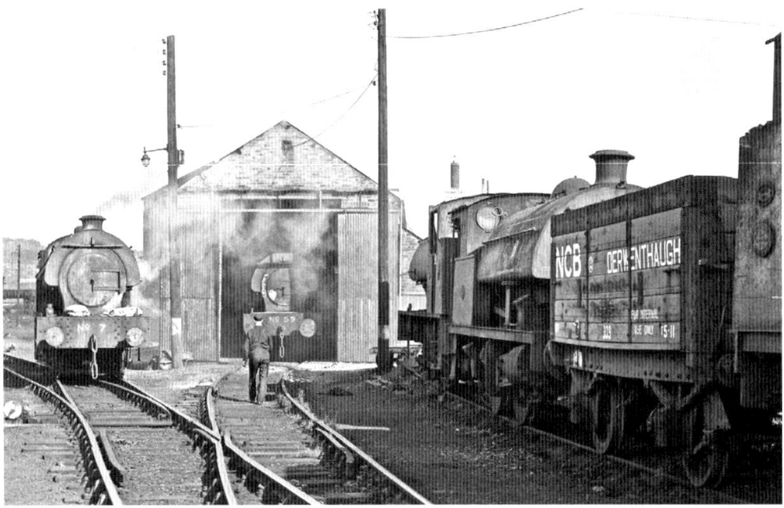

Left: Early morning at Derwenthaugh loco shed, during the late summer of 1969, with former Lambton Railway Austerity 0-6-0 saddle tanks Nos 7 and 59 already prepared for their day's duties. Both had been transferred there in March 1969 upon dieselisation of the Lambton Railway at Philadelphia, and they saw further service on the Derwenthaugh Railways system until scrapped in October 1972. Already dumped on the 'scrap line' are (left to right) Austerity 0-6-0 saddle tank (Hunslet No. 3689 of 1949), Robert Stephenson & Hawthorns 0-4-0 saddle tank No. 78 (W/No. 7538 of 1949) and an unidentified Austerity 0-6-0 saddle tank. They would all meet their fate by March 1971. (Tony Brown)

Opposite page: Hunslet Austerity No. 7 'brewing up' while taking on water, alongside the Derwenthaugh loco shed's elevated coaling gantry, leaving a smoke screen across Dunston and the Tyne Valley. (Tony Brown)

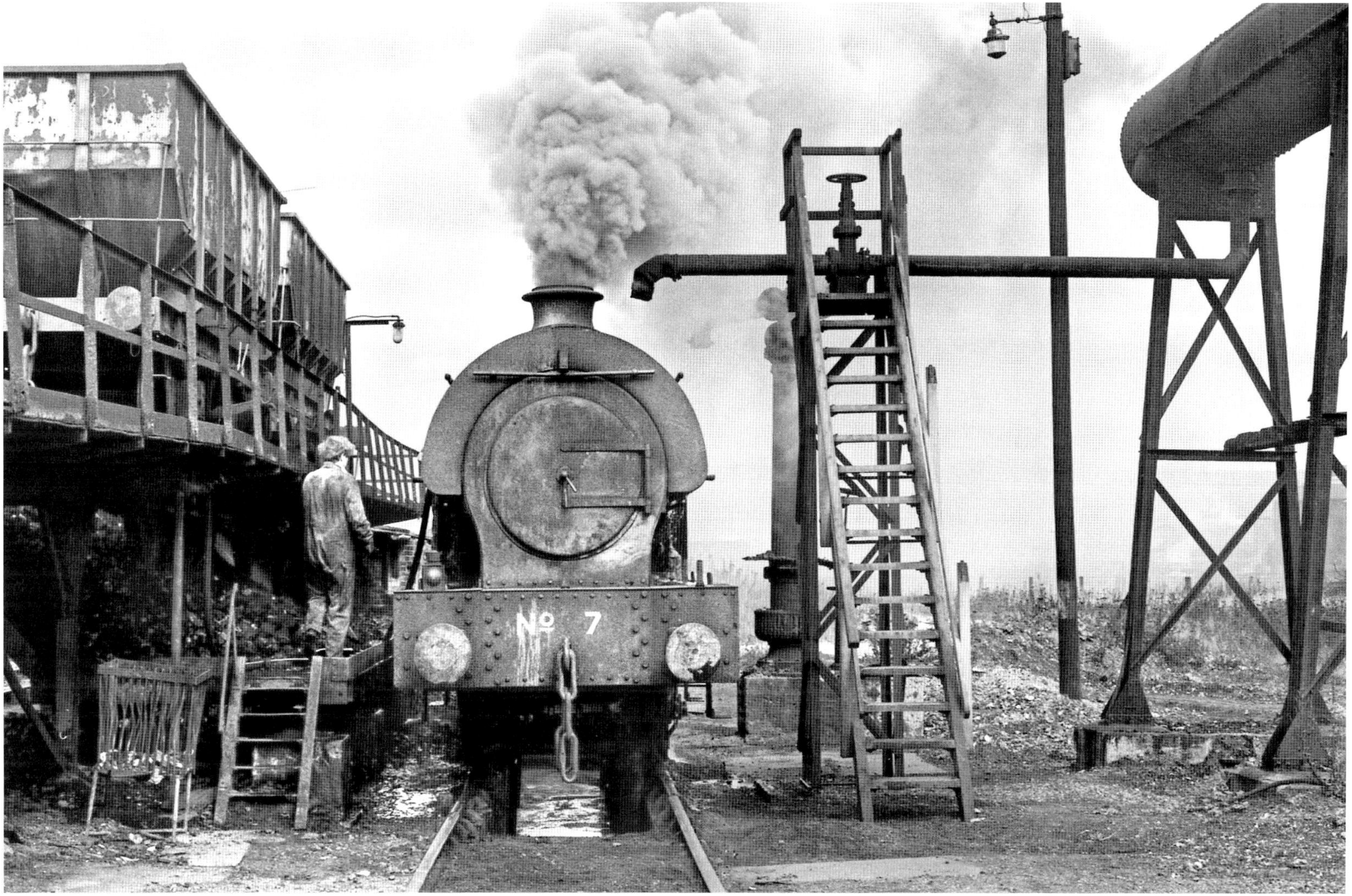

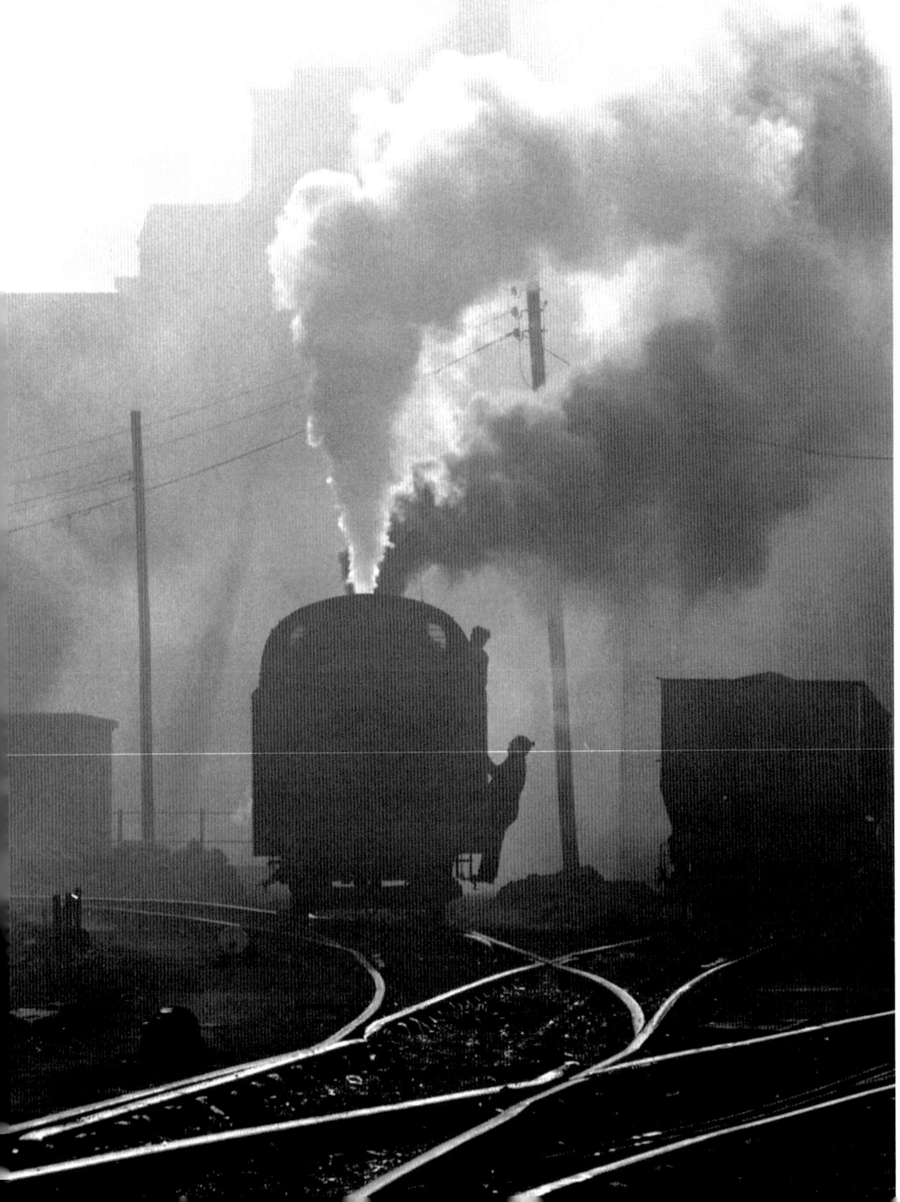

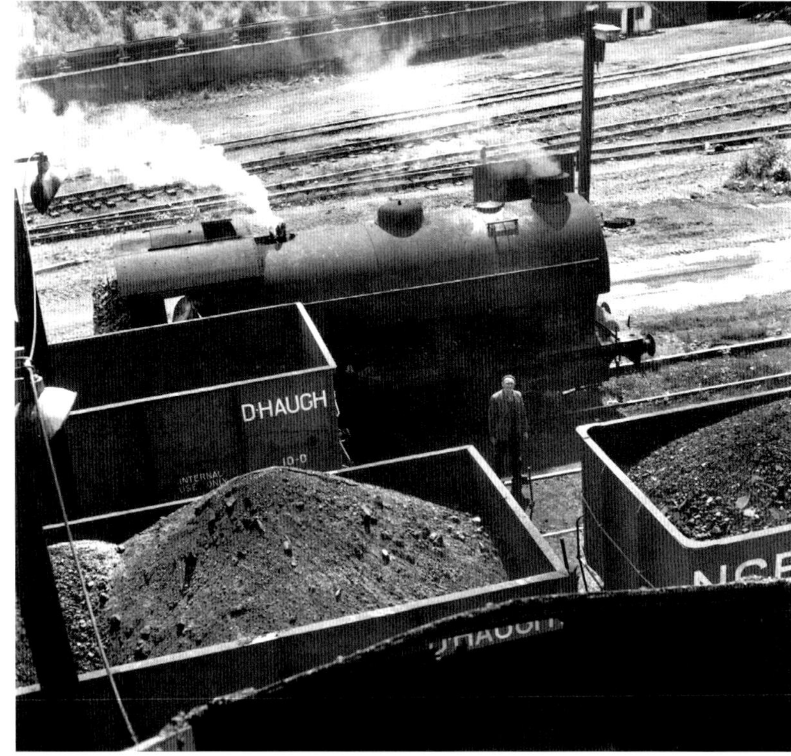

Left: The distinctive Lambton Railway-style cut-back cab of Vulcan Foundry-built Austerity No. 59 is unmistakeable in this backlit early morning scene of it shunting Derwenthaugh coking plant in late summer 1969, shortly after its transfer from Philadelphia. (Tony Brown)

Above: Newcastle-built Robert Stephenson & Hawthorns 0-6-0 saddle tank No. 6 (W/No. 7603 of 1949) of Derwenthaugh loco shed stands at the Clockburn drift mine loading point in late summer 1969. It had been transferred from Boldon colliery in July 1968 but was scrapped at Derwenthaugh in October 1972. (Author's collection)

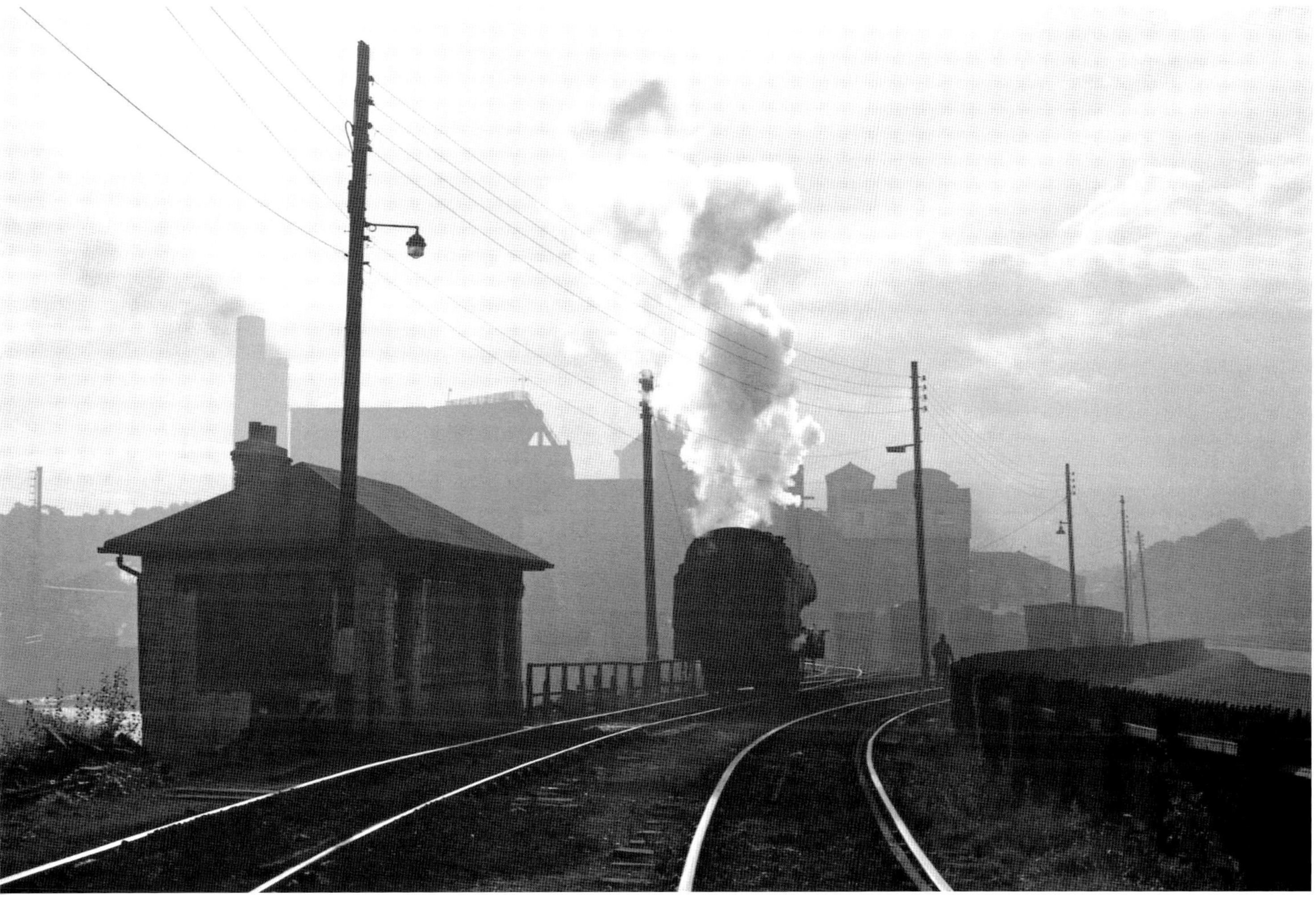

Vulcan Foundry-built Austerity No. 59 standing by the railway yard hut at the north end of Derwenthaugh coking plant in late summer 1969. (Tony Brown)

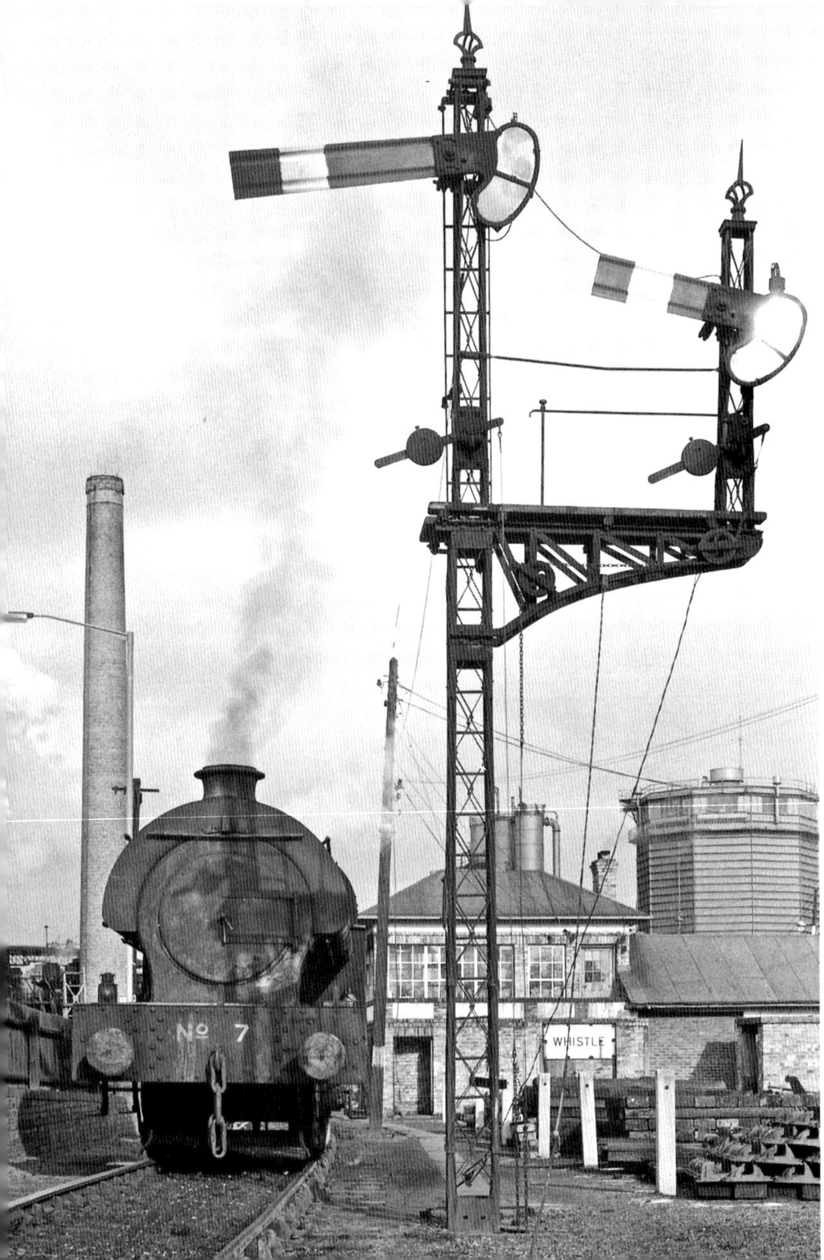

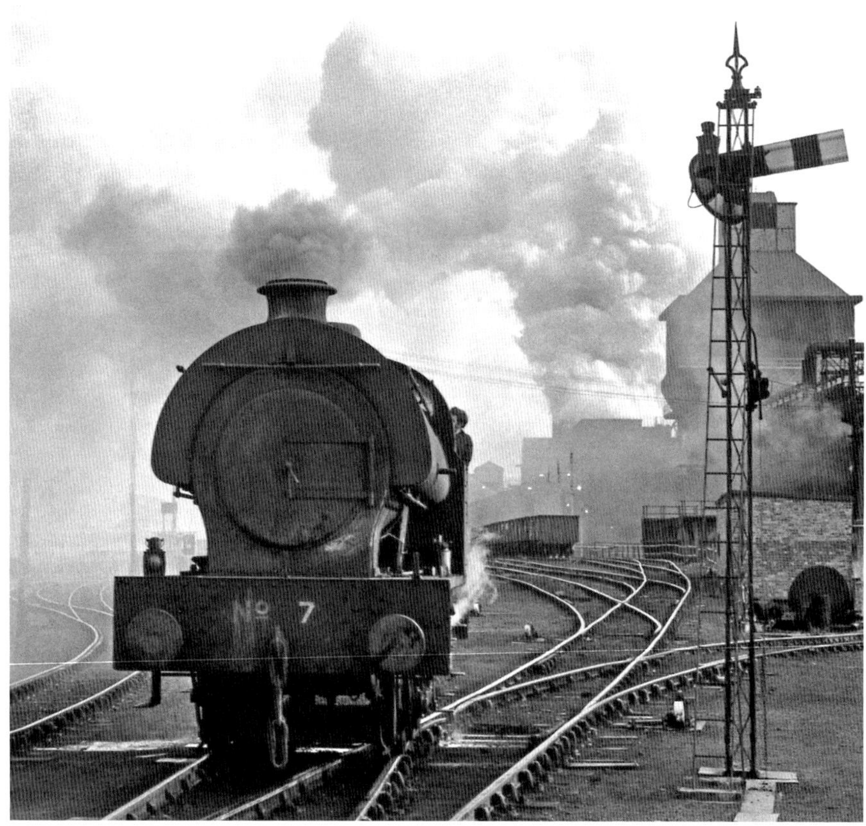

Left, above and opposite page: Scenes of the impressive signalling aspects that graced the railway around Derwenthaugh coke works, installed for the Consett Iron Company Ltd with the construction of the plant in 1929. The signalman in this spacious box at the extreme west end of the site controlled both the main level crossing access road to the coking plant and all rail movements on the main running line, as well as within the coke works sidings themselves; in this case, Austerity 0-6-0 saddle tank No. 7 is in action there on a summer's morning in 1969. (All Tony Brown)

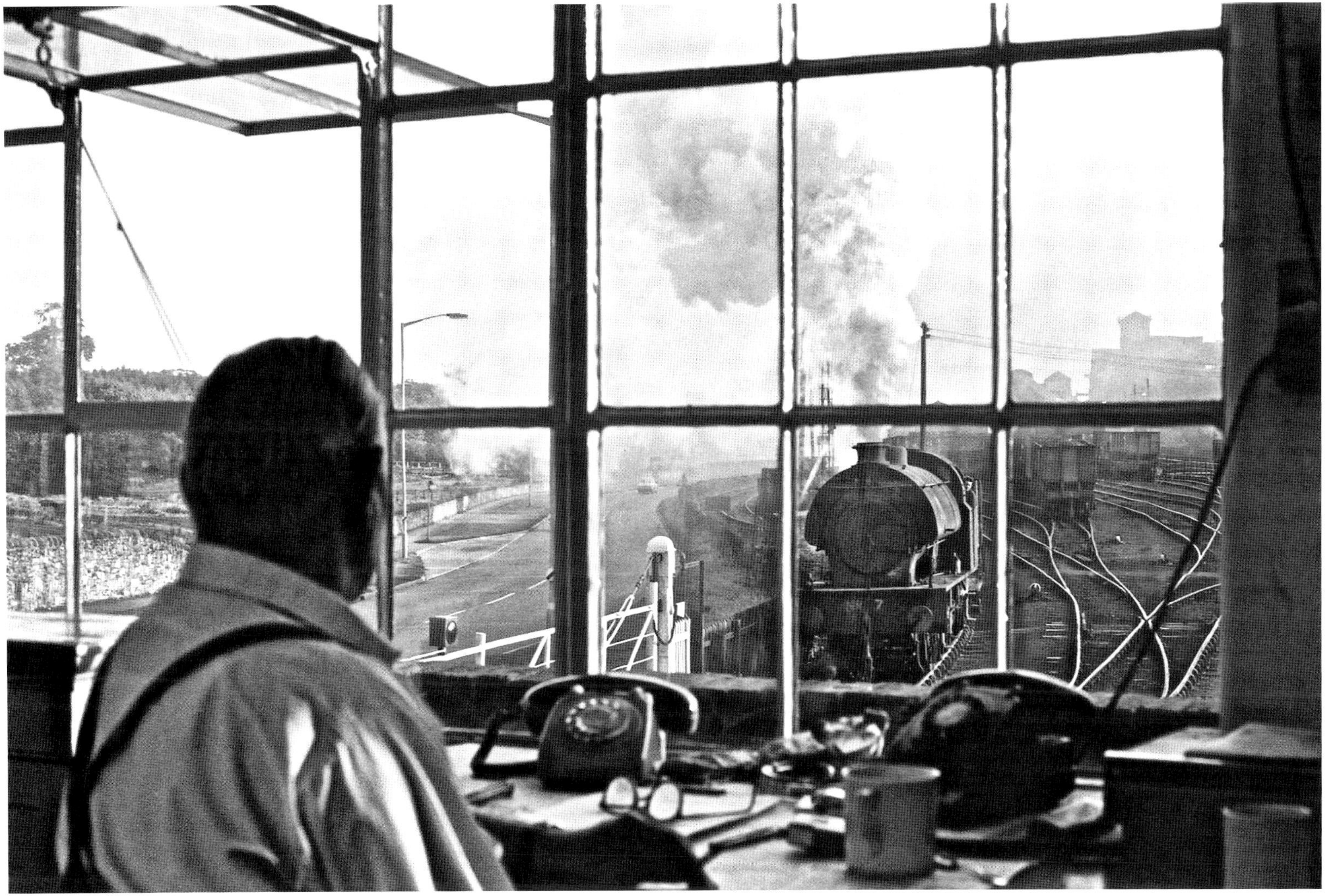

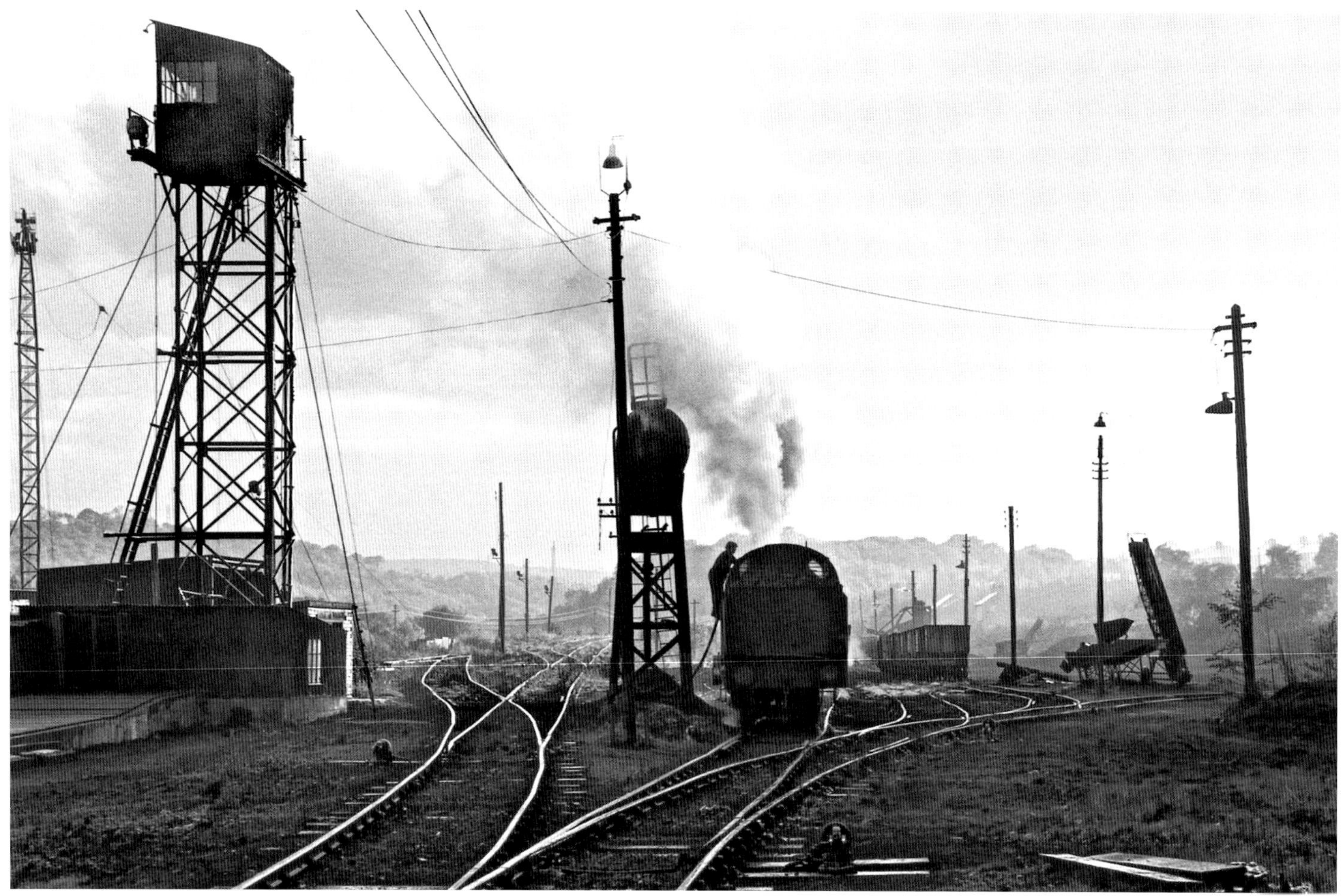

Another 'transferee' from Philadelphia, recognisable by its Lambton Railway cut-back cab, was Vulcan Foundry Austerity No. 58 (W/No. 5299 of 1945), seen taking water from the torpedo tank at Clockburn drift mine yard in late summer 1969. The yard control tower appears to be a precarious outpost for the incumbent! (Tony Brown)

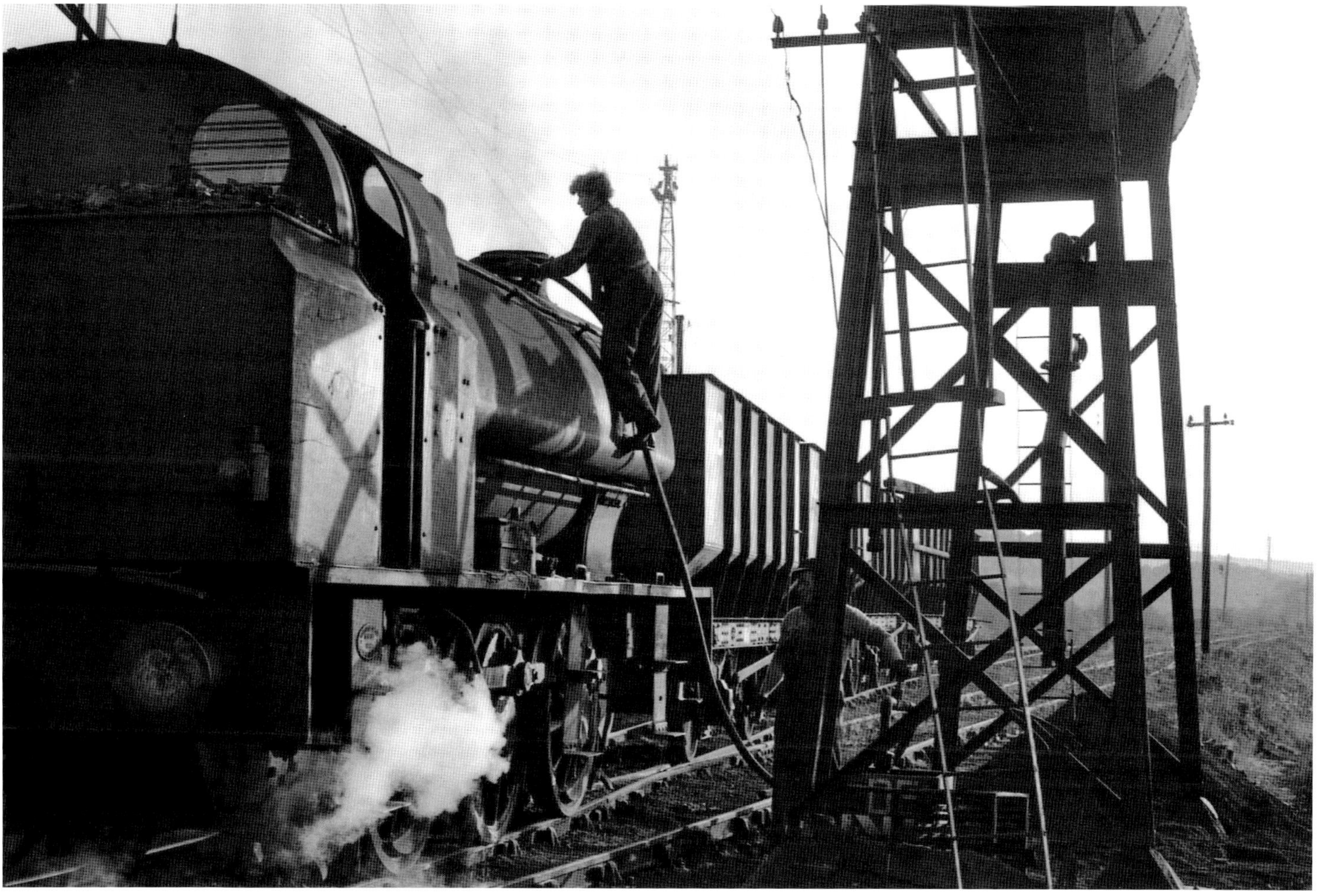

Austerity No. 59 taking on water at Clockburn drift mine from the torpedo tank, a one-time Lancashire boiler and ideal for its 'semi-retired' use as an elevated water tank for the locos. (Tony Brown)

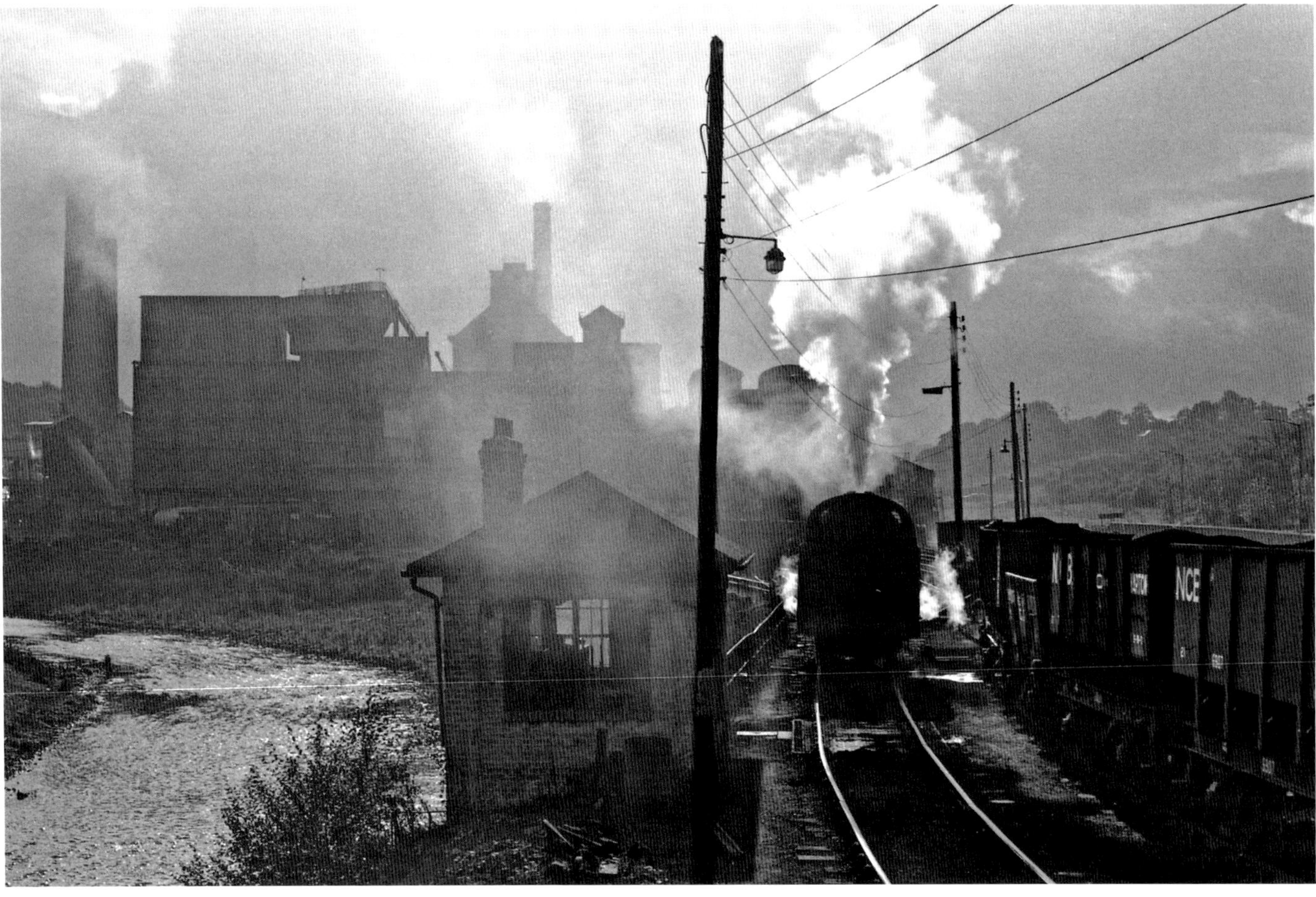

Austerity No. 59 going about its routine daily business at Derwenthaugh coking plant in the late summer of 1969. Photographer Tony Brown appropriately comments: 'Derwenthaugh coking plant would have come under the category of "dark satanic mill", and it would seem a paradox to make something "artistic" of such a grim scene, but I didn't have to work there of course!' But all too soon the place fell silent, and in any case, there wasn't a soul to be seen working there following its closure in 1985. (Tony Brown)

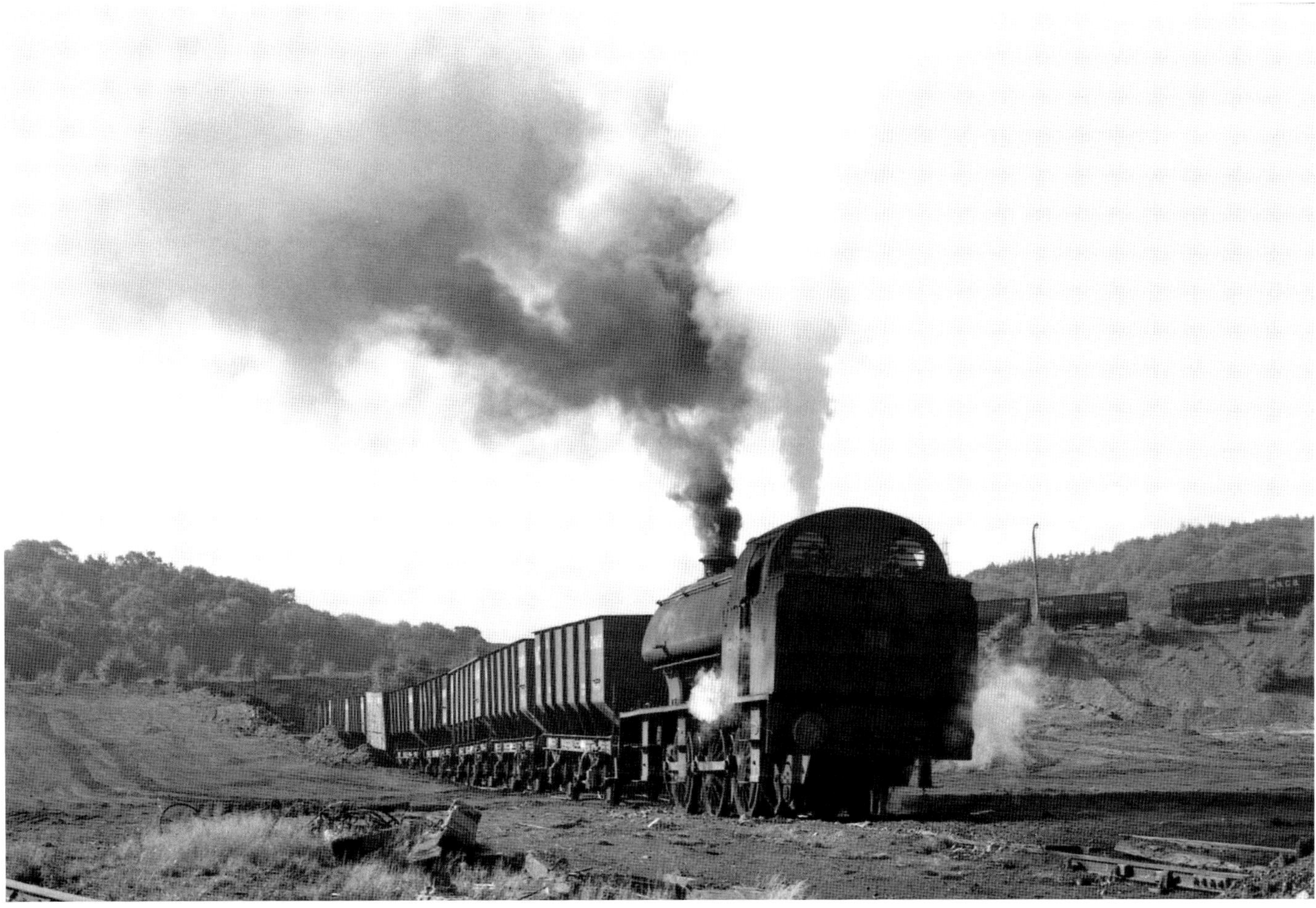

In late summer 1969, Derwenthaugh's Austerity No. 59 gets to grips with a mixed rake of internal hoppers at the south-western end of Clockburn drift mine yard, where excess raw coal was discharged or stockpiled. During the latter years of the Derwenthaugh Railway, redundant internal wagons were sent to Derwenthaugh for further use, notably from Consett Ironworks and from the Lambton Railway. (Tony Brown)

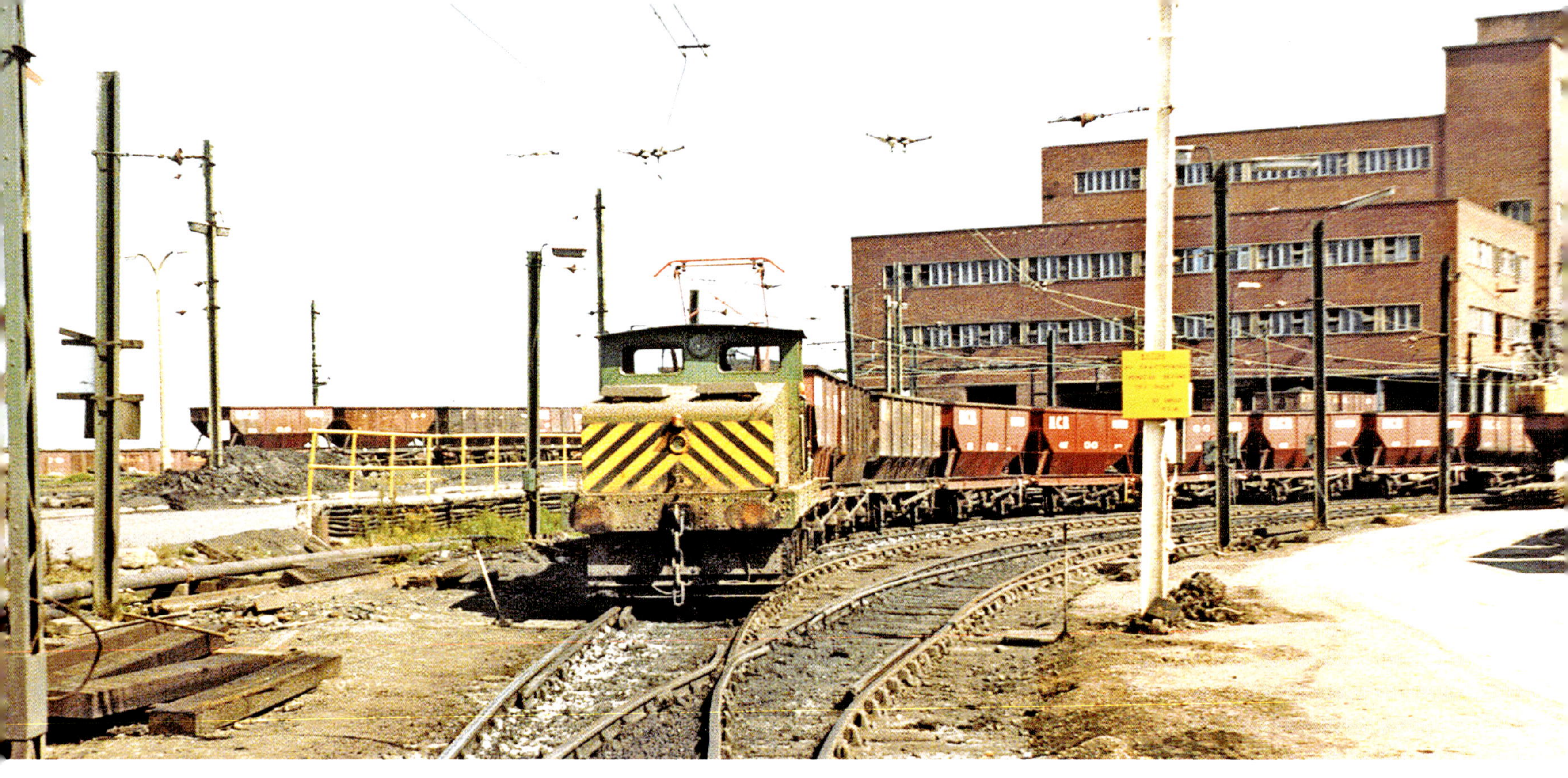

The 550 V DC Harton Railway at Westoe colliery at South Shields in summer 1982. Here, the Bo-Bo 400 hp electric No. 11 (English Electric W/No. 1795 – Baguley W/No. 3351 of 1951) was one of five 50-ton locos built between 1951 and 1959 by E. E. Baguley, with parts supplied by English Electric. The Harton Coal Company electrified almost its entire railway with a 550 V DC system in 1908. Ten locos were supplied from new: seven by Siemens, two by Kerr Stewart and one by AEG. These all survived into the 1960s, augmented from the 1950s by the new Bo-Bo electrics numbered 11 to 15. The large bow-collectors on the locos enabled the significant difference in height to be negotiated, with a variation of over 10 feet in places around the system. The loco shed was located at Westoe colliery, the epicentre of the railway, with three separate lines radiating out to Harton Low Staiths, Harton colliery and a non-electrified line to Whitburn colliery, the latter of which subsequently closed in 1968. Widespread electric working on the system ended in March 1988, after which just locos Nos 12 and 13 were retained for working the remaining section between St Hilda sidings and the Low Staiths on the Tyne. The surviving electrified system closed on 19 July 1989, after the last stone train worked to the Harton Low Staiths. Westoe colliery, which had opened in 1913, finally ceased winding coal in May 1993. (Colin Alexander)

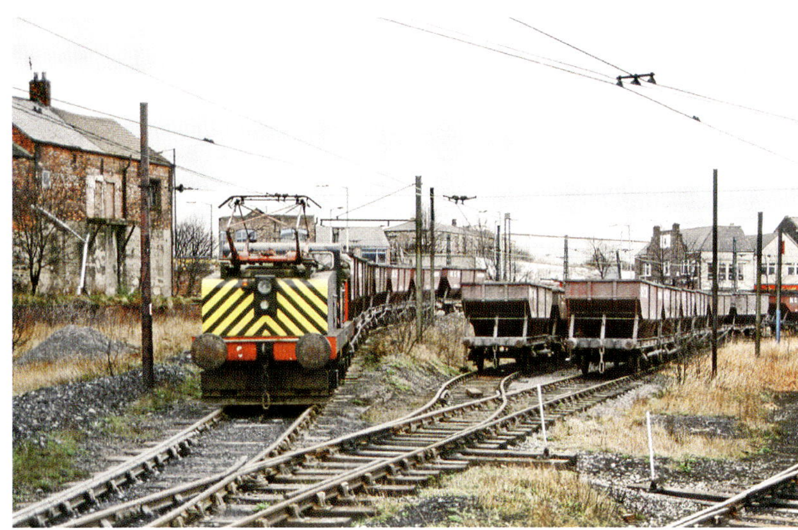

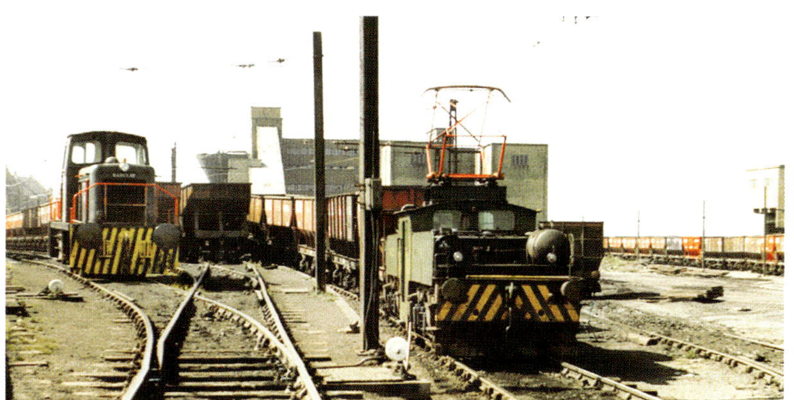

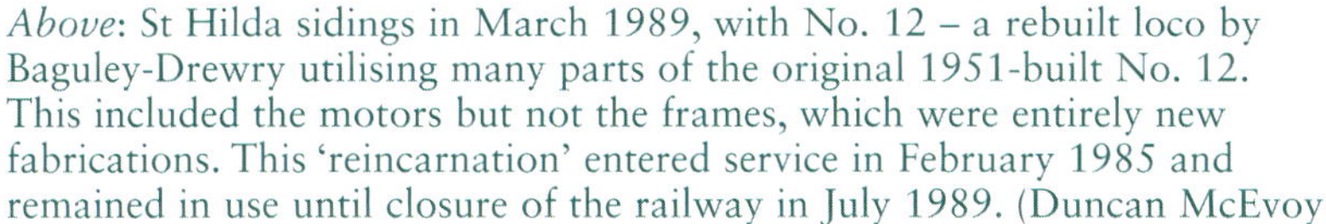

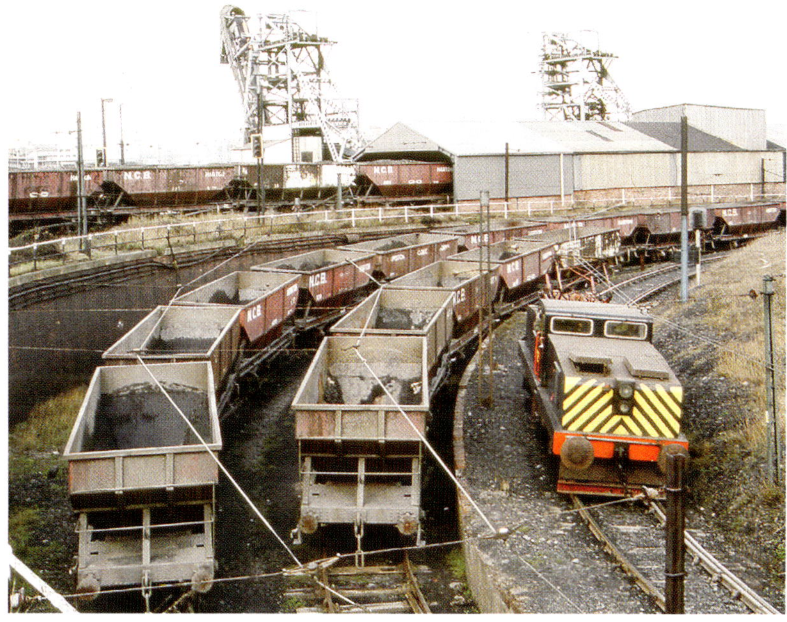

Above: St Hilda sidings in March 1989, with No. 12 – a rebuilt loco by Baguley-Drewry utilising many parts of the original 1951-built No. 12. This included the motors but not the frames, which were entirely new fabrications. This 'reincarnation' entered service in February 1985 and remained in use until closure of the railway in July 1989. (Duncan McEvoy)

Above right: Andrew Barclay 0-6-0 diesel-hydraulic No. 67 (W/No. 549 of 1967) and vintage AEG, Berlin-built Bo-Bo electric No. 9 (W/No. 1565 of 1913) in the concentration sidings at Westoe colliery in summer 1982. Despite its squat appearance, No. 9 was the most powerful loco to work on the system and hailed from a fleet that originally comprised some fifteen electric locos of nine varied types. Its squat design and power output were essential for negotiating the line to Low Staiths, via the 1 in 28 gradient, through a confined tunnel and riverside spirals. (Colin Alexander)

Right: In March 1989, No. 12 stands at Harton Low Staiths alongside internal-user empties destined for St Hilda sidings. Visible behind is the teeming shed, where incoming coal was acccpted prior to its transfer to ships by the conveyors on the dockside beyond. (Duncan McEvoy)

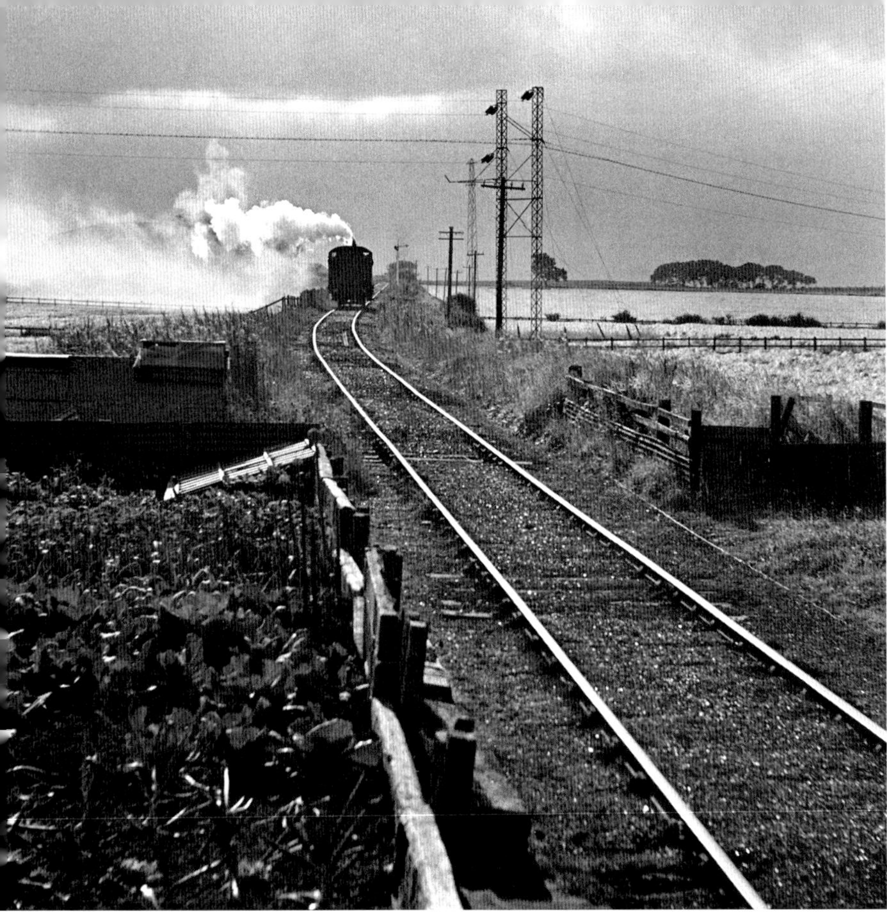

4

NORTHUMBERLAND

COAL

Left: Robert Stephenson & Hawthorns 0-6-0 saddle tank No. 35 *Clive* (W/No. 7299 of 1946) runs light engine between Burradon and Holywell in August 1969, approaching a level crossing keeper's well-tended and productive allotment. The NCB Burradon and Backworth railway systems were connected by this link line via Fisher Lane crossing, which opened in 1951, enabling through running between Weetslade, Hazlerigg, Burradon, Holywell (on the Blyth & Tyne line) and Backworth. Burradon colliery had ceased winding in November 1975, coinciding with the end of steam traction on the Backworth system, and this line was eventually taken out of use in November 1977. (Jon Marsh)

Above right: Rising Sun colliery, Wallsend, in April 1968, during the mine's last full year of production, with Robert Stephenson & Hawthorns 0-4-0 saddle tank No. 41 (W/No. 7674 of 1951) setting back onto a loaded rake of BR 21-ton hopper wagons. The colliery was served by a 1¼-mile-long connection with the BR Blyth & Tyne line, just north of Percy Main, and was closed on 24 April 1969. The Newcastle-built loco was supplied new to Rising Sun and spent its entire career there until its closure. Moved to Burradon shed around June 1969, where it saw little use, it was scrapped during the following August. (Jon Marsh)

Below right: On a wet 1960s day, Robert Stephenson & Hawthorns 0-6-0 saddle tank No. 60 (W/No. 7812 of 1954) stands beneath the fine signal gantry at Percy Main on the Backworth Railway. By this time the complex network of railway lines along the Blyth & Tyne railway corridor, which had seen much coal traffic for over two centuries from the outlying collieries via the Backworth, Cramlington and Seaton Burn Railway systems, was witnessing its swan song, with the inevitable NCB rationalisation following numerous colliery closures. As volumes further declined, the last staiths at Percy Main were taken out of use in 1971, leading to the closure of the NCB line from Backworth – although the BR line continued in use until 1983, after which time it was dismantled, ending over 200 years of railway use on the Blyth & Tyne corridor. Sections of the Seaton Burn Waggonway and Backworth Railway alignments saw track relaying in 1975, heralding its use by the Tyne & Wear Metro test centre. Test trains for the planned Tyne & Wear Metro system operated until 1979 from facilities at Middle Engine Lane at West Chirton. The Stephenson Railway Museum, managed by Tyne & Wear Museums, now occupies these buildings and occasional heritage services are operated over the 1¾-mile line to Percy Main village. On what is now called the North Tyneside Steam Railway, this runs along the original 1822 alignment of the former Cramlington Colliery Railway, which served the staiths on the River Tyne. The principal exhibit at the Stephenson Railway Museum is *Billy*, built in Newcastle around 1816 by Robert Stephenson & Company, one of the last of George Stephenson's designs of so-called 'Killingworth Travelling Engines' to be built. In use for over fifty years, it was the forerunner of many of the Robert Stephenson & Co. Ltd (and their successors') products supplied from the Forth Bank works in Newcastle for industrial railway use locally, countrywide and overseas. (Author's collection)

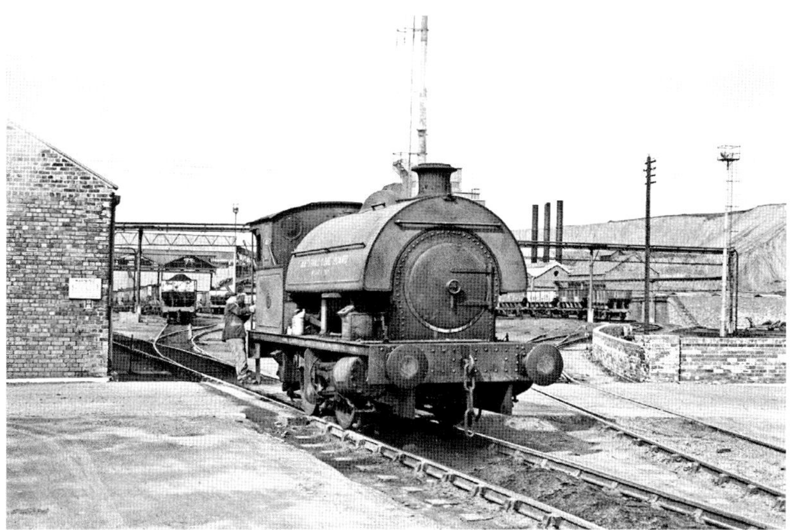

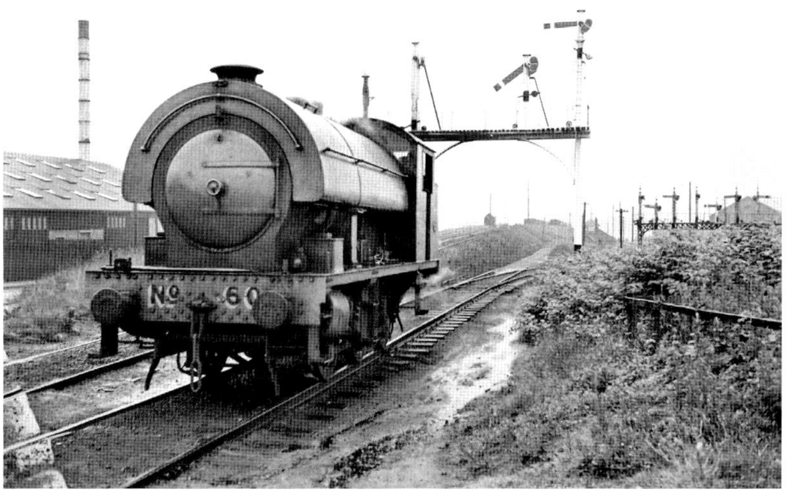

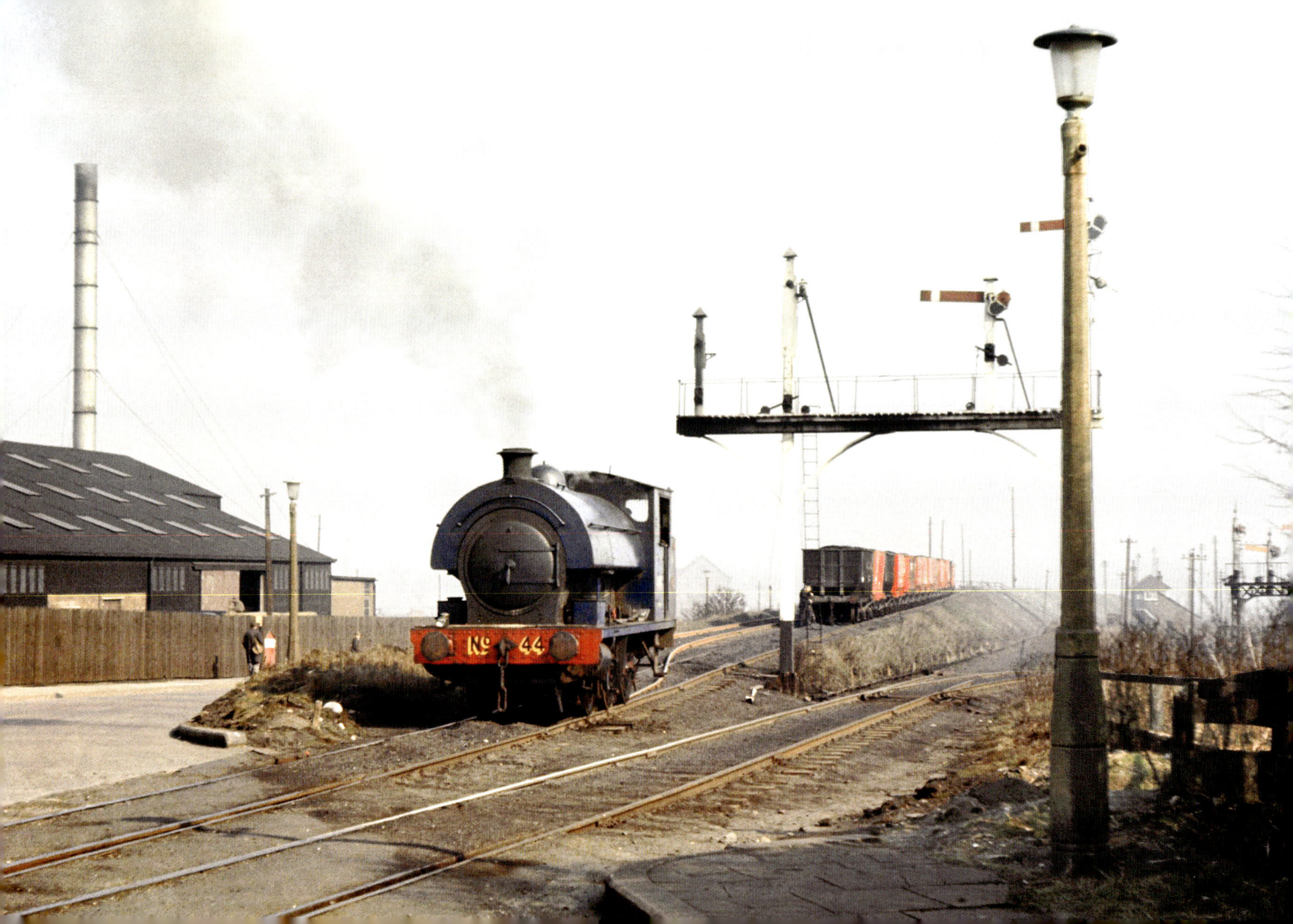

Nº 44

Opposite page: The same signal gantry featured on the previous page, at the Howdon Road crossing at the Tyne Improvement Commission's Quay at Percy Main, but on a somewhat brighter day in the late 1960s. Backworth shed's Robert Stephenson & Hawthorns 17 x 24-inch cylinder 0-6-0 saddle tank No. 44 (W/No. 7760 of 1963) is setting back onto a loaded train to propel on to the staiths at Whitehill Point. The line falling away to the right descended to the Tyne Improvement Commission's Railway. (Jon Marsh)

Above right: On 1 September 1971, BR English Electric Type 3 No. 6792, complete with shunter's pole and shunter, has arrived from Earsdon Junction for a load of 21 and 24-ton coal hoppers for tripping to Blyth power station. The Backworth system's Fenwick colliery branch leads away to the left of the picture and the BR Earsdon signal box can be seen between the two locos. This controlled the flat crossing of the NCB East Holywell branch between Backworth and Fenwick colliery, which crossed the BR Blyth & Tyne line. Robert Stephenson & Hawthorns 0-6-0 tank No. 29 (W/No. 7607 of 1950) and its crew take a break from shunting the stocking site sidings, this and the waste train workings to Seghill tip being its duties for the day. No. 29 was unceremoniously consigned for scrap at Backworth in September 1972. As for the BR Type 3 No. 6792, later Class 37/0 No. 37092, it survived until May 1996, when it was withdrawn from Toton Traction Maintenance Depot. It was not disposed of until October 2001, by T. J. Thomson at Stockton (*see page 120*). (Author)

Below right: In September 1969, William Bagnall Austerity 0-6-0 saddle tank No. 6 (W/No. 2749 of 1944) is positioning empty internal-user wooden-bodied hopper wagons at Fenwick colliery. This colliery was closed on 31 August 1973 and the railway east of Earsdon Junction, as portrayed in the above photo, was lifted. Following Fenwick colliery's closure, a new east to west spur was installed, thus ending the practice of frequent shunting moves back and forth across the increasingly busy B1322 road at Bankfoot cabin, and along the stub of the truncated line that formerly served the staiths at Whitehill Point at Percy Main until 1969, as depicted on the opposite page. (Author's collection)

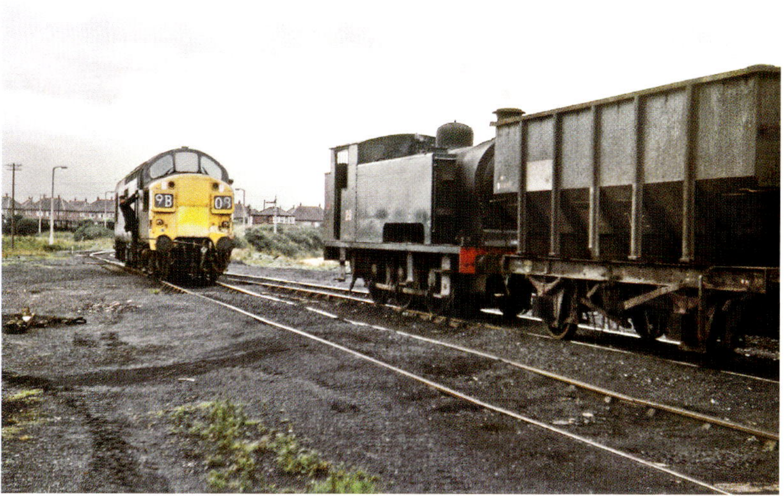

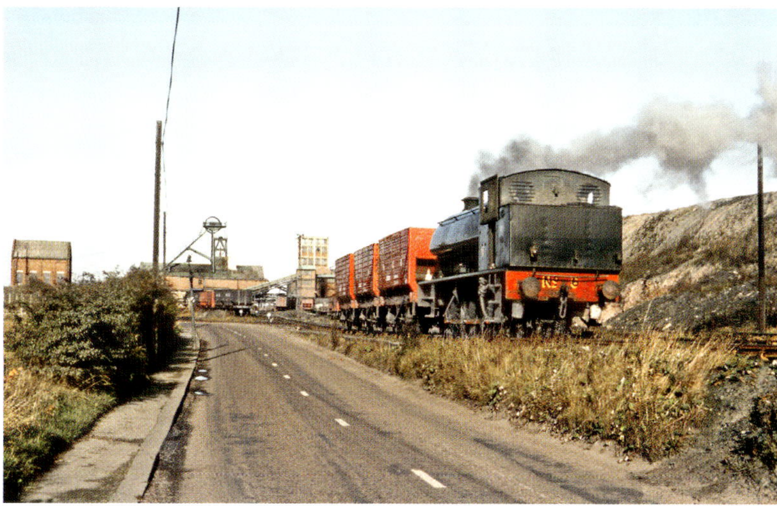

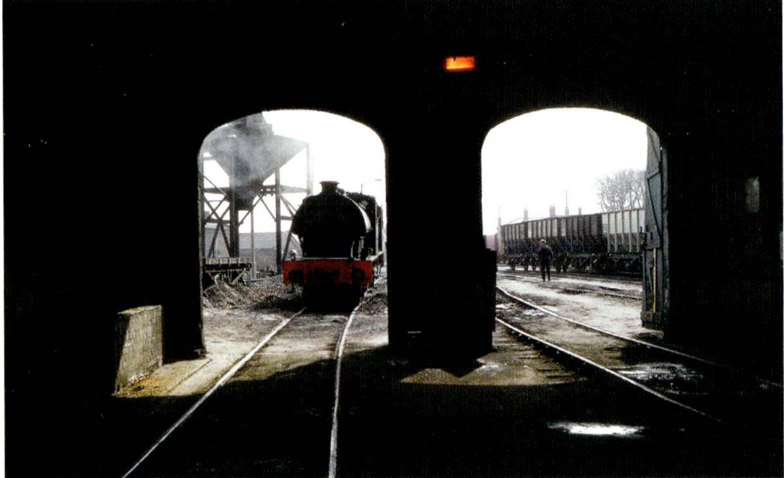

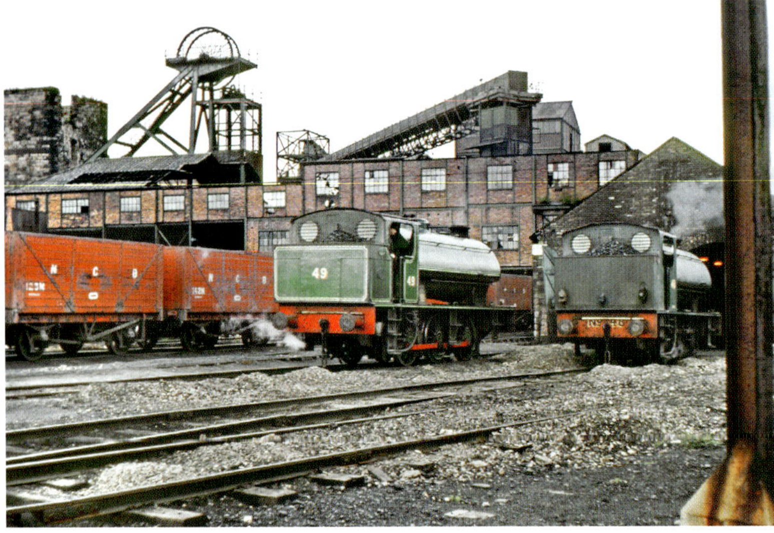

Above left: The impressive and very well-appointed brick-constructed Backworth loco shed on 23 March 1973, with Hunslet Austerity No. 48 (W/No. 2864 of 1943) in steam standing outside the double-arched two-road entrance. Visible alongside the Austerity is the conveyor-fed coal hopper used for quickly and effectively replenishing the locos' bunkers at this principal shed of the once extensive Backworth Railway. (John Sloane)

Below left: The Backworth system's loco shed was situated alongside Eccles colliery. On 25 June 1971, Robert Stephenson & Hawthorns Austerity 0-6-0 saddle tank No. 49 (W/No. 7098 of 1943) and Hunslet Austerity No. 48 are in residence. By this time the shed's commitment was to provide four locos in steam daily, this being reduced to just two towards the end of steam traction on the remnants of the once extensive system. Backworth had been one of the two last outposts of steam traction in the North East, but in January 1976 diesels were introduced and the steam locos were put into store to await scrapping or preservation. In 1977, traffic to Weetslade coal preparation plant ended and the line to Burradon was subsequently lifted. The line to Seghill disposal point was also abandoned at this time and stone tipping then took place in a field at the start of the line to Burradon, the track being slewed to enable this to commence. The end was now in sight and Eccles colliery, the last of the highly productive former Backworth Coal Company's pits to be worked, closed in May 1980, with all rail traffic ceasing on 17 July 1980. This brought not only an end to the Backworth Railway, but also to deep mining in the Backworth area, after an unbroken history of more than 167 years. (Author's collection)

Opposite page: In its usual smartly presented condition during the latter years of its NCB service, Robert Stephenson & Hawthorns Austerity 0-6-0 saddle tank No. 49 is positioning BR 21-ton hoppers onto the weighbridge at Eccles colliery on 1 September 1971. Following its withdrawal from service at Backworth shed at the end of 1975, the celebrity NCB North East Area Austerity was to be found a home in preservation on the Tanfield Railway at Marley Hill in County Durham. (Author)

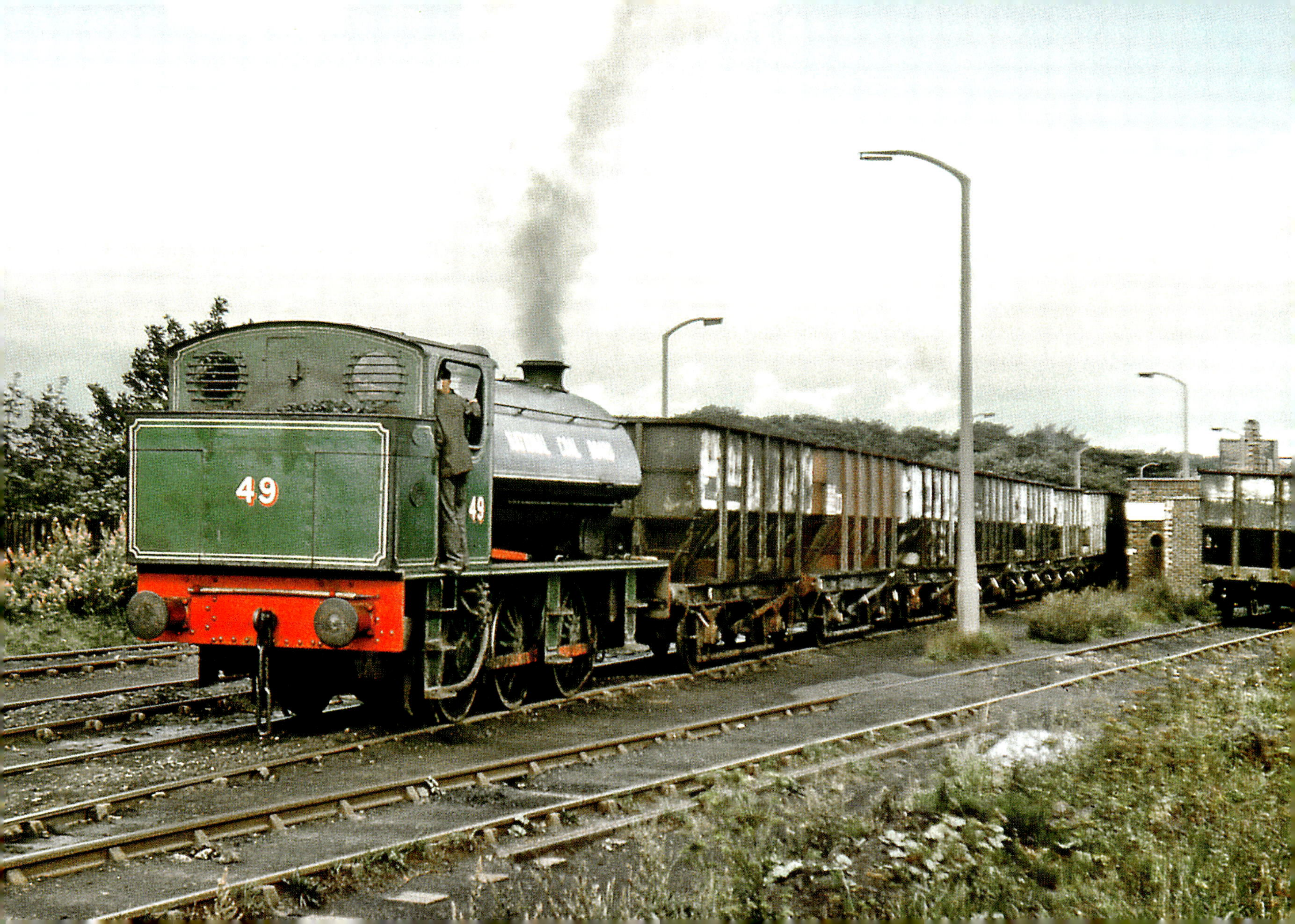

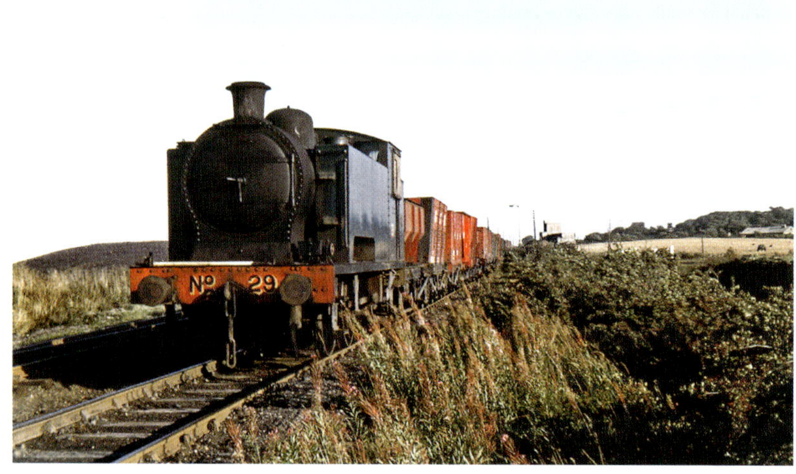

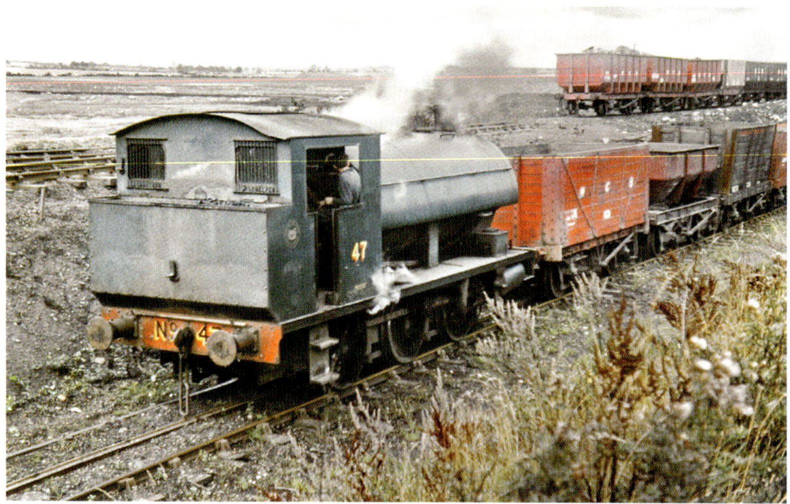

Above left: During the early evening of 1 September 1971, Robert Stephenson & Hawthorns Newcastle-built 0-6-0 tank No. 29 is seen close to the Seghill disposal point at the head of a mixed rake of internal-user NCB wagons containing colliery shale and stone for tipping. This chunky and powerful 18 x 26-inch cylinder workhorse, by this time the regular Backworth loco employed on this duty, was one of five side tanks originally supplied new to the NCB for use on the extensive Ashington system, which included working the miners' passenger services. It was transferred from Ashington to Backworth shed in June 1969, where it saw three further years of use. (Author)

Below left: On 1 September 1971, Newcastle-built Robert Stephenson & Hawthorns 0-6-0 saddle tank No. 47 (W/No. 7849 of 1955) is waiting for its spoil wagons to be discharged at the Seghill disposal point. This tip was on the site of the Backworth 'C' pit, which had closed as long ago as 1895, and for the stone waste trains to gain access to the tipping lines at Seghill they had to cross over the Holywell to Burradon branch line at Fisher Lane crossing. No. 47 was originally supplied new to the Backworth Colliery Railway as an oil-burner, one of very few NCB locos so fitted. After an extended return visit to the builder's Forth Bank works in Newcastle between 1956 and 1957, No. 47 returned as a conventional coal-burner. It was to spend almost its entire NCB working career on the Backworth Railway until its move to Whittle colliery in December 1971 for its final years of NCB service. It was eventually acquired for preservation in September 1973, today being found on the Embsay & Bolton Abbey Steam Railway. (Author)

Above right: Gradually taking over from the steam workings, several former BR 650 hp Class 14 0-6-0 diesel-hydraulics found further employment on the Backworth and Burradon railway system. On 1 September 1971, D9555, still in its original BR two-tone green livery, is seen at Burradon village, 2 miles west of Backworth, working a lightly loaded train of BR 21-ton coal hopper wagons from the Weetslade coal preparation plant. D9555 was taken into BR traffic from Swindon works in October 1965 but was withdrawn from BR service as early as May 1969 and sold on from Landore TMD in March 1970. Acquired by the NCB for further use at Burradon, it was allocated the fleet running number 9107/57. D9555 was the last of its class and holds the distinction of being the last of the Western Region diesel-hydraulic locos built between 1958 and 1965, of which there were a total of 365. It is also the very last loco built by the famous Swindon works for BR service. Worthy of preservation, it was initially found a home at the Rutland Railway Museum, when sold by the NCB in 1987, but it is now to be found operating in the area where some of the class worked during their exceptionally short days in BR traffic, at the Dean Forest Railway. (Author)

Below right: Shortly after D9555 had passed along the Burradon system from Weetslade Central Coal Preparation Plant on 1 September 1971, work-stained Robert Stephenson & Hawthorns 0-6-0 saddle tank No. 43 (W/No. 7758 of 1953) was found shunting a splendid collection of assorted NCB internal-user wagons at the plant, located near Wideopen. The A189 Newcastle to Bedlington road is visible to the right. This washery facility and the large co-located coal concentration depot, which supplied most of Tyneside with household coal, had been developed in the 1960s, replacing numerous smaller landsale depots in the region. The associated BR interchange sidings were located alongside the Newcastle–Edinburgh main line, north of the former Killingworth station and around half a mile east of the Weetslade complex. NCB traffic was handled by locos from Burradon shed until its closure in January 1976, when a new shed was provided at the plant itself. Backworth locos also worked to Weetslade until July 1977 and shale and stone for disposal from Weetslade was worked to Seghill until November 1977, when the line east of Weetslade was completely closed. Rail traffic to the extensive coal depot ceased in the summer of 1979, with the whole system closing during March 1981. (Author)

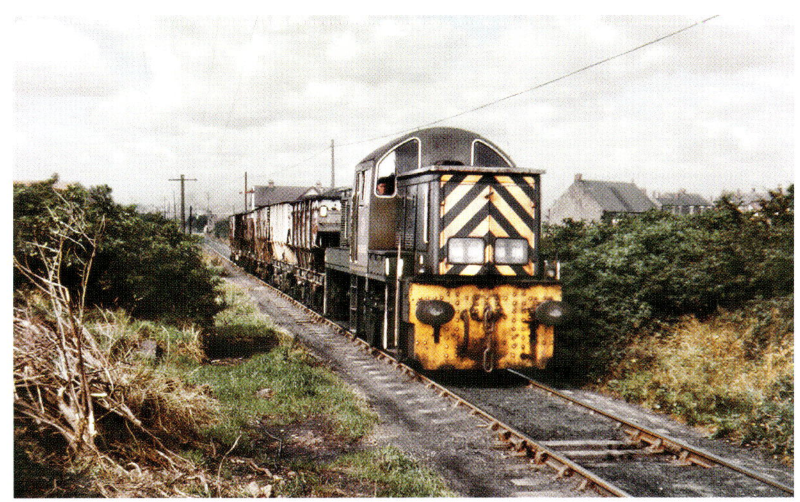

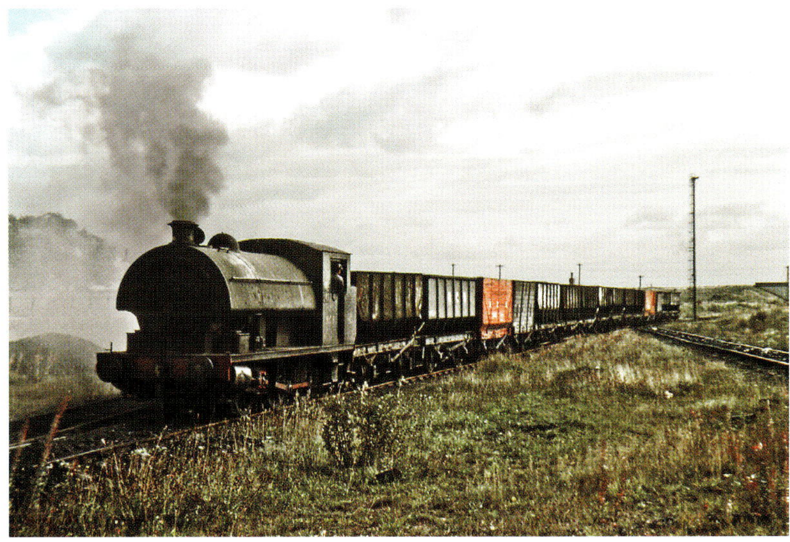

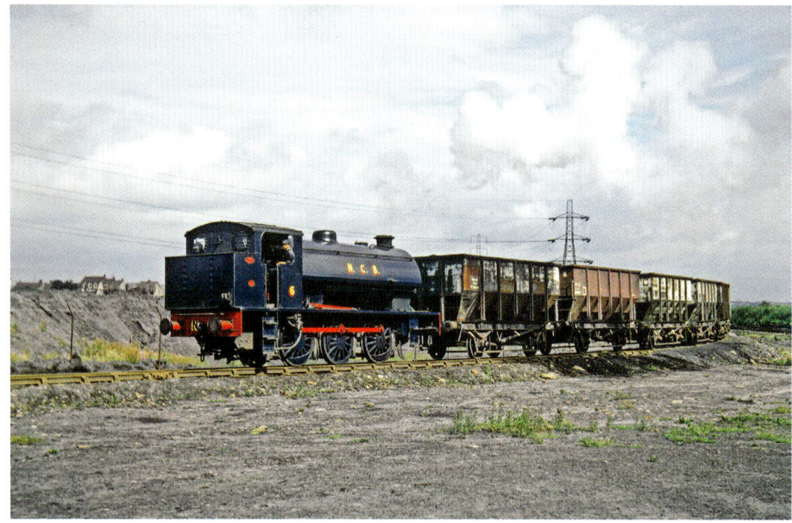

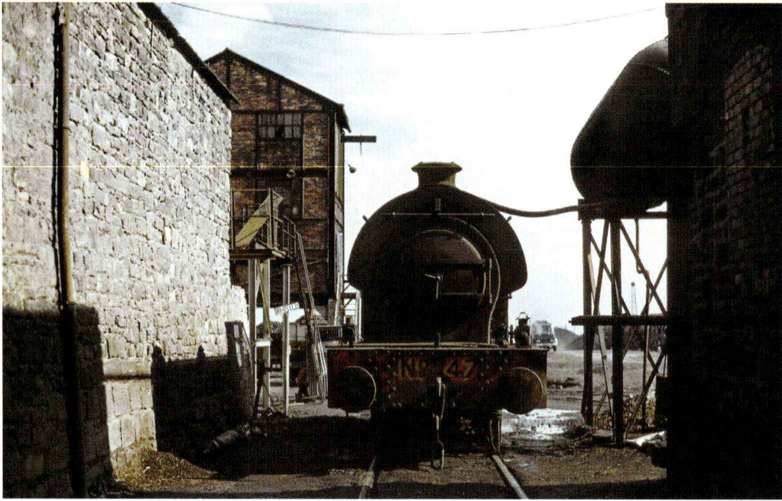

Above left: A final look at the Backworth system; between the Eccles colliery stockpile sidings and the Fenwick colliery line was a curve to the north to one of two sets of exchange sidings with the BR Blyth & Tyne line. These were known as the New Sidings, having been commissioned in the late 1960s, and they were controlled by the BR Holywell signal box, which also granted access to the Burradon colliery branch. On 10 July 1973, William Bagnall Austerity 0-6-0 saddle tank No. 6 (W/No. 2749 of 1944) swings away from the New Sidings with a rake of empty wagons for refilling at Eccles colliery. The Blyth & Tyne line is just visible on the right of the picture. Although Backworth locos had always been kept reasonably clean, by the time of this visit they were immaculately presented, all seeming to have been recently repainted, and to a very high standard too, despite being in their final years of commercial industrial service. Indeed, they were a great credit to the Backworth Railway staff concerned. There is little wonder that many of Backworth's locos found homes in preservation, this example now being found on the Caledonian Railway, at Brechin in Angus. (Richard Stevens)

Below left: The compact site of Netherton colliery, also known as Howard Pit, some 3 miles south of Morpeth, near Bedlington, was served by a 1-mile branch from the BR Bedlington–Morpeth line, a quarter of a mile north-west of Choppington station. Hunslet Austerity 0-6-0 saddle tank No. 47 (W/No. 3166 of 1944) takes a break from its shunting duties while being replenished with water from the torpedo water tank by the colliery shed on 23 March 1973. After closure, the Austerity succumbed to the scrap man in September 1974. (John Sloane)

Opposite page: Earlier on the same day, Hunslet Austerity 0-6-0 saddle tank No. 47 was found shunting the screens at Netherton colliery. (John Sloane)

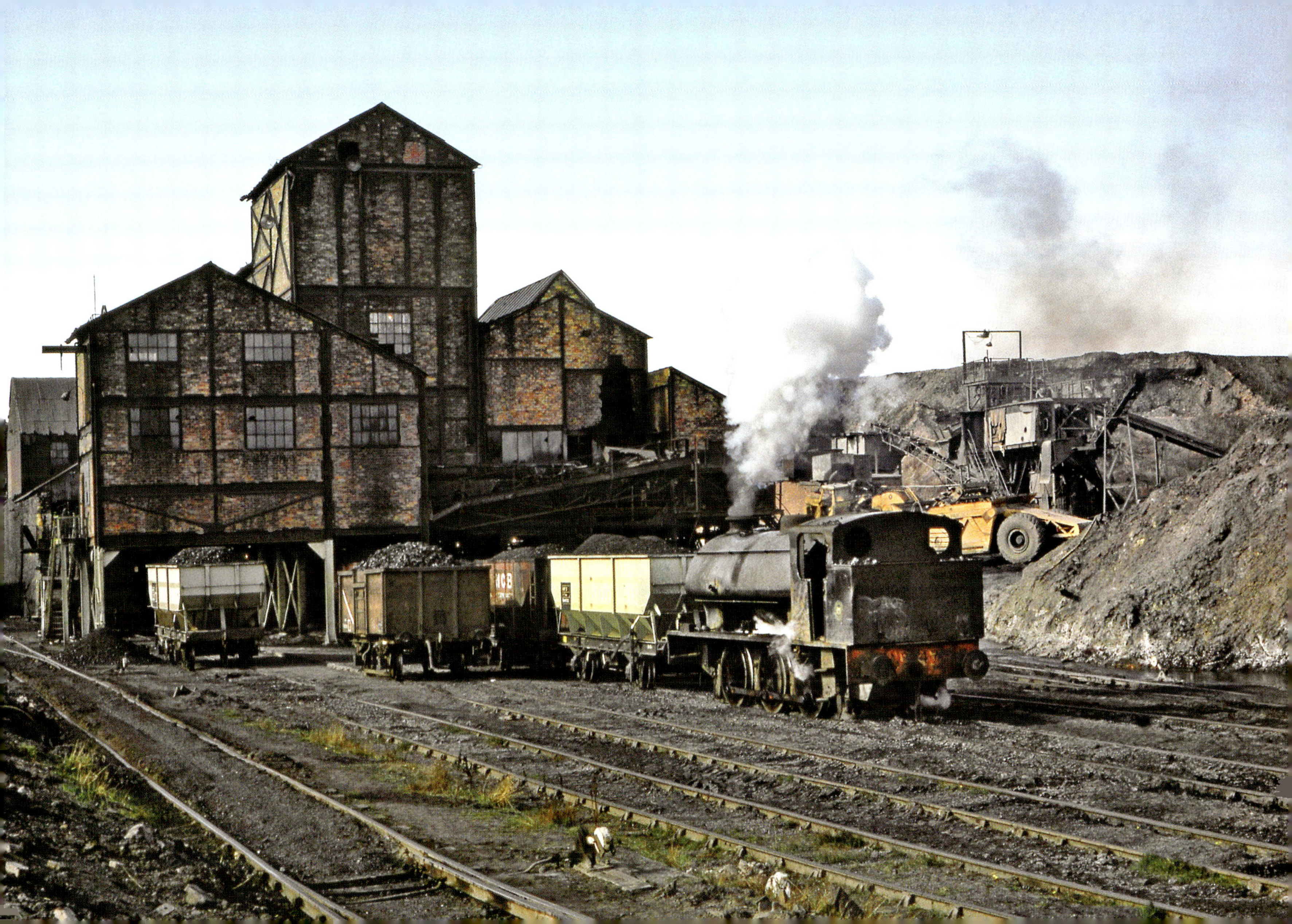

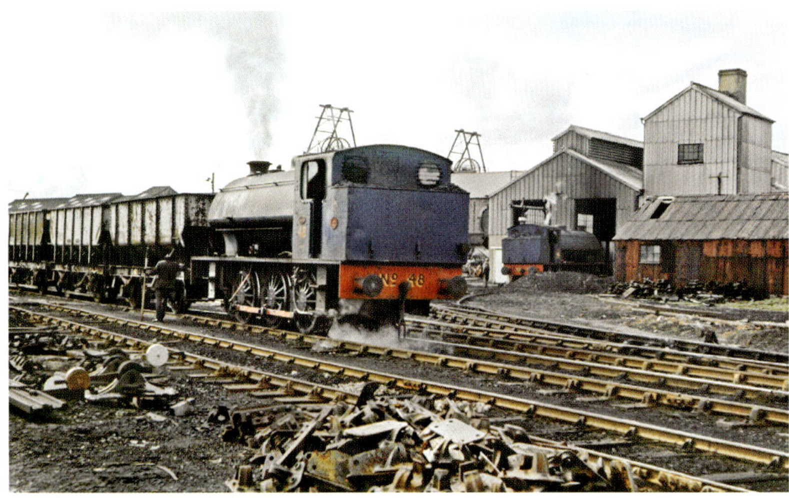

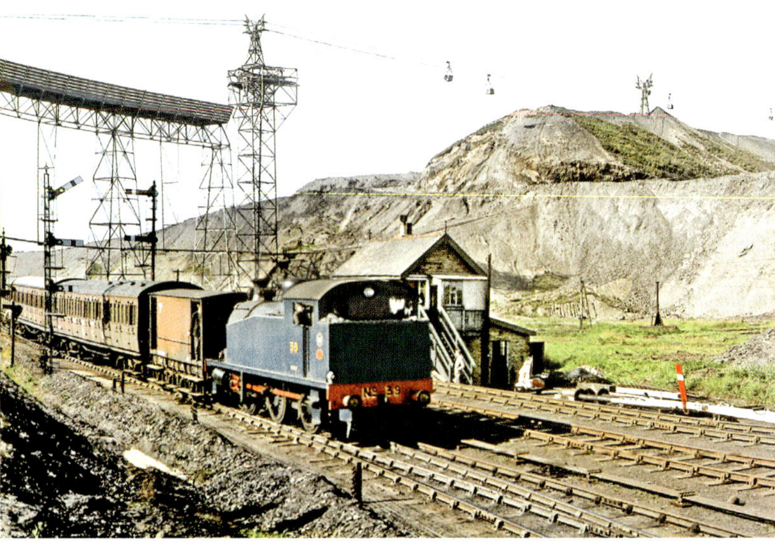

Above left: Ashington in April 1968, with Hunslet Austerity No. 48 (W/No. 3172 of 1944) coupling up to BR 21-ton hopper wagons, while simmering on shed to the right is sister Hunslet Austerity No. 46 (W/No. 2878 of 1943). (Jon Marsh)

Below left: On 10 June 1967, Newcastle-built Robert Stephenson & Hawthorns 0-6-0 tank No. 39 (W/No. 7764 of 1954) heads the 'S.L.S./M.L.S. Ashington Railtour' special charter train using former miners' 'Paddy Train' coaches, seen at Ashington No. 1 Loop signal box, near Hirst Platforms station, between Linton and Ashington. Former main line coaches of North Eastern Railway and Furness Railway origin were purchased by the NCB and its predecessors and were used for their services operating between Ashington, Linton and Ellington collieries. This double-track section comprised a circular route of around 20 miles with several branches running off, and served Woodhorn, Newbiggin, Lynemouth and Linton collieries, as well as Longhirst drift mine. The fully signalled route was not entirely completed until as late as August 1956, when a new link line was opened between Woodhorn and Lynemouth, thus completing the circuit, with halts at Ashington, Ellington, Linton and North Moor. The passenger service had ceased running on 16 May 1966. Part of this section, retained by Network Rail, is now used by main line freight services to and from Lynemouth power station and until recently the Alcan aluminium smelter, before its closure. The Ashington Group Railway, as it was known, required Board of Trade inspection and a signalling system, using both lower and upper quadrant signal types. The 18 x 24-inch outside cylinder tank locos, Nos 39 and 40 (*featured on page 86*), were built especially for hauling the system's workmen's services, although in practice these locos were not used exclusively on the 'Paddy Trains'. Some locos, including those used on the passenger services, were fitted with steam-powered generators and directional lights front and rear, to enable working around the clock. (Author's collection)

Opposite page: Between working the miners' 'Paddy Train' services, Newcastle-built Robert Stephenson & Hawthorns 0-6-0 saddle tank No. 38 (W/No. 7763 of 1954), also fitted with headlamps, stands on the chord leading to Ashington colliery, adjacent to the Hirst Platforms station. The passenger coaches are just visible at one of the station's bleak platforms, which were located on the northern fringe of Ashington town. The long cable run to the immense spoil tip is a noteworthy feature. (Colour Rail)

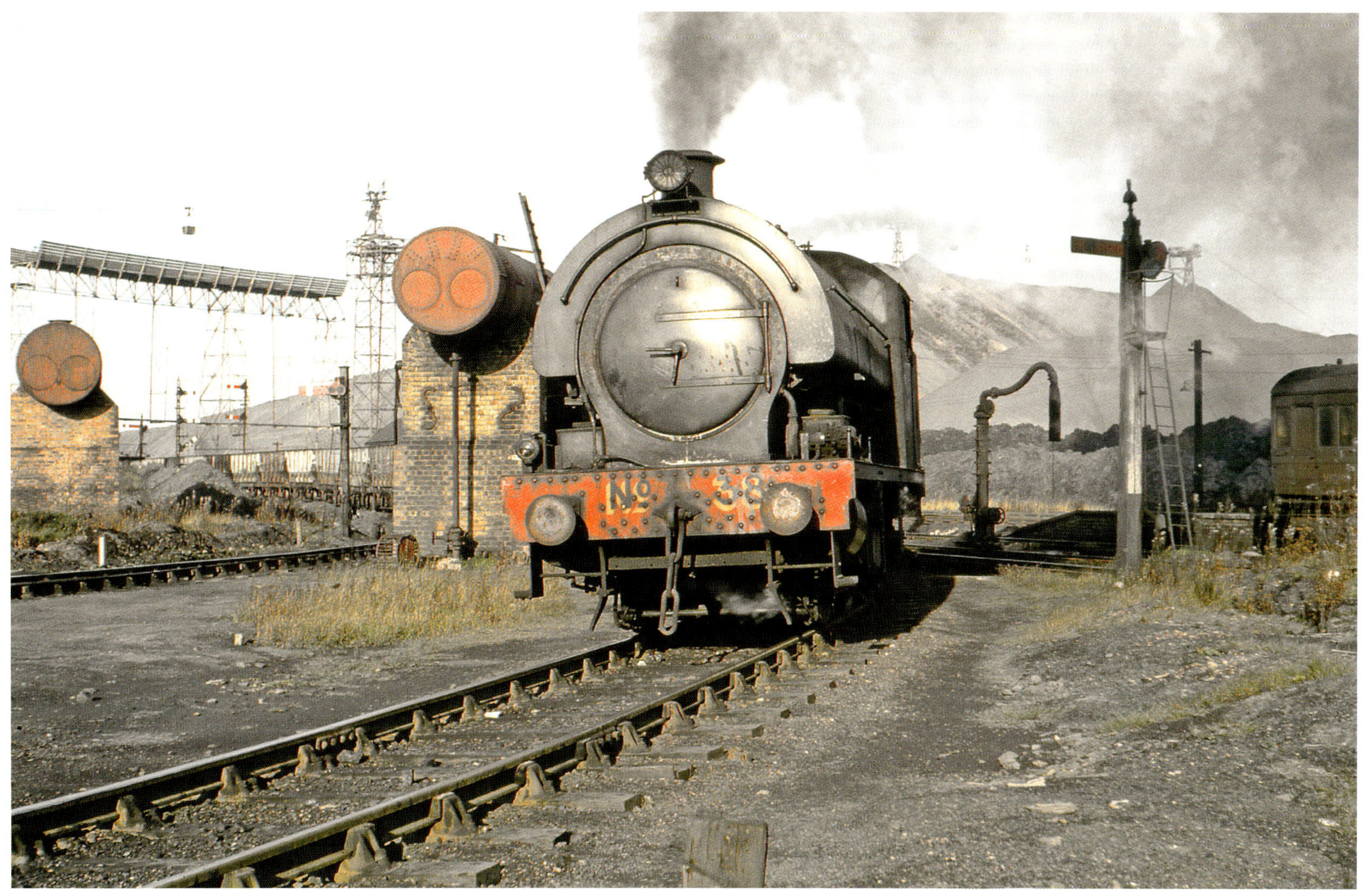

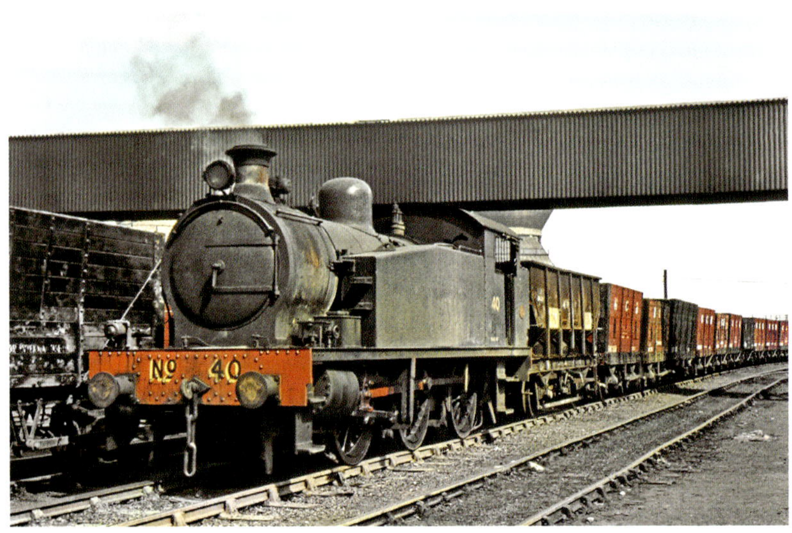

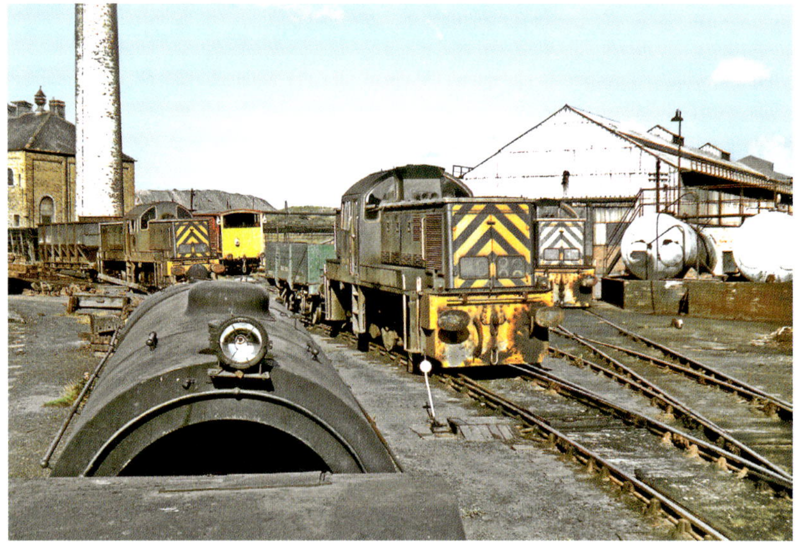

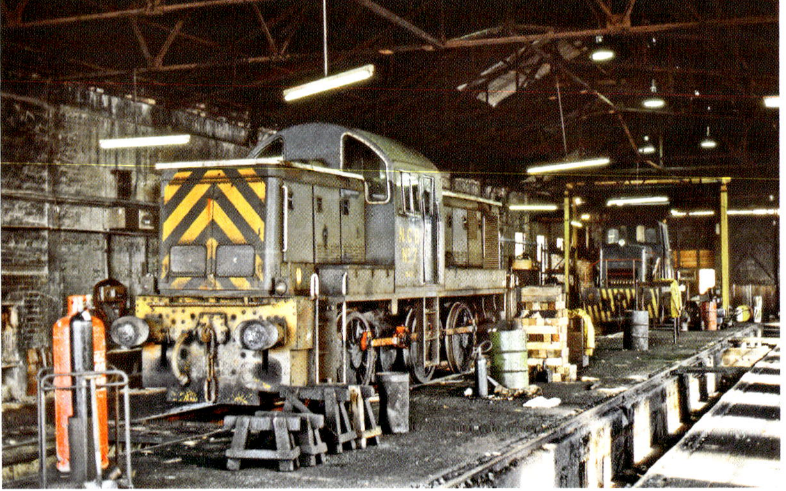

Above left: Newcastle-built Robert Stephenson & Hawthorns 0-6-0 tank No. 40 (W/No. 7765 of 1954) is seen at rest between duties at Ashington colliery in the late 1960s. (Author's collection)

Above right: The transitional period from steam to diesel traction on the Ashington system, at the loco shed and general workshops on 1 September 1971, with (left to right) former BR Class 14s D9518, D9508 and D9536. In the foreground are the remains of a Robert Stephenson & Hawthorns saddle tank, some of the last remnants of the steam era at Ashington. (Author)

Below left: A glimpse inside the former steam running shed at British Coal Ashington on 25 March 1986. Despite the facility having been given over to diesel from steam traction some fifteen years earlier, the primitive conditions are evident, not unlike those found on BR following the demise of its steam traction. However, by this time the shed was in its eleventh hour, with Ashington colliery closing in 1988. Former BR Class 14 (previously BR D9518) NCB No. 7 and Andrew Barclay 311 hp 0-6-0 diesel-hydraulic No. 2120/211 (W/No. 514 of 1966) stand inside the former steam running shed. (Author)

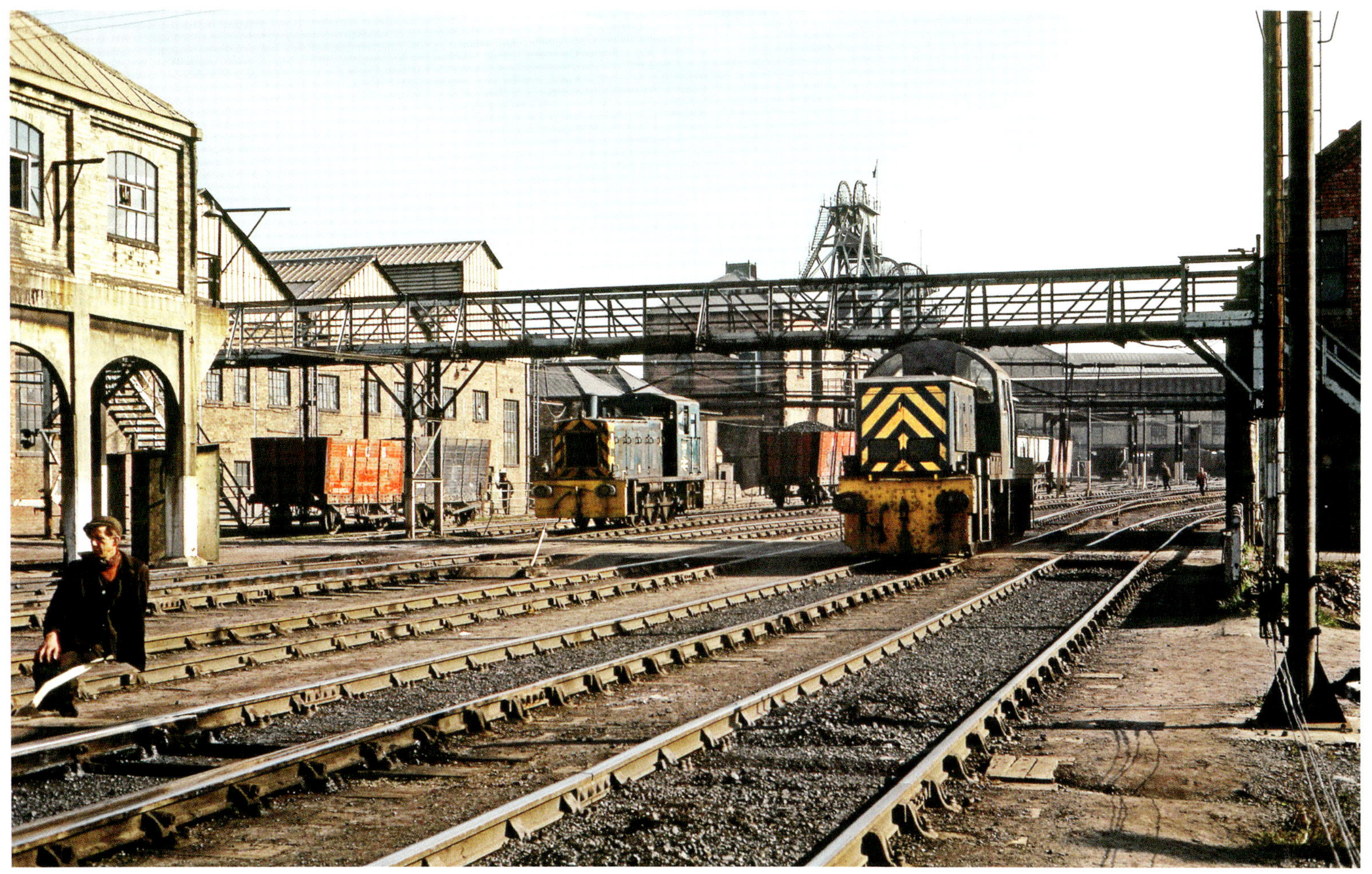

Ashington colliery on 23 March 1973, with Gateshead-allocated BR Class 03 No. 2110 (yet to bear the assigned TOPS number 03110) and No. 1 (ex-BR Class 14 D9528) busily engaged in shunting activities. (John Sloane)

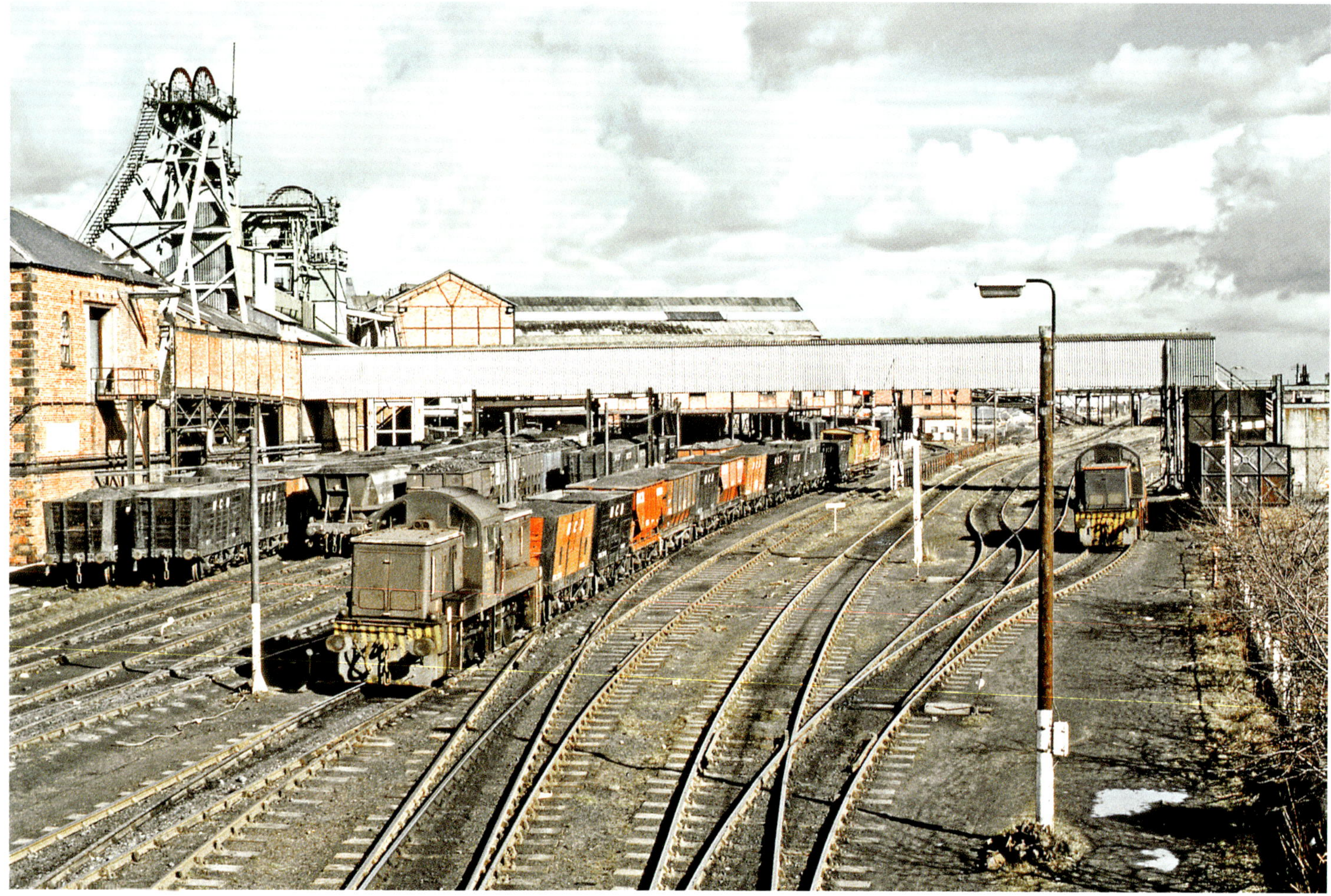

Former BR Class 14 D9500 passes sister loco D9521 at Ashington colliery while heading a short coal train from Lyncmouth Colliery on 25 March 1986. (Author)

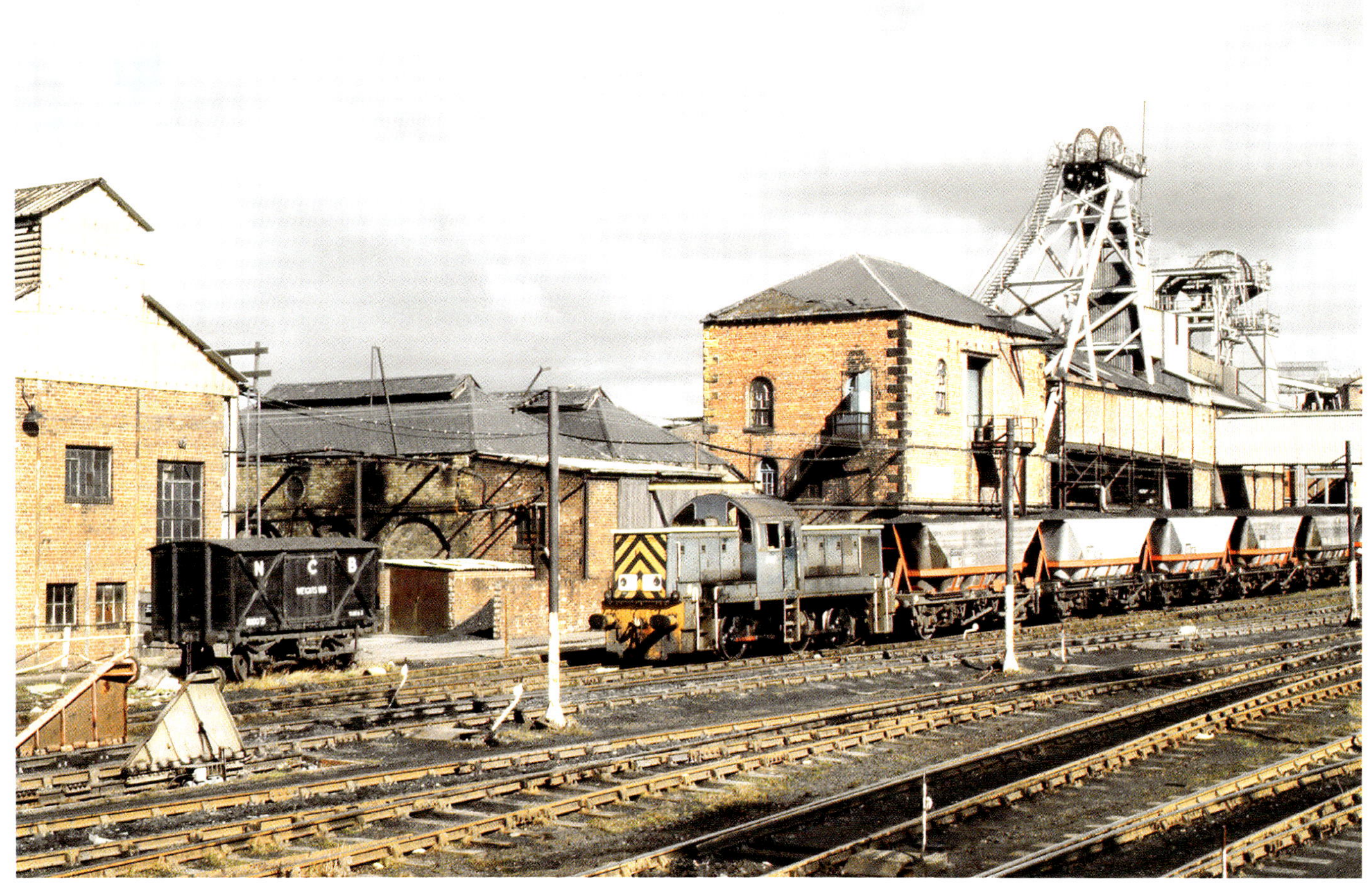

On 25 March 1986, No. 507 (ex-BR Class 14 D9525) heads loaded MGR wagons past the Ashington colliery headstocks and what looks like a former gunpowder van. Upon purchase by the NCB from BR Hull Dairycoates depot in November 1968, D9525 was initially deployed to the Philadelphia system. Unlike its time with BR, it experienced a somewhat peripatetic existence with the NCB, spending time at Burradon, Backworth, Weetslade Coal Preparation Plant and Ashington. (Author)

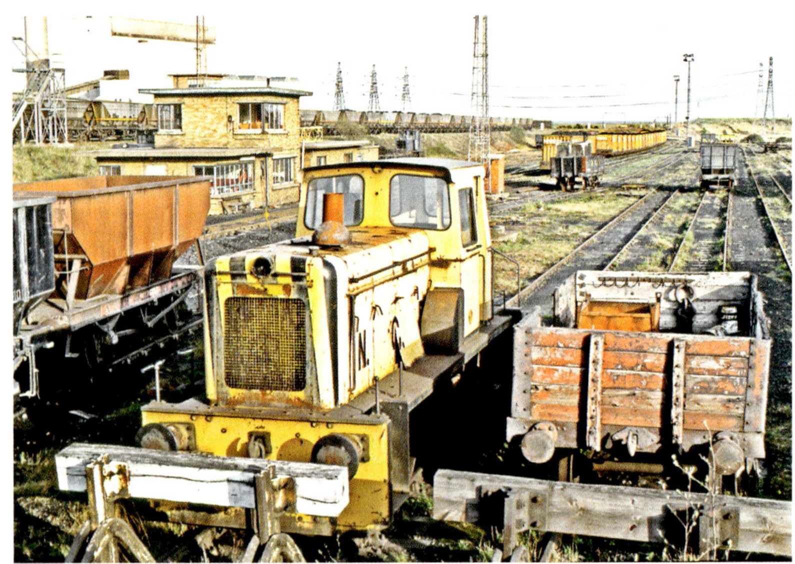

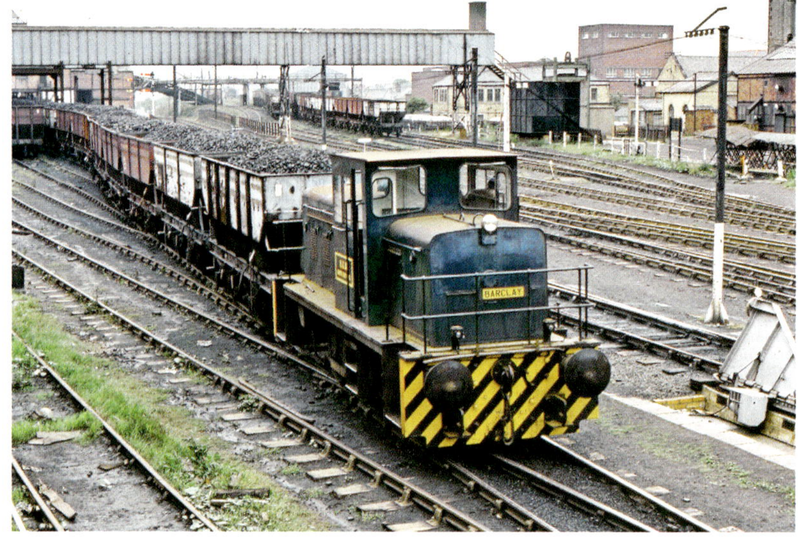

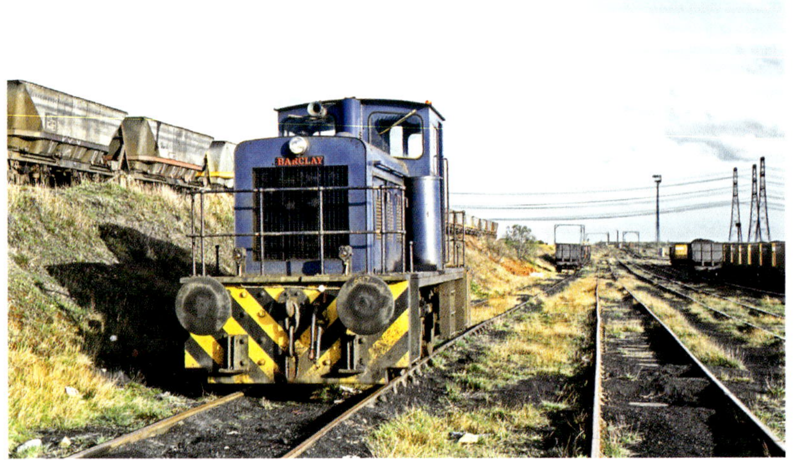

Above left: Andrew Barclay 0-6-0 diesel-hydraulic No. 2304/59 (W/No. 488 of 1964) was to see no further commercial industrial work, set aside at British Coal's Ellington Coal Preparation Plant, Lynemouth, on 24 April 1992. The varied collection of wagons, both internal and main line-certified, is of interest; the loaded Cawood's containers were destined for Ellesmere Port and subsequent shipment to Ireland. (Author)

Above right: An unidentified Andrew Barclay 0-6-0 diesel-hydraulic loco shunting at Ashington colliery on 23 June 1978. (John Sloane)

Below left: Out of use at Lynemouth on 24 April 1992 was Andrew Barclay 0-6-0 diesel-hydraulic No. 2100/521 (W/No. 584 of 1973 – rebuilt by Andrew Barclay in 1987 as W/No. 6718 and in 1990 by Hunslet Barclay W/No. 6917). Its shunting days are over at 'Big E', as Ellington colliery was affectionately known. It was subsequently transferred to Gascoigne Wood colliery for further use. Sadly, under the watch of UK Coal, the almost century-old mine, the last deep mine in the north of England, was closed in 2005. (Author)

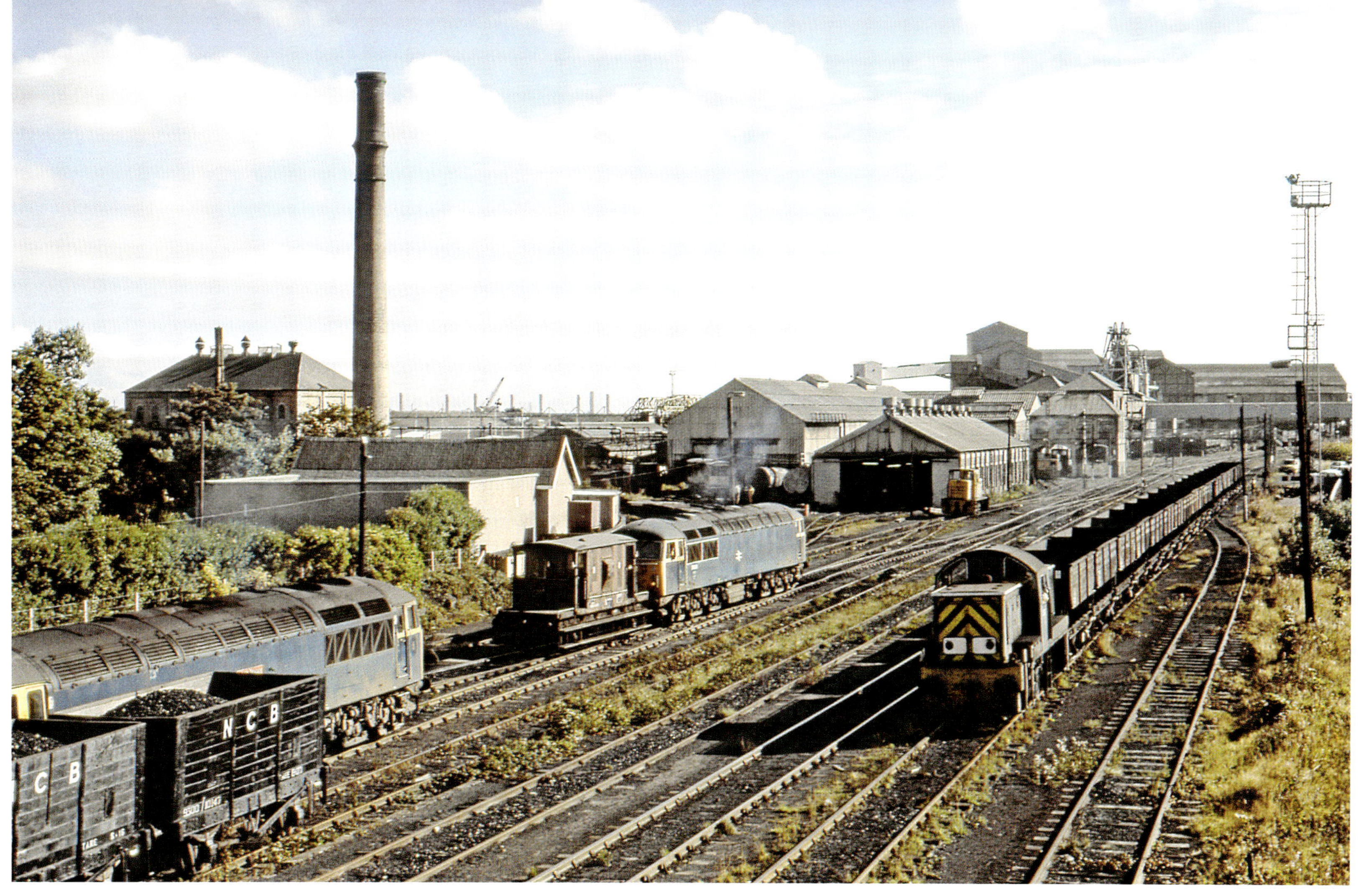

A busy scene at Ashington on 17 September 1986, with Class 14 0-6-0 diesel-hydraulic No. 507 moving a rake of BR 21-ton hopper wagons. BR Class 56 locos Nos 56081 and 56076 *Blyth Power* are active in the exchange sidings. (Roy Burt)

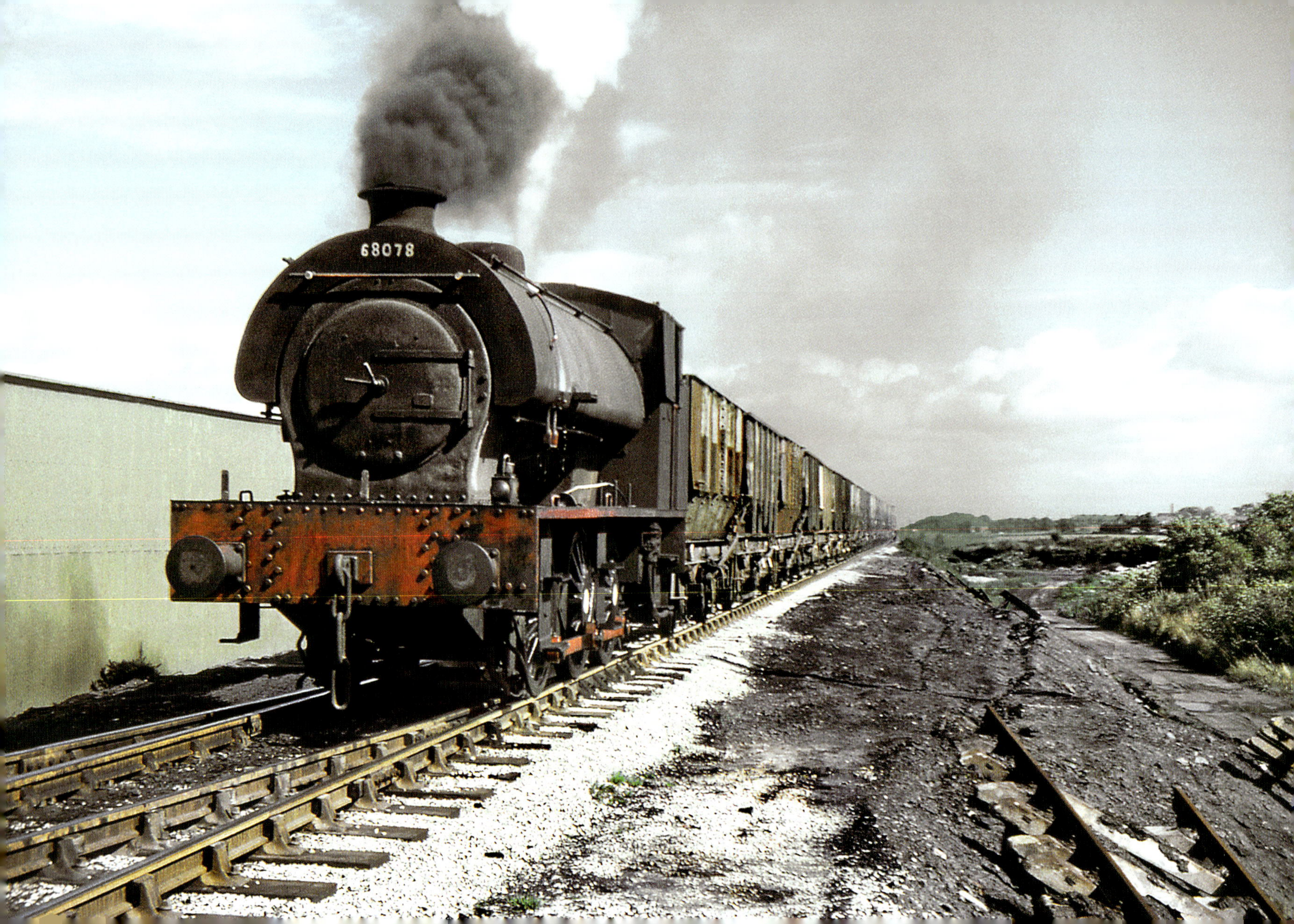
68078

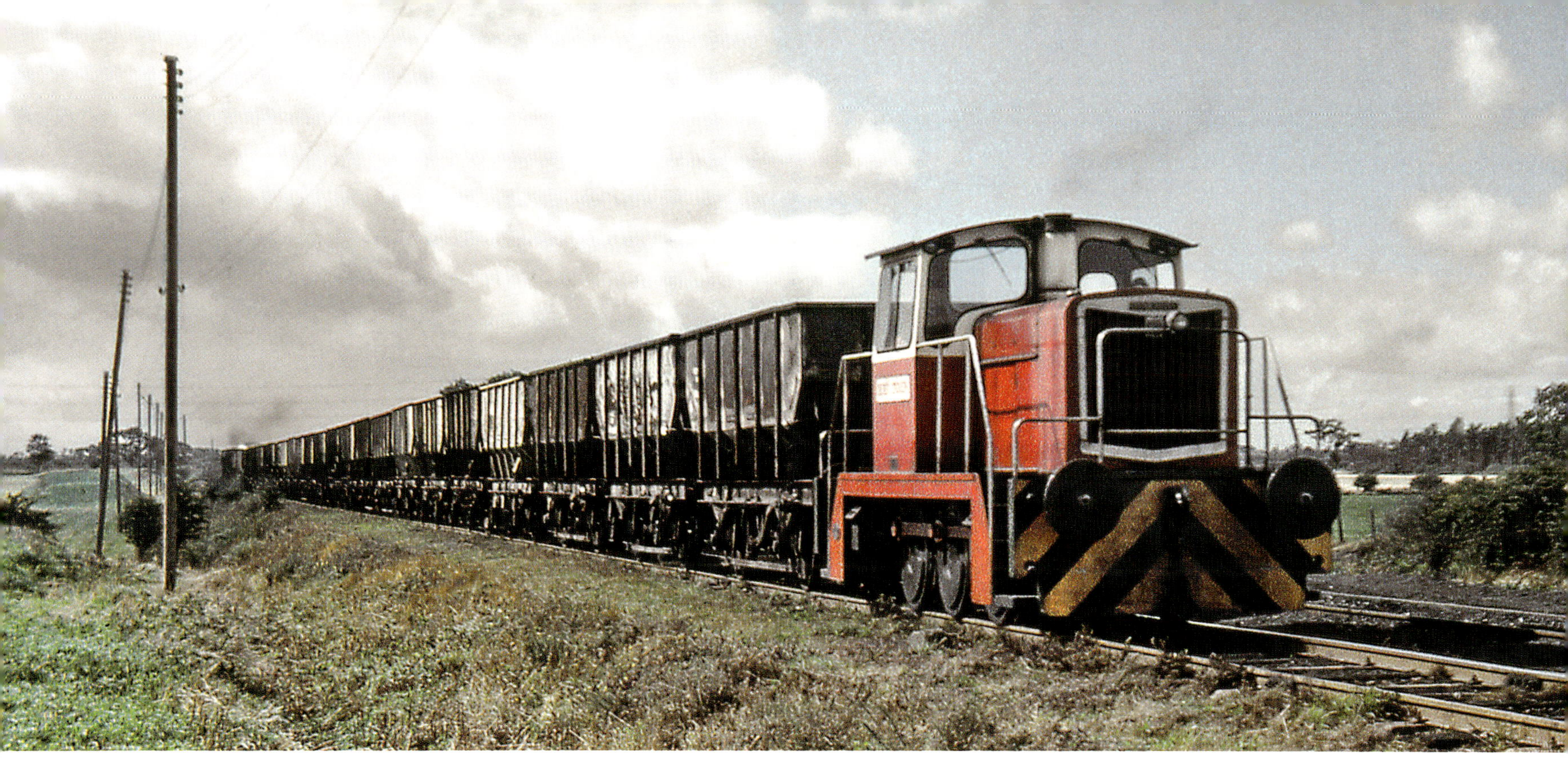

Opposite page: About 5 miles north of Ashington could be found the large opencast working at Widdrington, situated about 1 mile east of the East Coast Main Line, with which this coal loading point was connected. It was supplied by road vehicles before the coal was crushed, blended and loaded into rail wagons for onward despatch. On 1 September 1971, former BR Austerity J94 Class 0-6-0 saddle tank No. 68078 gets a heavy train underway, bound for the BR interchange sidings. Sub-contracted by Hunslet and built by Andrew Barclay in 1946 (as W/No. 2212), No. 68078 was one of only five Austerity saddle tanks built by Barclay, to the order of the Ministry of Supply, out of a total of 377 built. For many years it was allocated to BR's Immingham shed, but it was finally withdrawn from Langwith Junction in March 1963, and sold on to a new life with the NCB Opencast Executive, ultimately claiming the distinction of being the last steam loco in commercial industrial use in Northumberland. (Author)

Above: On 1 September 1971, English Electric Vulcan Works 0-6-0 diesel-hydraulic *Derek Crouch* (W/No. D1201 of 1967), the regular motive power by this time, heads a rake of empty BR 21-ton hopper wagons back to the Widdrington Disposal Point, with former BR Class J94 Austerity No. 68078 attached at the rear. (Author)

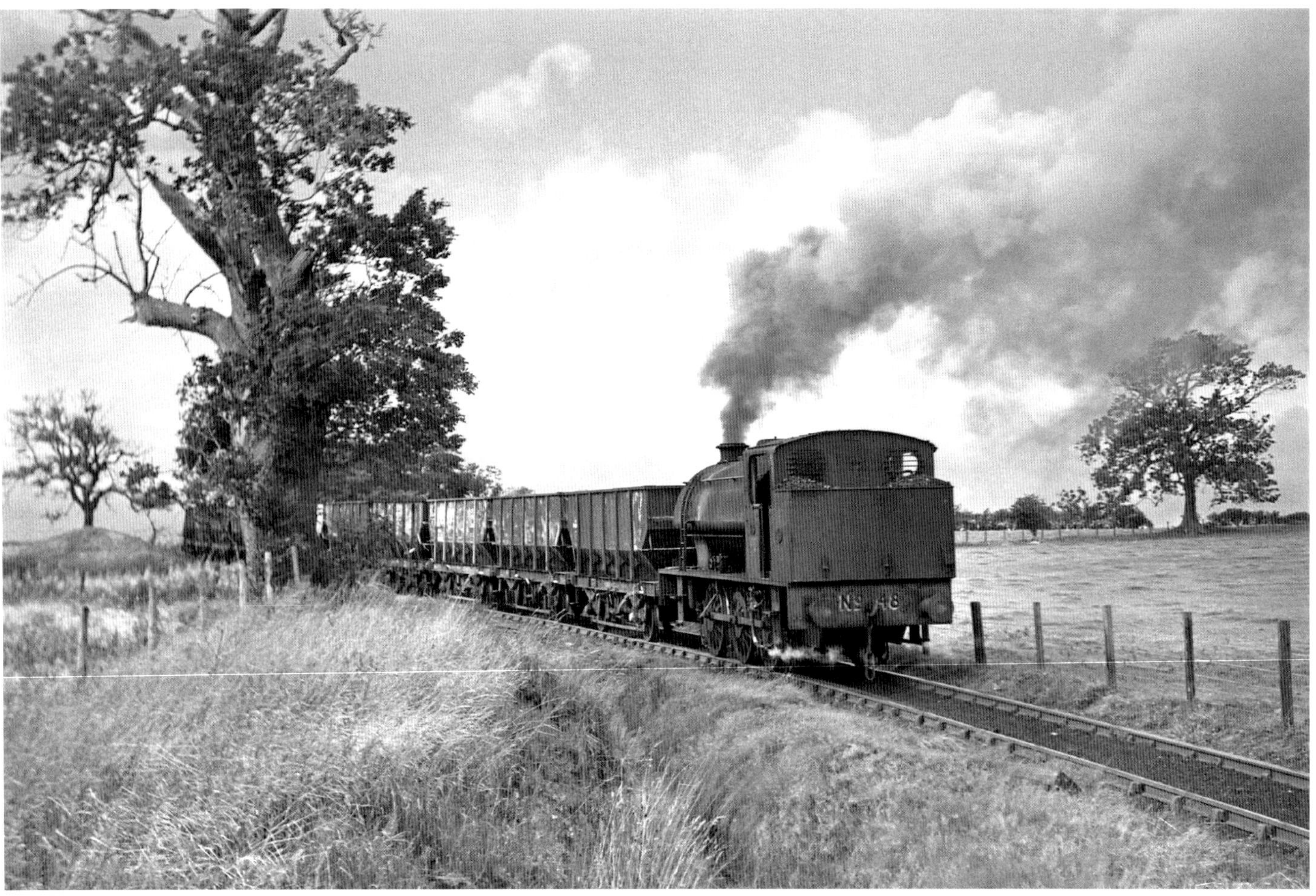

Shilbottle was the NCB's northernmost colliery in Northumberland and was connected to the East Coast Main Line south of Alnmouth by a branch line of a couple of miles in length, passing through pleasant countryside and worked by NCB locos. On 17 September 1970, Hunslet Austerity 0-6-0 saddle tank No. 48 (W/No. 3172 of 1944) pushes its train of empties up a pleasantly wooded, sinuous and steep part of the branch. (Richard Stevens)

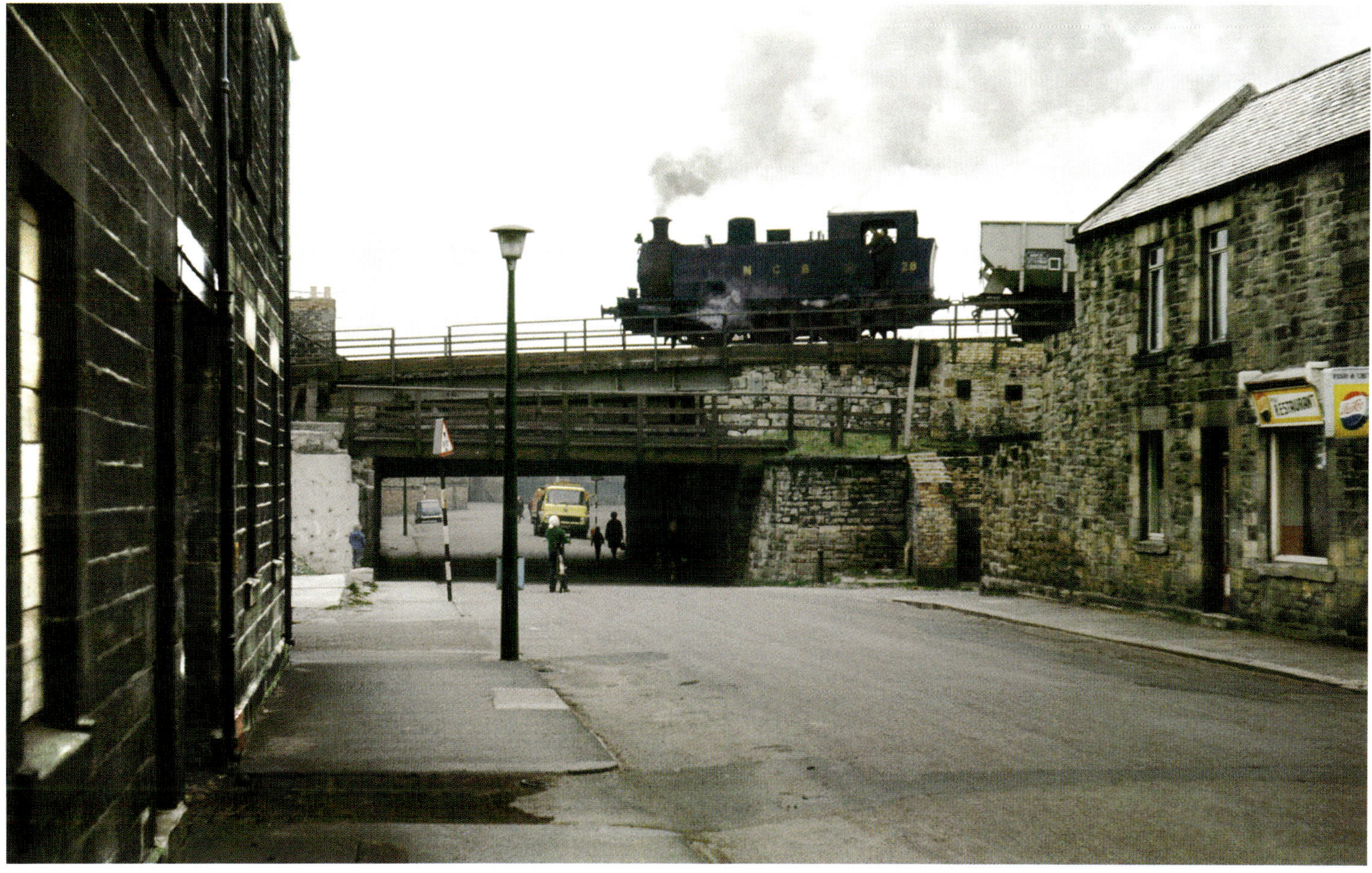

In April 1968, Hudswell Clarke 0-6-0 tank No. 28 (W/No. 1825 of 1949) of Broomhill NCB loco shed returns empty BR 21-ton hopper wagons from Amble staiths to the BR reception sidings, crossing Church Street in Amble. Following the closure of Broomhill colliery in February 1961, NCB locos used one of the two tracks of the BR branch to Amble to reach the staiths, which handled coal brought in by BR from Shilbottle and Whittle collieries. These staiths finally closed in September 1969. (Jon Marsh)

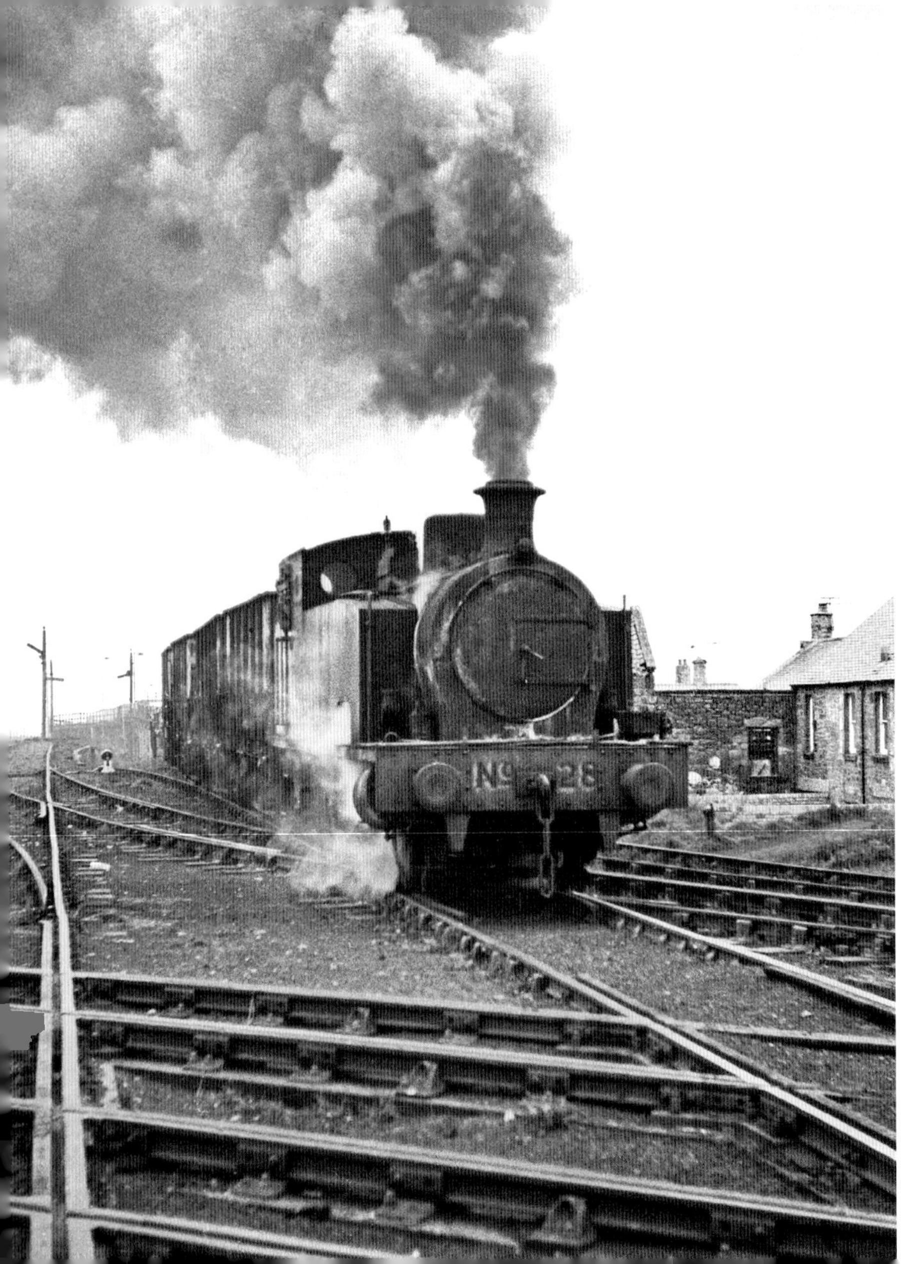

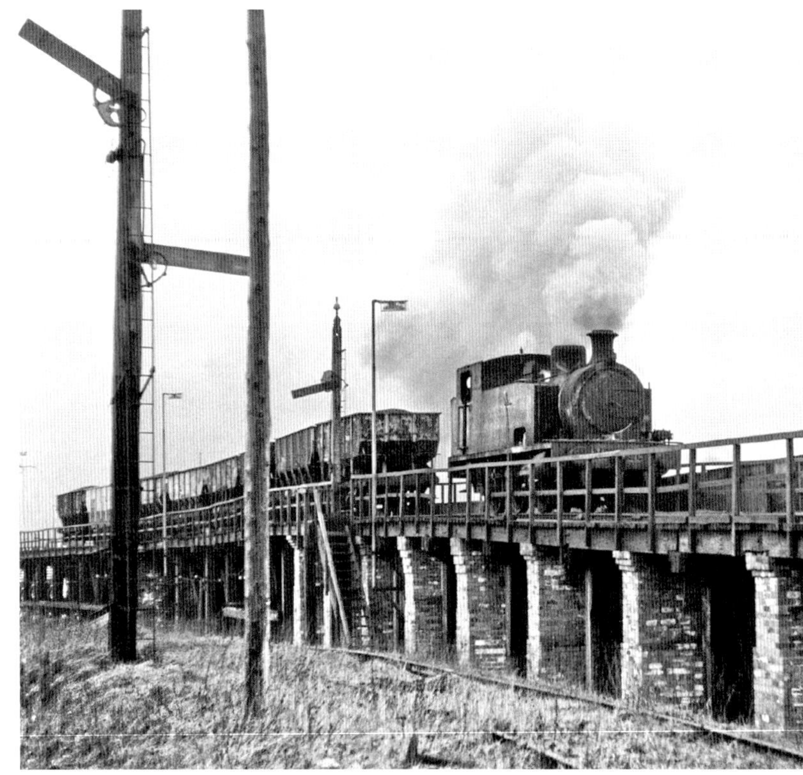

Left: In April 1968, No. 28 is working hard away from Amble staiths, negotiating the complex network of lines that once served Hauxley colliery. (Jon Marsh)

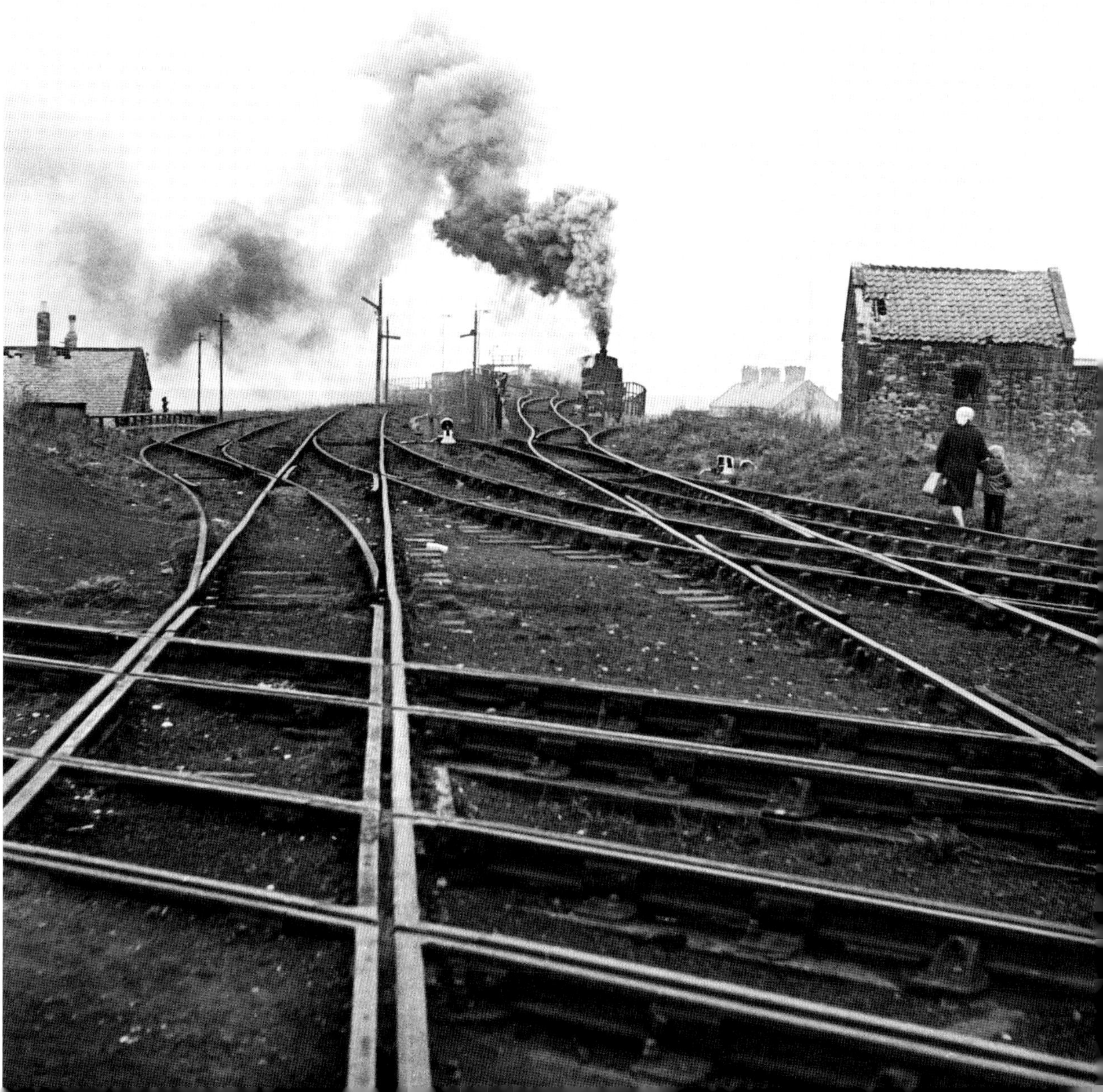

Opposite page: In April 1968, former Ashington colliery Hudswell Clarke 0-6-0 tank No. 28 is seen 'brewing up' on Amble staiths, a location which was originally referred to as Warkworth harbour. (Jon Marsh)

Right: Amble staiths were worked by locos provided by Broomhill colliery loco shed. From 1954, the more indirect NCB line between Broomhill colliery and Amble staiths, via the former Radcliffe colliery, was abandoned in favour of using one of the lines of the direct two-track BR line. Although Broomhill had ceased winding in February 1961, the loco shed remained open to provide locos for shunting traffic from Hauxley and to work Amble staiths, as well as handling coal brought in by BR from the nearby Whittle and Shilbottle collieries. Hauxley colliery closed in November 1966, but shunting of the coal from Whittle and Shilbottle continued at Amble staiths until September 1969. Although Broomhill had a Hunslet Austerity saddle tank at its disposal by this time, the six-coupled side tank No. 28 was found in action in April 1968, and it is seen working away from the staiths at Amble, with the complex of lines and the crossover for the 1-mile Hauxley branch in the foreground. Both the Hudswell Clarke side tank and the Hunslet Austerity saddle tank were cut up in January 1970 following the closure of the staiths. (Jon Marsh)

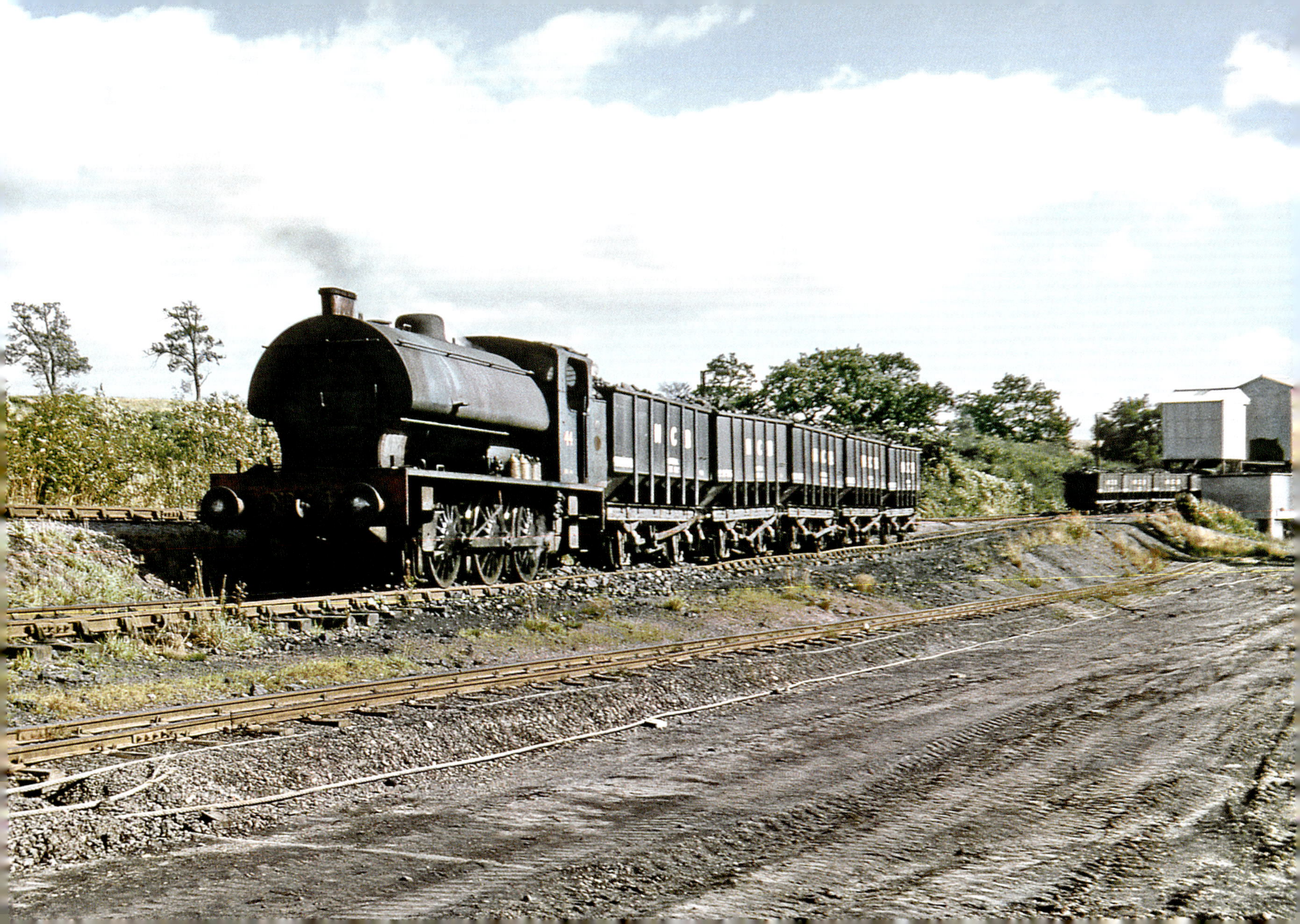

Opposite page: The 4½-mile rural branch, connecting Whittle with exchange sidings on the Newcastle–Edinburgh main line at Southside, between Warkworth and Acklington, was steeply graded in parts with several level crossings over country lanes. On 1 September 1971, Giesl ejector-fitted Robert Stephenson & Hawthorns Austerity 0-6-0 saddle tank No. 44 (W/No. 7104 of 1943) moves loaded internal hopper wagons away from the conveyor-fed drift mine loading point, installed in the mid-1960s for screening and washing. Closure under the NCB came in 1987 when it became uneconomic to cut coal from the ever decreasing thickness of the seams. (Author)

Above right: Shilbottle colliery was approximately 3 miles south-east of Alnwick and, as a modest landsale concern of the Shilbottle Coal Company, had been acquired along with nearby Whittle in 1917 by the Co-operative Wholesale Society Ltd. It was taken over by the NCB on Vesting Day in 1947, when it was producing high-quality steam coal, as well as coal for domestic and coking purposes. It dispensed with steam traction in early 1973, when three 350 hp shunters were purchased from BR, but its underground connection with Whittle colliery saw rail traffic cease in February 1978. This 23 March 1973 scene shows Robert Stephenson & Hawthorns Austerity 0-6-0 saddle tank No. 45 (W/No. 7113 of 1943), Robert Stephenson & Hawthorns 0-6-0 saddle tank No. 38 (W/No. 7763 of 1954) and Hudswell Clarke 0-6-0 tank No. 38 (W/No. 1823 of 1949) dumped alongside the colliery, awaiting disposal following the arrival of the diesels. The two furthest locos survived into preservation at Marley Hill, but the Austerity was scrapped within days of this picture. (John Sloane)

Right: Bardon Mill drift mine was situated virtually in the middle of mainland Britain in a rural setting, adjacent to the Tyne Valley railway line, totally isolated from the main Northumberland area pits by the 1970s. It processed coal from other nearby drift mines as well as from its own drift, with much of its output being destined for Willowholme power station in Carlisle. On 26 August 1971, Andrew Barclay 0-4-0 saddle tank No. 40 (W/No. 2280 of 1950) was the colliery's solitary motive power, but it had encountered a mechanical problem and was being retired to the shed for fitter's attention, and the driver clearly wasn't at all happy! The 14 x 22-inch cylinder Barclay was supplied new to NCB Hazlerigg Colliery, Gosforth, also working at Burradon colliery, Seaton Burn, from 1964 before ending its days at Bardon Mill. It needed a heavy repair and was withdrawn from service in March 1972, eventually being scrapped in June 1973. The modest-sized colliery closed in 1973, with the loss of 240 jobs. (Author)

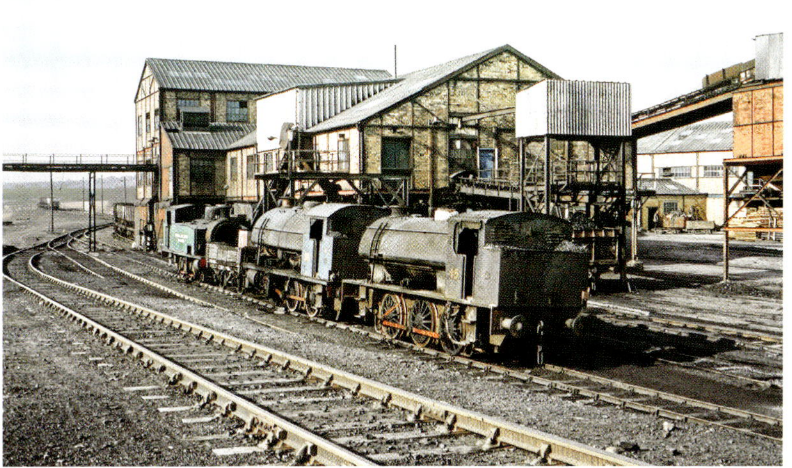

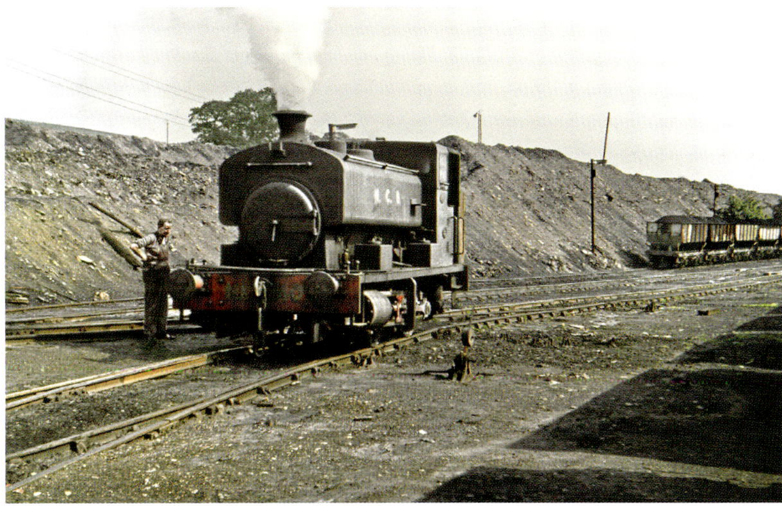

5

INDUSTRIAL MISCELLANY

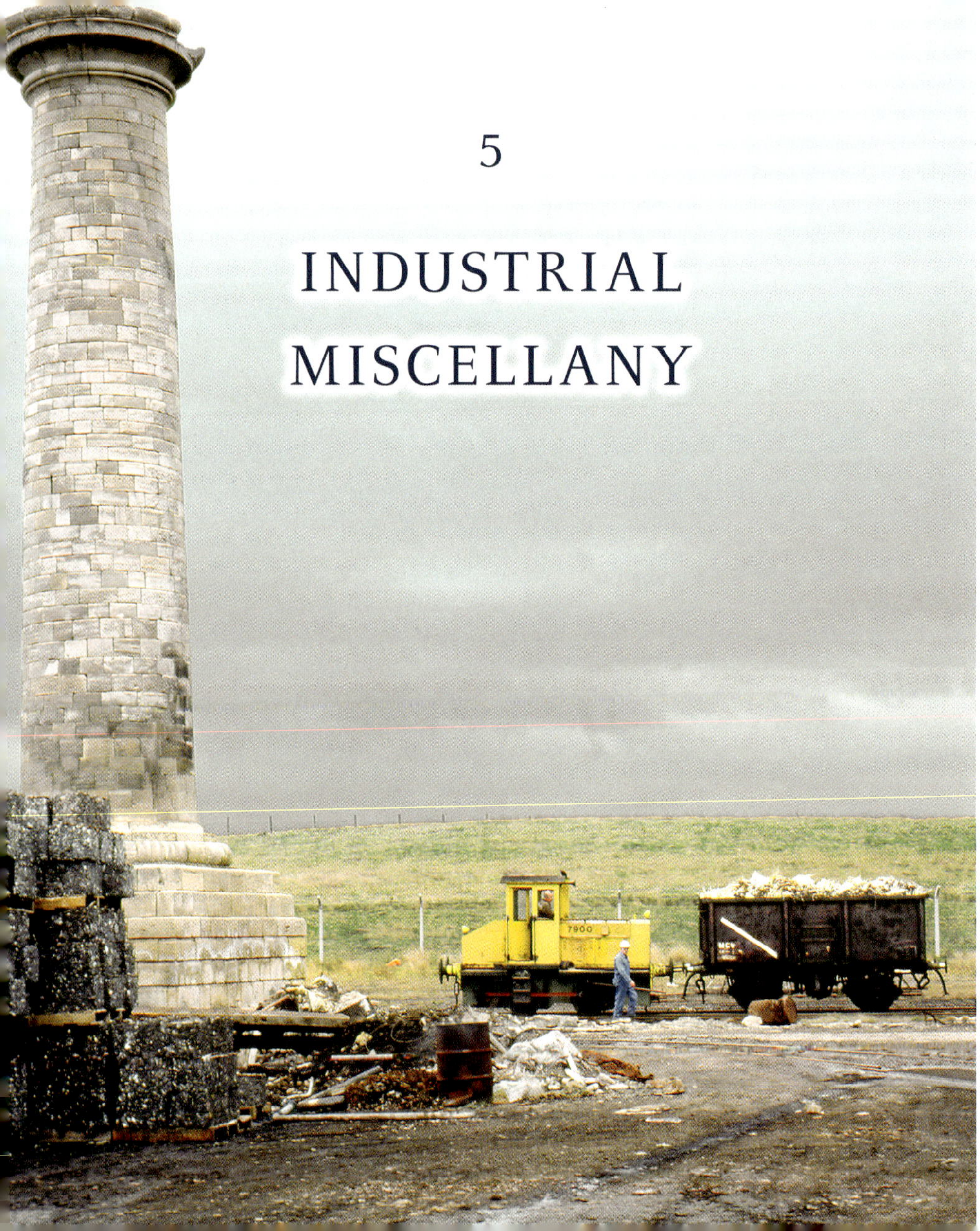

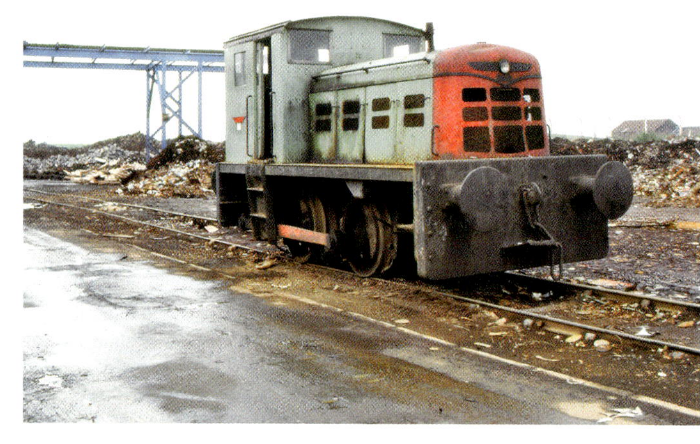

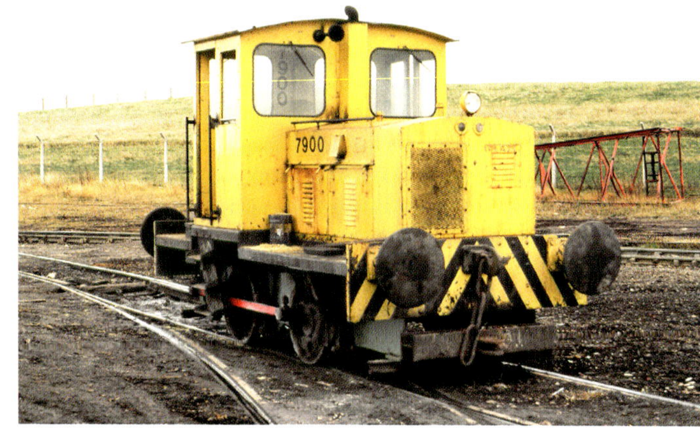

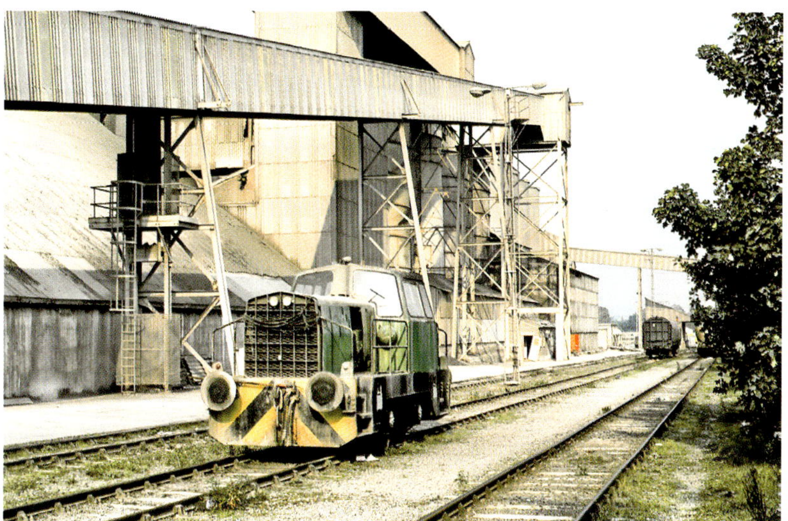

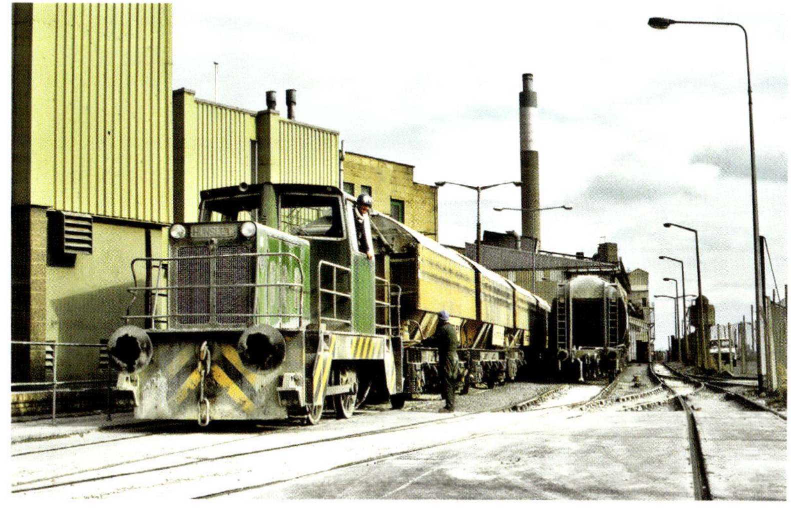

Opposite page left and below right: A Newcastle-built Robert Stephenson & Hawthorns 'Husky' 107 hp 0-4-0 diesel-mechanical (W/No. 7900 of 1958) at Vulcan Materials, Hartlepool Tinplate Works, Longhill, on 18 March 1983. It was one of only fifteen 'Husky' locos to be built, of which seven examples were exported. It was sold on to A. V. Dawson Ltd at Middlesbrough, where it was used for a couple of years before being externally restored and plinthed outside the company's head office at the automotive coil store at Ayrton road. (Roy Burt)

Opposite page above right: The other loco used at Vulcan Materials was a John Fowler 150 hp 0-4-0 diesel-mechanical (W/No. 4210136 of 1958), seen standing in the yard on 24 September 1986. (Kevin Lane)

Above right: This Rolls-Royce four-wheel diesel-hydraulic (W/No. 10197 of 1965) was one of a pair of identical Sentinel locos at the Weardale cement works of Blue Circle Industries Ltd near Eastgate, located at the western extremity of the then 19-mile freight-only branch from Bishop Auckland, the former North Eastern Railway branch from Bishop Auckland to Wearhead. Rail traffic was intermittent by the time of this photograph on 30 August 1991, when the Sentinel was found out of action in the works exchange sidings. Rail traffic finally ceased during 1993, following the withdrawal of BR's 'Speedlink' service, upon which Blue Circle relied at Eastgate. The works manufactured specialist cements including sulphate resistant products and continued production up until 2002, when final closure came about. (Author)

Below right: The Steetley Refractories manganese plant at Hartlepool was opened in the late 1930s to produce magnesium. It was accessed from the Durham coast line via Cemetery North Junction. Magnesium was produced by reacting magnesia from sea water with dolomite, a high grade material available nearby at the Coxhoe quarry. The product was in high demand well into the 1960s, being used for refractory bricks and tiles, and the chemical grade magnesia was used in the manufacture of many household products. A visit in September 1986 found Hunslet 0-4-0 diesel-hydraulic (W/No. 7425 of 1981) shunting PAA wagons used to carry dolomite from the quarry at Thristlington. The works closed in 2005. (Kevin Lane)

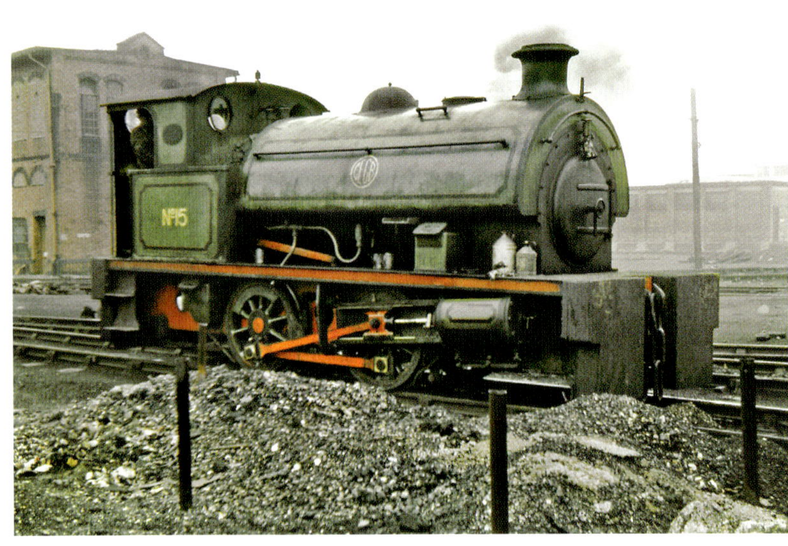

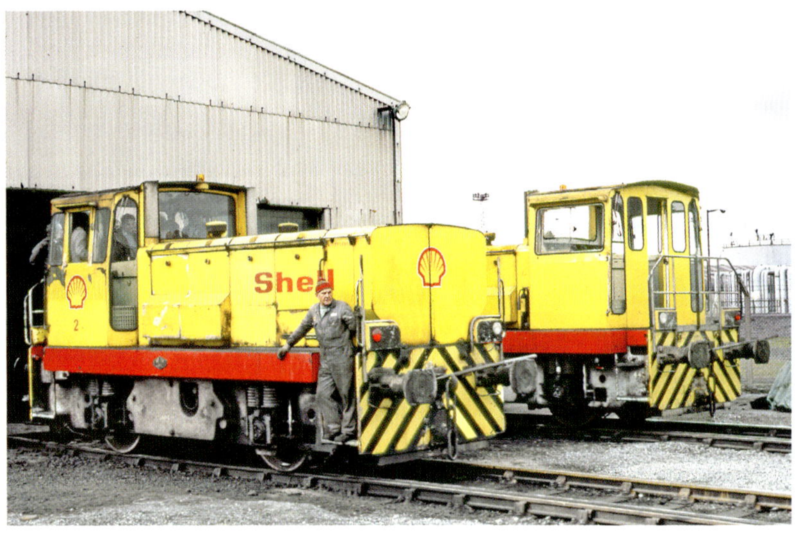

Above left: Robert Stephenson & Hawthorns, Newcastle-built 0-4-0 saddle tank No. 15 (W/No. 7063 of 1942) at the loco shed disposal point at CEGB Dunston power station on 24 August 1971. (Author)

Above: The Teesport refinery of Shell UK Oil Ltd at Grangetown, Middlesbrough, had three identical four-wheel diesel-electric locos, built in France by Moyse. No. 2 (W/No. 1364 of 1976) is seen at the loco shed with a sister loco (W/No. 1464 of 1979) standing behind on 17 March 1983. (Roy Burt)

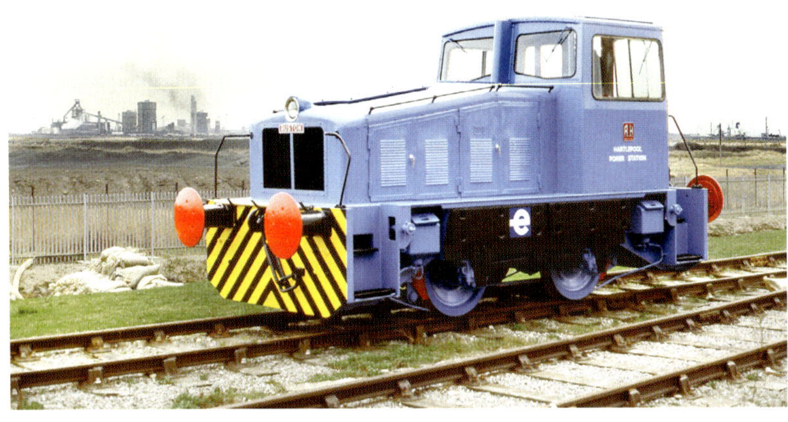

Left: Immaculately turned-out, as would be expected of the nuclear electric industry seeking to foster good public relations, this Ruston & Hornsby Class LLSH four-wheel diesel-hydraulic (W/No. 544996 of 1968) poses at Hartlepool power station, Seaton Carew, on 18 March 1983. This was one of only four locos of this class built at the Lincoln works, and was the third to last loco built by Ruston & Hornsby. The Redcar blast furnace and coke ovens can be seen in full production across the Tees Estuary. (Roy Burt)

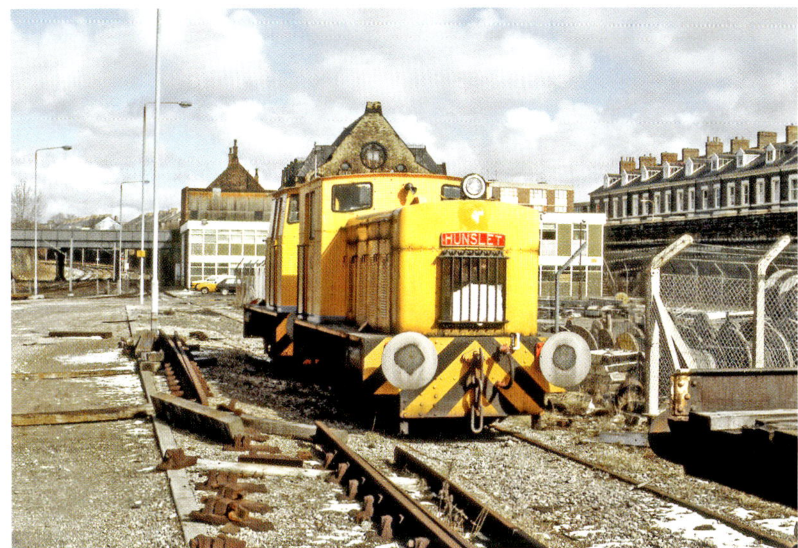

Left: Two diesel locos used on the engineers' trains during the construction of the Tyne & Wear PTE Metro system, Hunslet 0-4-0 diesel-mechanical locos HL7 (W/No. 4212 of 1950) and, behind, HL6 (W/No. 4264 of 1952), stand at the Permanent Way depot at New Bridge Street, Newcastle, on 25 March 1986. HL6 had been purchased in 1974 from Track Supplies & Services Ltd at Wolverton and had originally worked at MoD (Navy Dept) Portsmouth Dockyard as *Yard No. 6954*. It was used for general maintenance work on the Metro test track between West Allotment and Chirton, on part of the former NCB route from Backworth to Percy Main, and had been based at the Middle Engine Lane test centre (*see page 75*). This test track was closed in June 1980 and the loco was then moved to the New Bridge Street engineer's sidings. HL7 was obtained from NEI-Parsons Ltd, at nearby Heaton, and was employed on the Metro extension works trains to South Shields. These two, plus another 1953-built Hunslet, were eventually cut up on site in February 1989. (Author)

Right: Several of the north Teesside chemicals works were served by a 2½-mile BR branch line from the Greatham Creek branch at Seal Sands Branch Junction. The line served an isolated location on the mudflats by the north bank of the Tees Estuary, an area developed by the chemicals industry from the 1960s. Hazardous products were conveyed along the line, hydrocyanic acid being one example. As the chemicals businesses grew, so did the branch line, requiring further extensions in 1977 and 1989. One company regularly using rail was Monsanto Chemicals (later operated by BASF and INEOS), producing acrylonitrile, a key ingredient for acrylic fibres used to make clothing and carpets, ABS plastics and carbon fibre. The branch line fell into disuse for regular chemicals traffic from around 2006, such products then being moved by road transport. On 17 March 1983, the Monsanto Chemicals Ltd shunter, English Electric Vulcan Works 0-6-0 diesel-hydraulic GM245 (W/No. 3870 of 1969), stands at their private connection with the BR branch, waiting for the next delivery of tanker wagons. (Roy Burt)

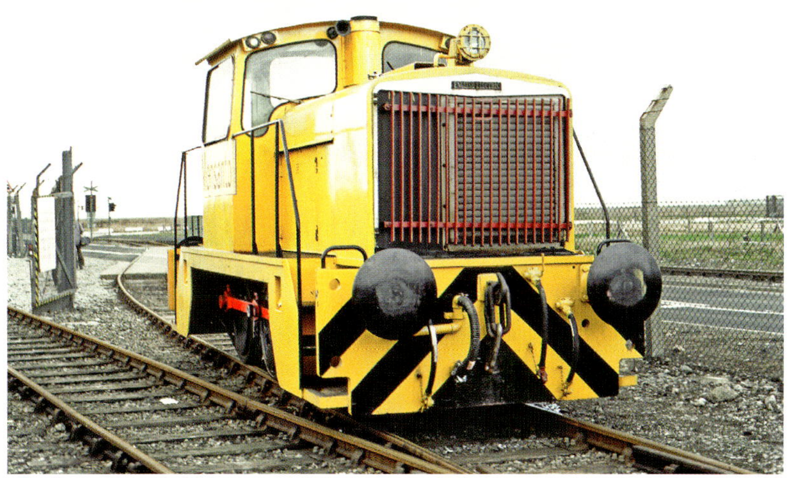

DANGER

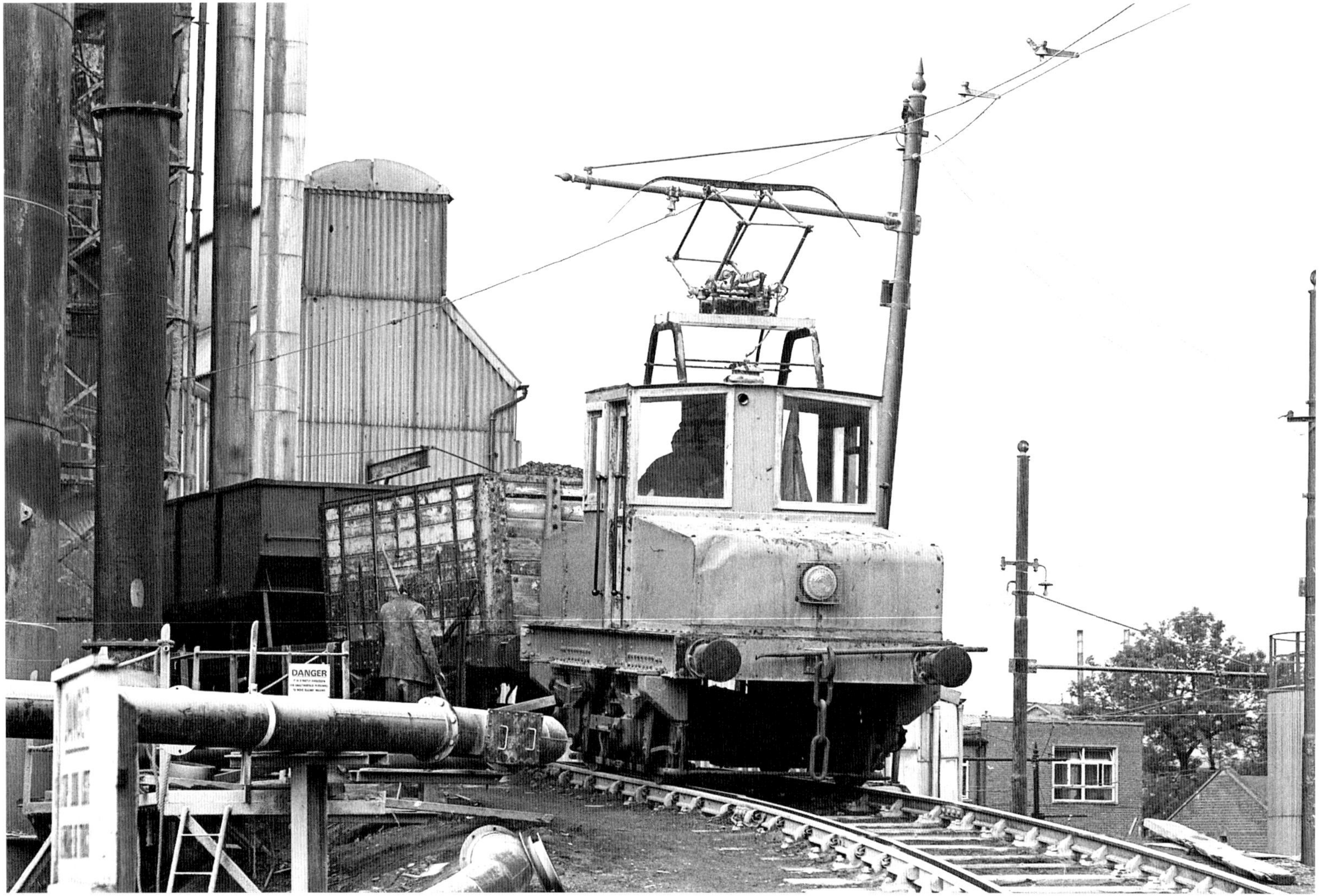

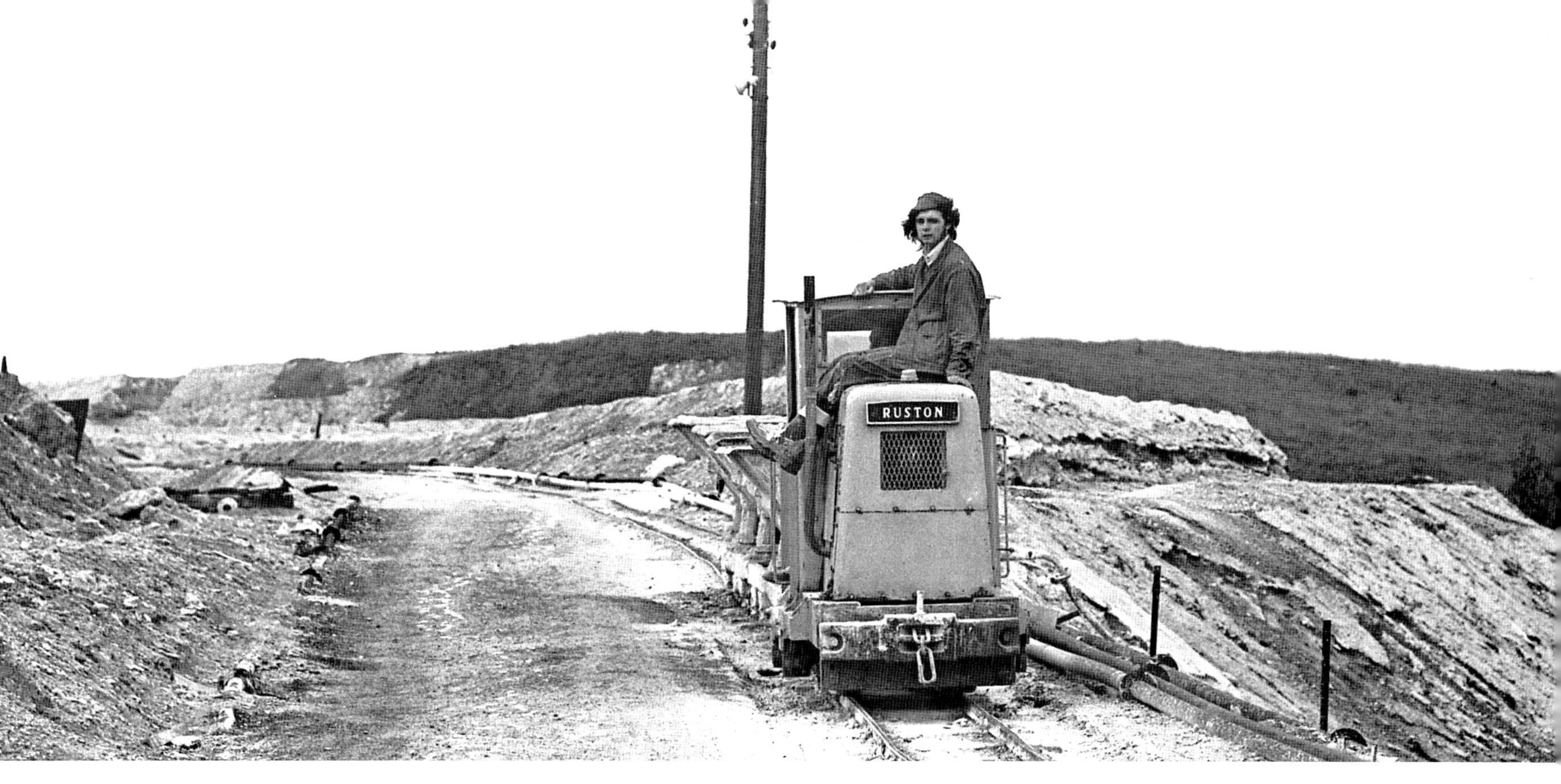

Above: The Chemical & Insulating Company Ltd's works at Faverdale, near Darlington, also known as 'Darchem', was opened in 1928 and manufactured inorganic insulating materials for six decades. It was located near Darlington North Road station, enjoying a connection with the line to Barnard Castle. As well as using standard gauge, it had two narrow-gauge systems. One was of 2-foot gauge located deep within the works, used for the charging and discharging of the indurating (pellet production) plant, and worked by a Greenwood & Batley battery loco (W/No. 2848 of 1957), now preserved on the private Ripon & District Light Railway. The other, a 1-foot 8-inch gauge line, was used for the handling of materials between sections of the processing plant, and it also ran out to a tipping area. Returning after tipping 'waste' material in June 1978 is Ruston & Hornsby four-wheel diesel-mechanical (W/No. 476124 of 1962) with a rake of 'V' skips. The consequence of such tipping was the contamination of the ground with asbestos, but despite these challenges the land was subsequently successfully reclaimed for housing and parkland in the early twenty-first century. A standard gauge line (*opposite page*) was worked by a vintage 1928-built General Electric Company 'steeple cab' four-wheel overhead wire electric loco. The loco is seen positioning coal wagons over the discharge point at the boiler house during the same June 1978 visit. (Both Kevin Lane)

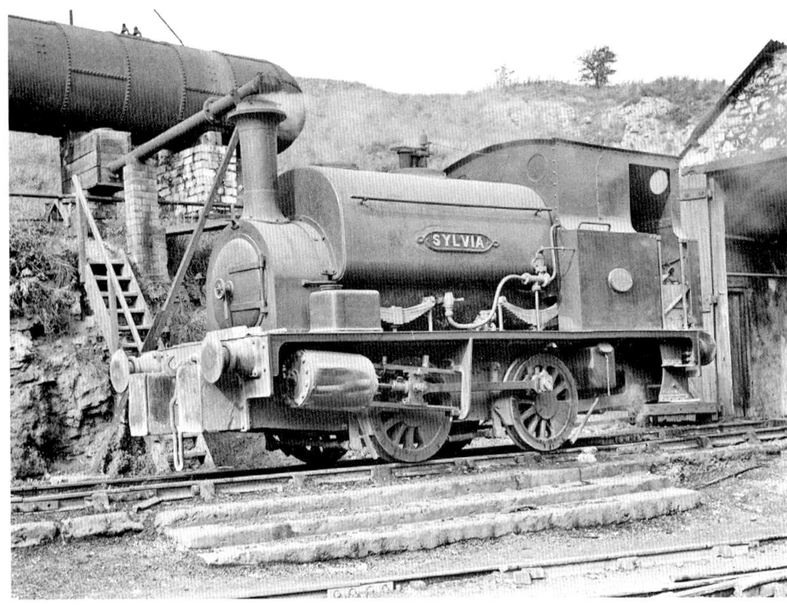

Left: The limeworks of Sir Hedworth Williamson had a long history dating back to the early eighteenth century, and the works eventually expanded into a huge complex, with a connection alongside the Gateshead–Sunderland railway, three quarters of a mile north of Fulwell station. The workings were known as Southwick and Fulwell quarries. In the mid-1950s Hudswell Clarke 0-4-0 saddle tank *Sylvia* (W/No. 1599 of 1927), one of a fleet of seven steam locos, stands in steam outside the loco shed. It was supplied new to the limeworks and was scrapped on site after the works closed in February 1957. Today, eight lime kilns survive as Grade II-listed structures. (Kevin Lane collection)

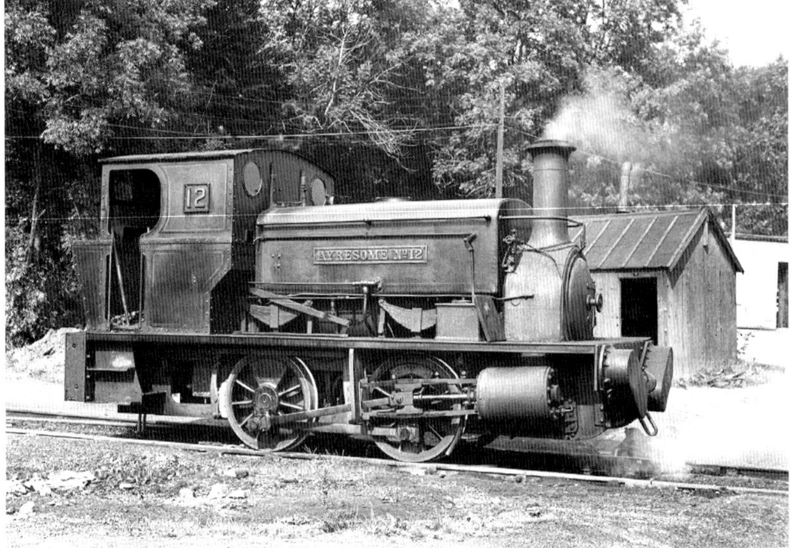

Right: The Aycliffe Lime & Limestone Company Ltd's magnesian limestone quarry was located west of the Durham–Darlington main line and, in latter years, the railway was worked by two Manning Wardle 0-4-0 saddle tanks. The older loco, built in 1881, was scrapped in 1956, but shortly before rail traffic ceased in 1961, a lonesome *Ayresome No. 12* (W/No. 1903 of 1916) was found resting between its duties. It was to face the cutter's torch during the following year, in April 1962. (Tony Brown)

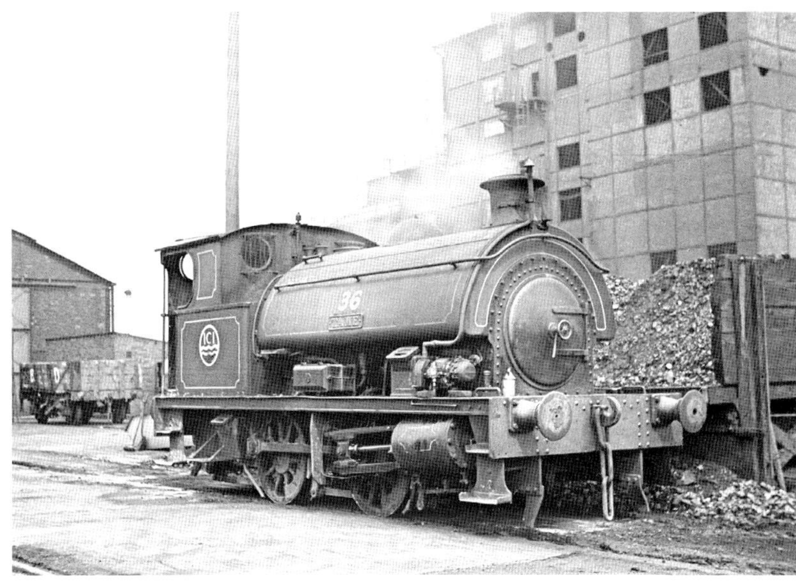

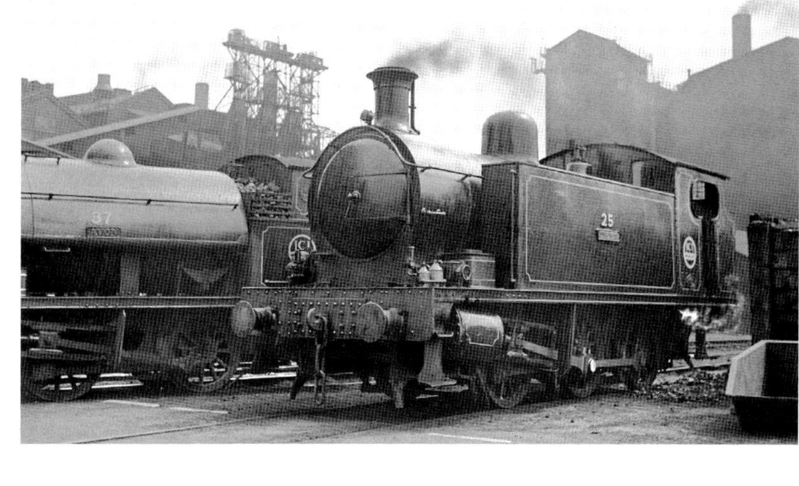

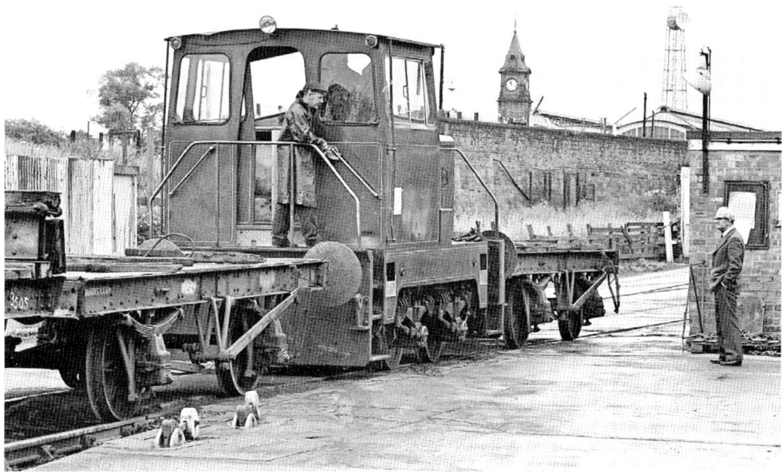

Above: Hawthorn Leslie 0-4-0 saddle tank No. 36 *Tame* (W/No. 3720 of 1928) at ICI Billingham in the late 1950s. The works at this time possessed a core fleet of around twenty-four six-coupled locos named after rivers in the United Kingdom but these were replaced from the late 1950s by new Yorkshire Engine Janus Class diesel-electric locos. (Tony Brown)

Above right: Hawthorn Leslie 0-6-0 tank No. 25 *Tees* (W/No. 3738 of 1928) standing on shed in the company of Hawthorn Leslie 0-4-0 saddle tank No. 37 *Avon* (W/No. 3567 of 1924) at ICI Billingham in the late 1950s. (Tony Brown)

Right: Thomas Hill 157 hp four-wheel diesel-hydraulic (W/No. 111C of 1961) was a conversion from a Sentinel vertical-boiler steam loco and was in use at the Darlington works of Cleveland Bridge & Engineering Co. Ltd on 1 July 1978. Located just north of Bank Top station, the company relocated to a new site in December 1981. The loco is now on the Foxfield Railway. (Kevin Lane)

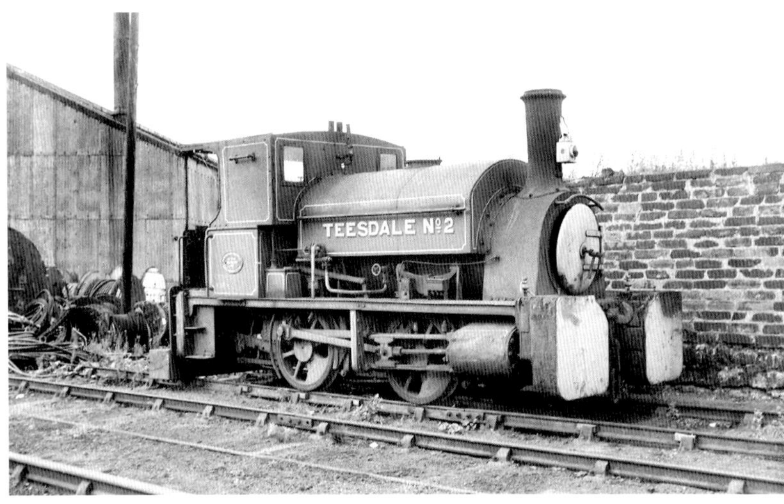

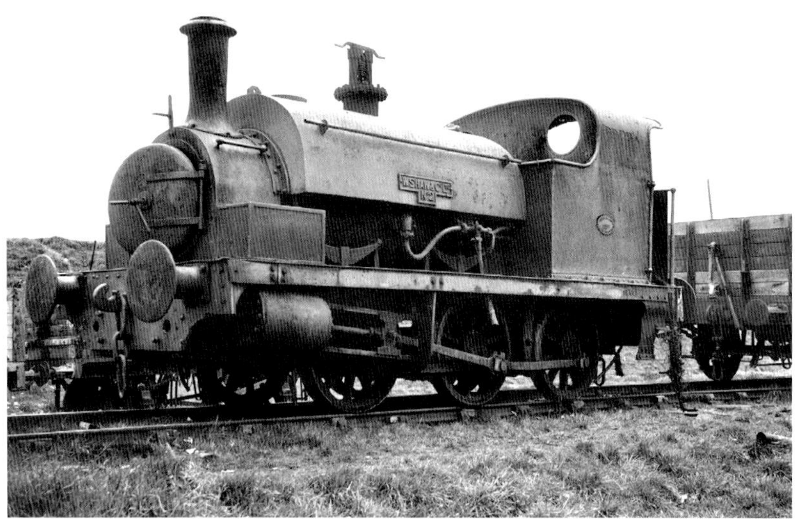

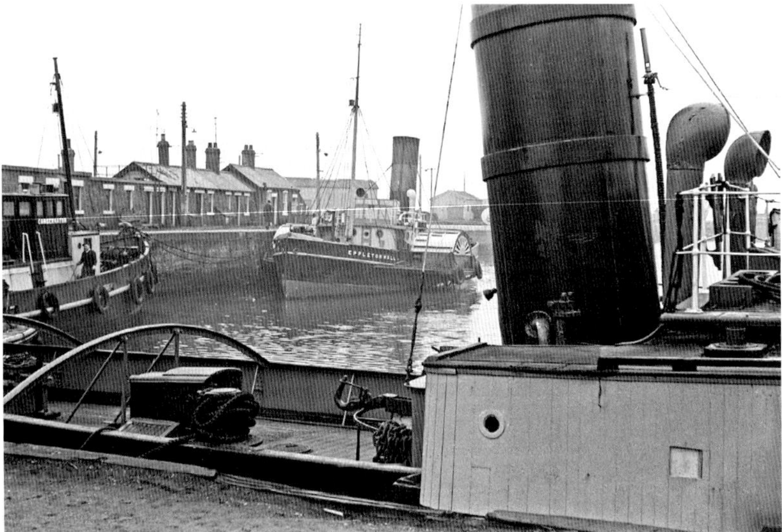

Above left: Head Wrightson of Thornaby used this veteran Black Hawthorn 0-4-0 saddle tank, *Teesdale No. 2* (W/No. 905 of 1887), which was out of use by the time of this photograph taken in 1964. (Author's collection)

Above: This 0-6-0 saddle tank, fully rebuilt by Ridley Shaw in 1941 and bearing the identity of *W. Shaw No. 2*, had its origins as a product of Robert Stephenson & Co. Ltd. It is seen at Thornaby Malt Works on 31 March 1957. (Author's collection)

Left: How could this photo be overlooked – after all, these tugs were associated with the railway at Seaham Harbour (*as previously noted on page 17*) for many years. A gathering of the Seaham tugs, with 1914-built Tyne paddle tug *Eppleton Hall* taking centre stage, during her last year of service in 1967, before being sold for scrap. Remarkably, she did survive, and is now preserved in San Francisco. (Jon Marsh)

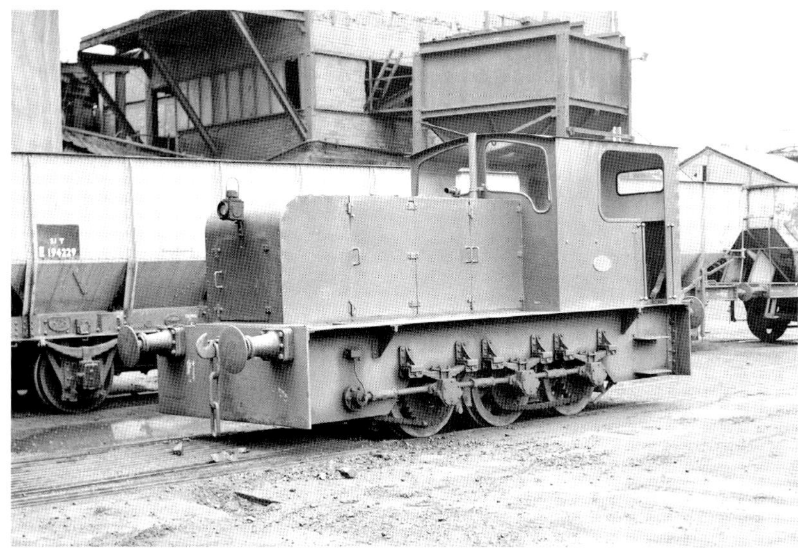

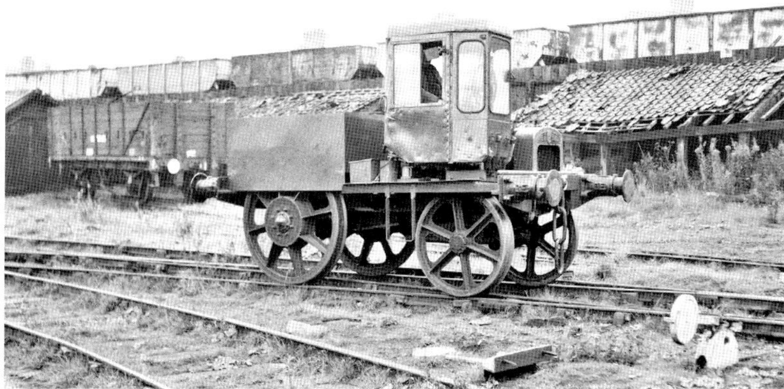

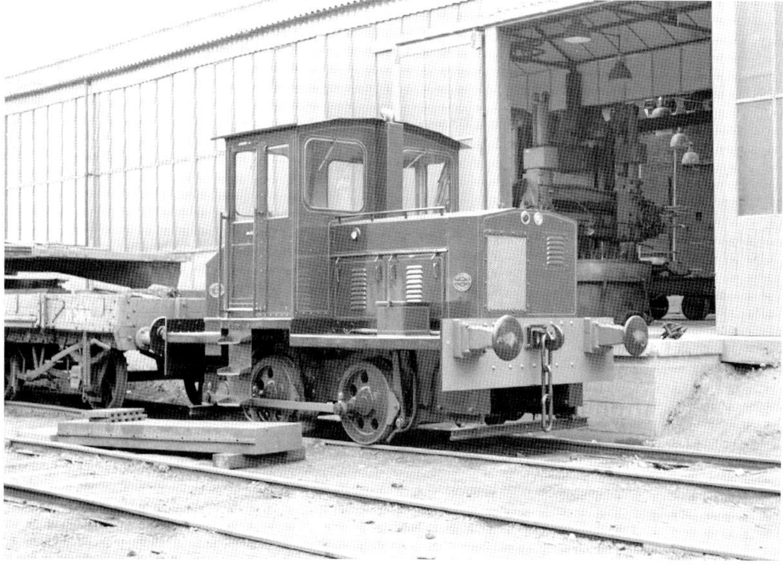

Above: A pioneer Kerr Stewart diesel product, 90 hp six-wheel diesel-mechanical (W/No. 4421 of 1929) at Wingate Grange colliery on 4 July 1962. Supplied new to the Ravenglass & Eskdale Railway, it was sold to the NCB in 1955, and sold out of NCB service from Deaf Hill colliery in December 1967 to Rom River Reinforcement Ltd at Lichfield. It survives today on the Foxfield Railway in Staffordshire. (Brian Webb – IRS collection)

Above right: NCB Lambton Workshops constructed this four-wheel diesel-mechanical in 1955, utilising parts from an Aveling Barford dumper truck. The 'XL5', as it was ironically known, was in action at Seaham Wagon Works on 9 October 1964, but was scrapped by September 1970. (Brian Webb – IRS collection)

Right: This anonymous Robert Stephenson & Hawthorns 'Husky' 0-4-0 diesel-mechanical (W/No. 7869 of 1956) was in use at their Darlington works on 11 June 1960 as a company hire/demonstrator loco. This was just prior to it being sold to the Northern Gas Board in Carlisle. (Brian Webb – IRS collection)

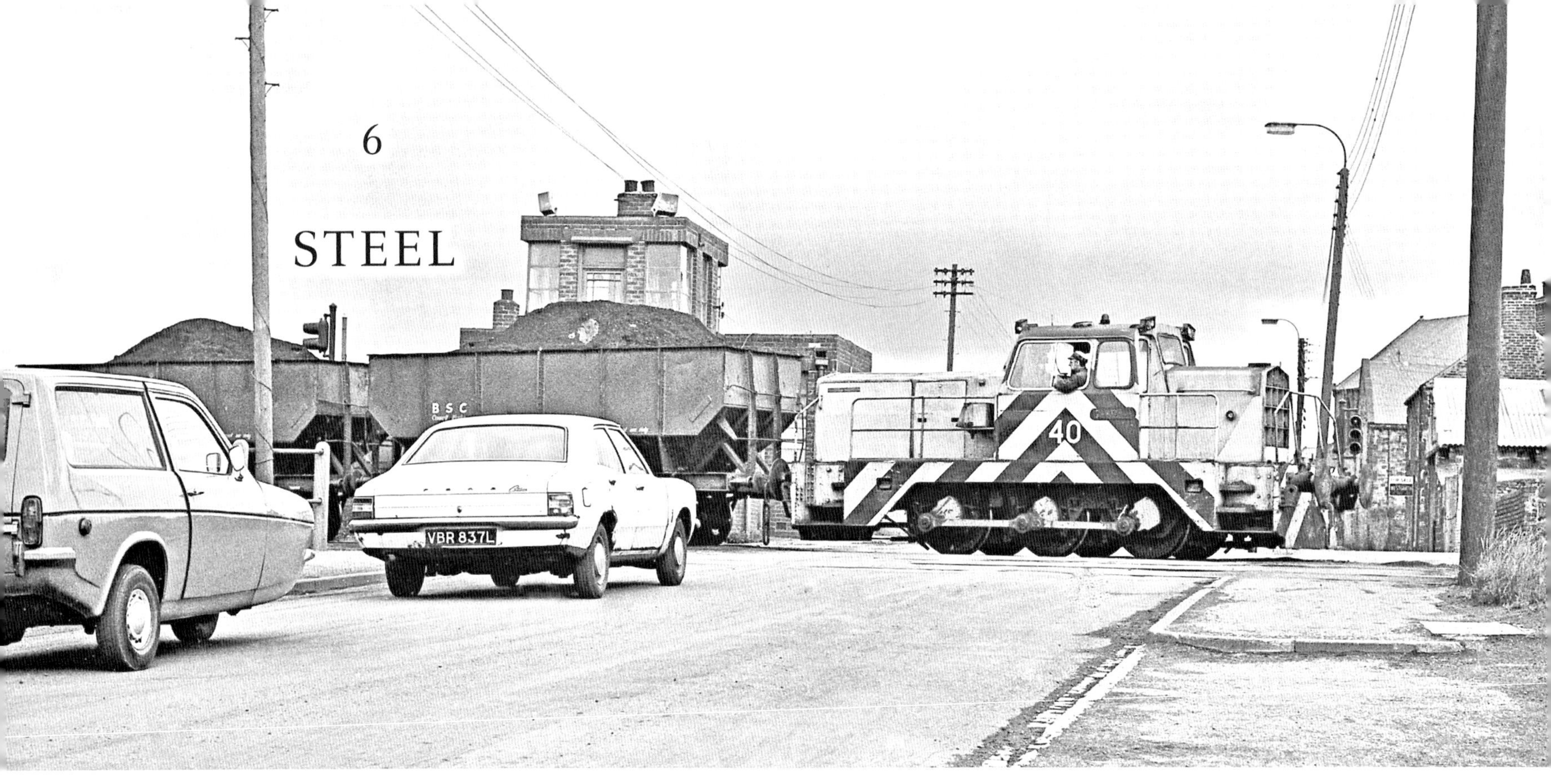

6

STEEL

The origins of the Consett iron and steelworks in County Durham can be traced back to 1840 and by around 1860 there were eighteen blast furnaces on the site, fed from the abundant local deposits of iron ore and coal. The Consett Iron Co. Ltd established collieries, coke ovens, byproducts plants, brickworks and quarries, all served by an extensive private railway system, which included the Whittonstall Railway and the Chopwell & Garesfield Railway. This latter railway enabled the Consett Iron Company's coal to access the staiths on the River Tyne via a self-acting incline, with locos provided from Derwenthaugh shed (*as previously discussed on page 60*). The company's coal mining interests and associated railways passed to the NCB on Vesting Day. The loco fleet was huge in order to serve the company's interests, with over twenty crane tanks of various types, four and six-coupled saddle tanks mainly from manufacturers in the North East and the distinctive 'long-boiler' 0-6-0 pannier tanks built to a design first produced for the company in 1872. The influx of diesel locos came early to Consett and the first of what would initially amount to a fleet of thirty locos was delivered from the Hunslet Engine Company in 1947. Further diesel deliveries from Sentinel and Thomas Hill arrived between 1969 and 1970, replacing some of the earlier Hunslet examples. In the 1870s, the company classified locos into three groups: the 'A' group comprised six-coupled locos, ultimately a group of 'long-boiler' pannier tanks; the 'B' group comprised four-coupled saddle tanks; and the 'C' group was for four small specialist four-coupled saddle tanks. Latterly added were the 'D' group for crane tanks and four-wheeled cranes, and the 'E' group, which was entirely of vertical-boiler cranes. All steam locos were scrapped by 1962, except for a solitary four-coupled Hawthorn Leslie, which had been converted to burn oil, and some of the vertical-boiler crane tanks, which served into the early 1970s. The steelworks was closed in 1980, resulting in over 3,000 job losses, leaving the sky around to be clear of the red oxide dust which had overshadowed the region for over a century.

Opposite page: The BSC works at Consett on 3 July 1978, with Rolls-Royce Sentinel 0-6-0 diesel-hydraulic No. 40 (W/No. 10290 of 1970) in charge of internal coal hopper wagons destined for the coking plant at Templetown. This was the last loco to be delivered to the Consett steelworks, but it had a short working life there. (Kevin Lane)

Above right: Robert Stephenson & Hawthorns, Newcastle-built 0-6-0 pannier tank *A No. 19* (W/No. 7029 of 1941) at the Templetown loco shed of Consett works on 3 April 1961. She was one of a trio supplied to the Consett Iron Company in 1941, built to the original 1872 Kitson design, and was cut up in March 1962, upon dieselisation of the Consett fleet. (Author's collection)

Below right: Consett Ironworks in 1968, with one of the two veteran 2-4-0 crane tanks, *E No. 1* (Black Hawthorn 897 of 1887). Designed jointly by Black Hawthorn and by the Consett Iron Company's Chief Engineer, it was employed for moving rail sections, and was able to lift a maximum of 12 tons. While *No. 2* was cut-up in 1964, *E No. 1* survived to see preservation at the Beamish Museum. (Jon Marsh)

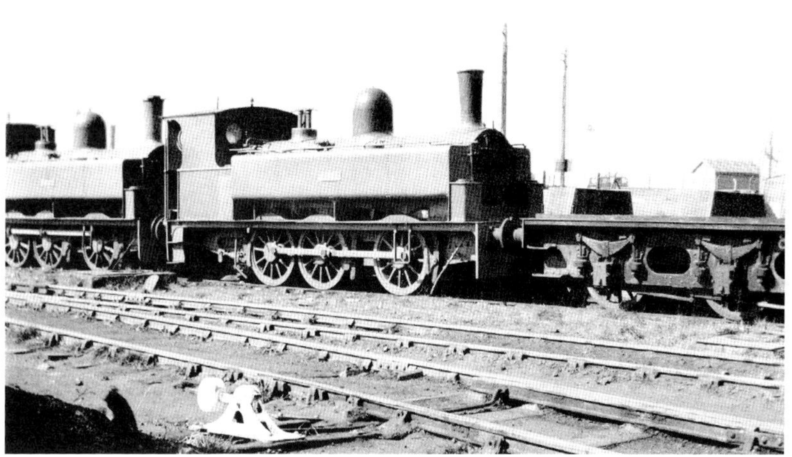

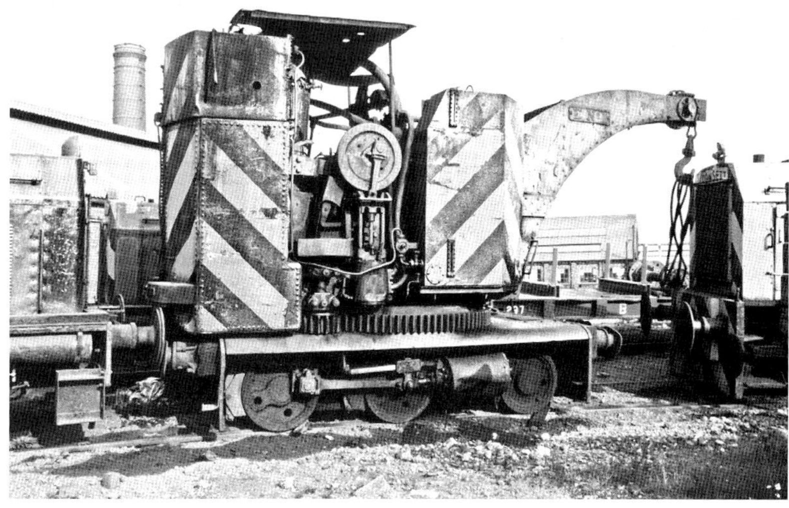

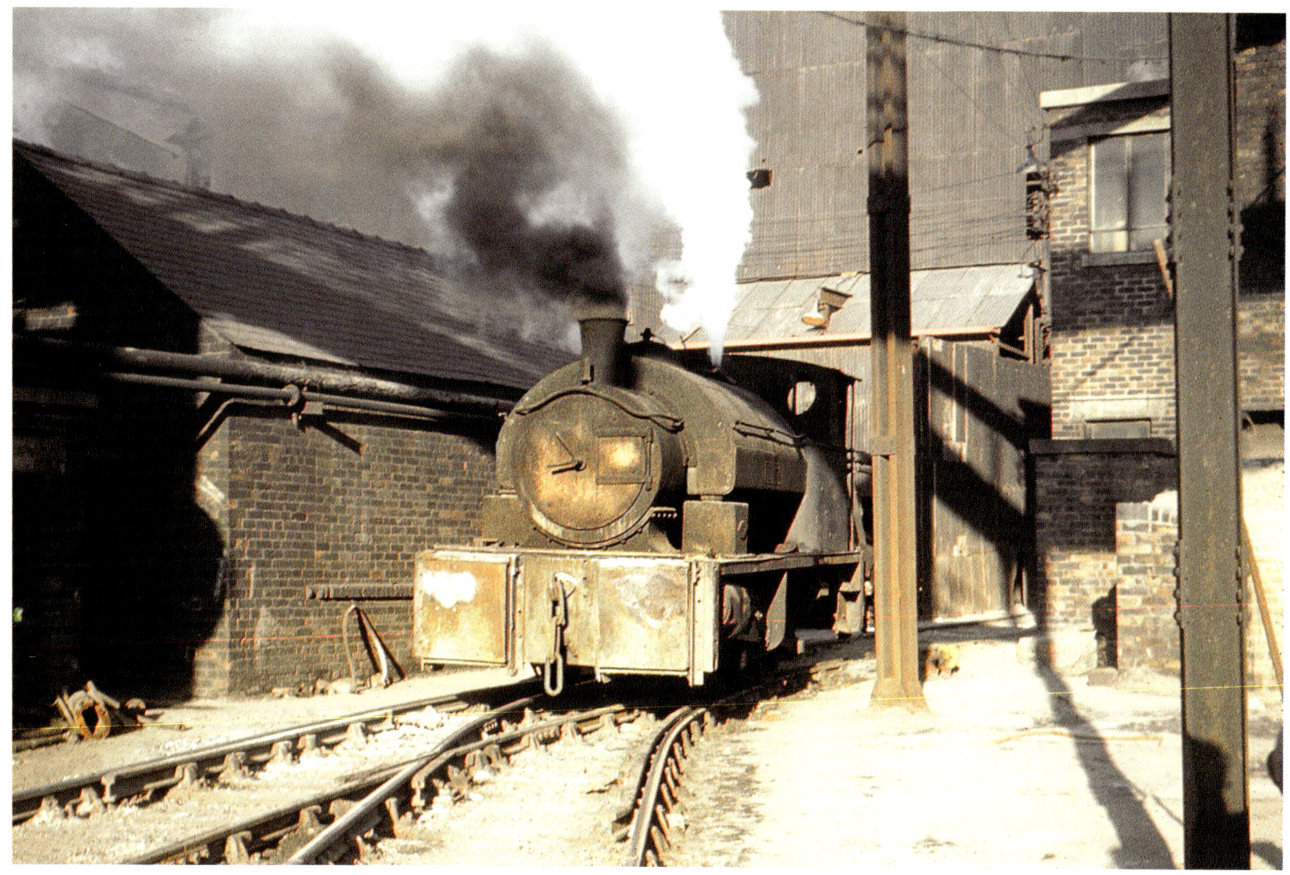

Robert Stephenson 0-4-0 saddle tank *Alfred* (W/No. 3674 of 1917), still showing a hint of its green livery beneath the grime, is seen at Skinningrove works on 19 January 1963. *Alfred* had been loyal to the works, principally being used on rolling mill shunting duties following its delivery from new to the Skinningrove Iron Company, but by 1963 it was nearing the end of its working days, being scrapped during the following spring. A fleet of new Sentinel diesel-hydraulics, delivered by rail from Shrewsbury, took over most of the duties from a fleet of around a dozen remaining steam locos in July 1963, except for just two fireless locos, which were retained for employment on specialist duties within the steel plant. They worked in that role until they too met their fate, in 1972. (Colour Rail)

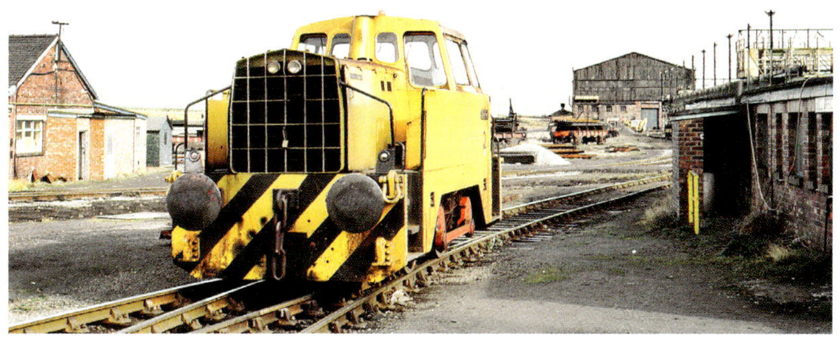

Left: Sentinel 311 hp 0-4-0 diesel-hydraulic No. 2 (W/No. 10126 of 1963), one of the first batch of diesels, working at BSC Skinningrove works at Carlin How on 17 March 1983. It was transferred to British Steel's Teesside works in February 1998. (Roy Burt)

Below: On 18 March 2017, dumped at the eastern extremity of British Steel Ltd's Skinningrove mill at Carlin How, high on the clifftop and forming a solid buffer stop, was this Yorkshire Engine Company 0-6-0 diesel-hydraulic (W/No. 2832 of 1962). It has been in this location for at least nine years. Before arriving at Skinningrove it had worked at Corus' Workington works in Cumbria, where it bore the running number 314. Perhaps it should be forgiven for being in such a deplorable condition, having previously endured the ravages of the Irish Sea at Workington, and now having to suffer those of the North Sea. Indeed, there cannot be too many industrial locos that have completed a coast-to-coast journey in England! Of note is that this Yorkshire Engine product was built at the Meadowhall works on the same production line as BR's Class 02 179 hp 0-4-0 diesel-hydraulic locos D2859 and D2860. (Author)

The Skinningrove Ironworks of the Loftus Iron Company was situated high on the cliff above the North Sea between Saltburn and Whitby at Carlin How, and produced its first pig iron in 1874. Iron ore was readily available from local mines in the Loftus area. The railway incline and jetty were both completed in 1887 for the new owners, the Skinningrove Iron Company, to enable their pig iron product to be shipped away from the tidal harbour, chiefly to Grangemouth for use in Glasgow and Falkirk factories, but later overseas. From the early twentieth century the integrated iron and steel works specialised in milling 'long products' such as rails, and post-war concentrated on angled steel and rails as well as steel colliery arches for the NCB. The works was nationalised in 1951, and under the rationalisation by the BSC the blast furnaces ceased operation during 1971. Open hearth steelmaking ceased soon afterwards, the steel being supplied by rail upon demand from the Lackenby works at Middlesbrough. Today, the works produces 'special profiles', recognised globally for the quality of the product, and a specialist plant was built adjacent to the mill in 1997 to produce Caterpillar track shoes for construction and mining equipment. Purchased from Tata Steel by Greybull Capital in 2016, the works now trades under the British Steel name, using steel supplied by rail from the company's Scunthorpe steelworks.

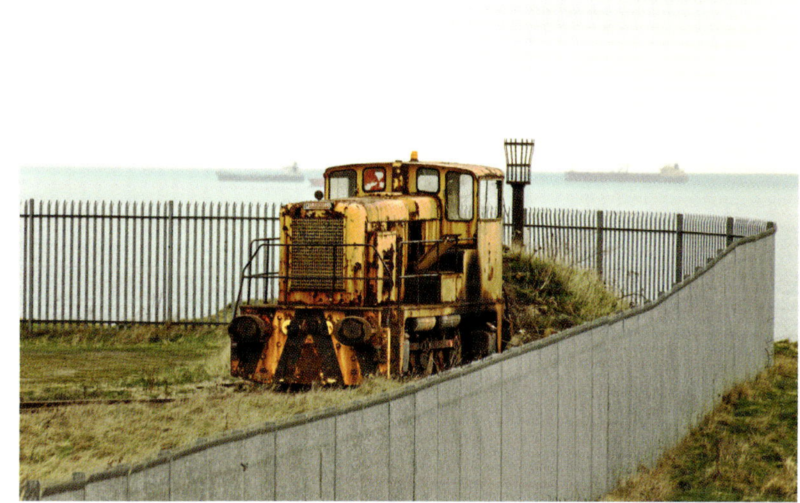

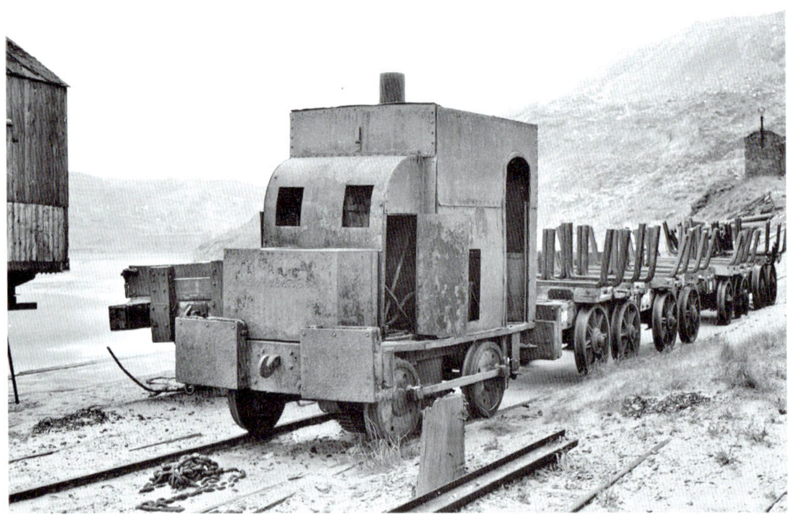

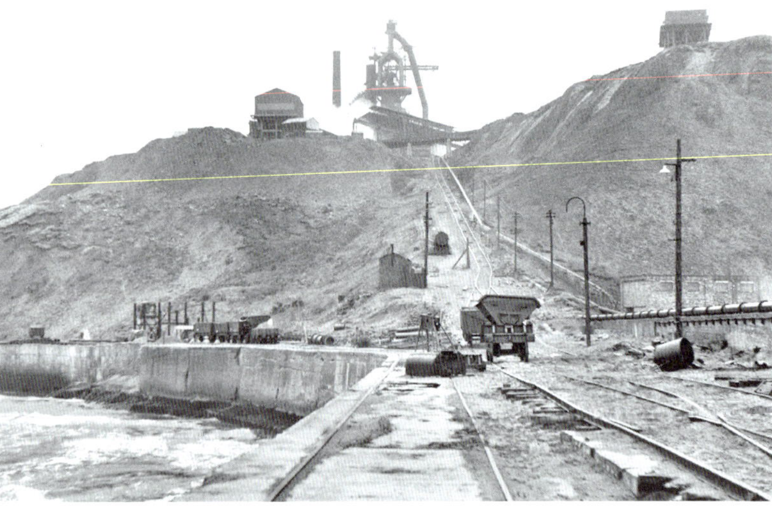

Above left: This strange contraption standing out of use on the Skinningrove jetty, taking on the appearance of an armour-plated war machine, was in fact a four-coupled vertical-boiler tank loco built by Cochrane & Co. of North Ormsby in 1871. It was first used at the ironworks in 1876, bearing the appropriate name *Coffee Pot*. The plating, a later addition, would have certainly offered protection from the unforgiving wind for the driver, if not the cold during the extreme winter months at this isolated location, and the sand over the trackbed is testament to the conditions that staff had to endure. It was scrapped around January 1954. (Kevin Lane collection)

Below left: The by then virtually abandoned Skinningrove cable-worked incline in the early 1950s, with the blast furnaces high on the clifftop above. Bogie wagons of pig iron were winched down the incline, the wagons positioned by the *Coffee Pot* loco, the waiting ships being loaded by steam crane. Shipments of pig iron ceased in 1936, after which the loco positioned sand wagons to the foot of the incline for winching up to the works. (Kevin Lane collection)

Opposite page above left: A mid-1950s photo of Peckett W4 Class 0-4-0 saddle tank *Rakie* (W/No. 583 of 1894) and Black Hawthorn 0-4-0 saddle tank *Rennie* (W/No. 1102 of 1896) on shed. Both were purchased from new and survived at Skinningrove until 1961 and 1957 respectively. (Kevin Lane collection)

Opposite page above right: *South Durham Malleable No. 5* in steam at South Durham Iron & Steel Co. at Stockton in the early 1960s. The 0-4-0 saddle tank is believed to have been built by the steel company at its Grange works in 1873, possibly using parts from a Black Hawthorn loco and other stock spare parts. It is now at the Beamish Museum. (Tony Brown)

Opposite page below left: Although Skinningrove works used a pair of Andrew Barclay 1950s-built 0-4-0 fireless locos like this, which were retained until 1972, this is in fact Andrew Barclay 0-6-0 fireless No. 9 (W/No. 2329 of 1952), seen at Dorman Long's Lackenby steelworks on Teesside in the 1960s. For such a loco type it had a relatively short life of only fifteen years, being scrapped in 1967. (Kevin Lane collection)

Opposite page below right: Black Hawthorn 0-4-0 saddle tank No. 40 (built in 1888 and rebuilt at Acklam Steelworks in 1919) working at Dorman Long's Acklam steelworks complex at Middlesbrough, quite possibly shortly before it was scrapped, around 1952. It carries the large distinctive and stylish number plates synonymous with Dorman Long's locos. (Kevin Lane collection)

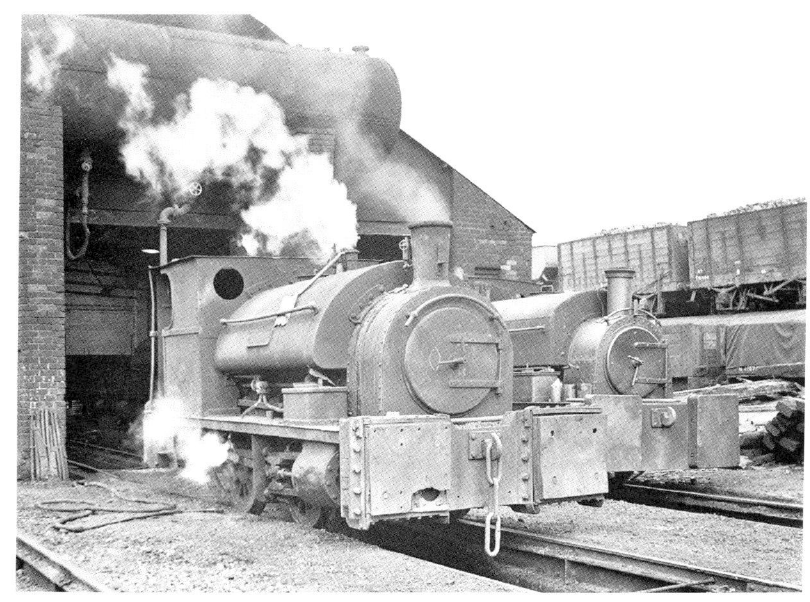

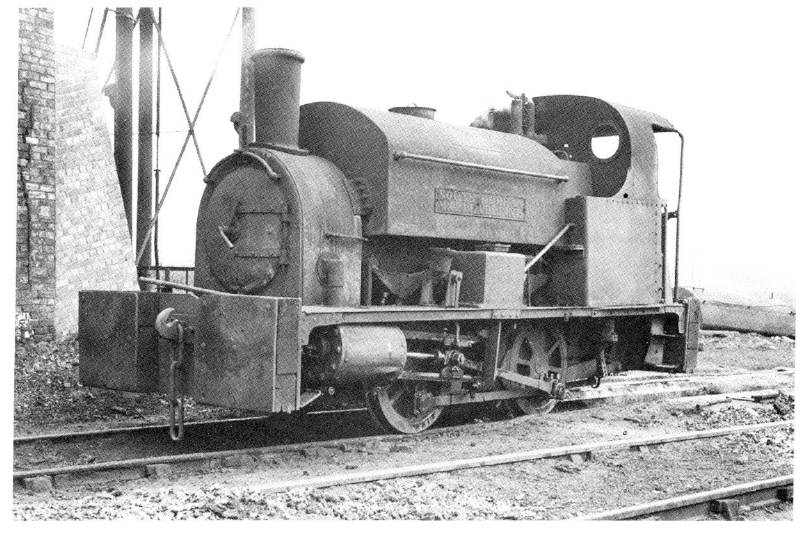

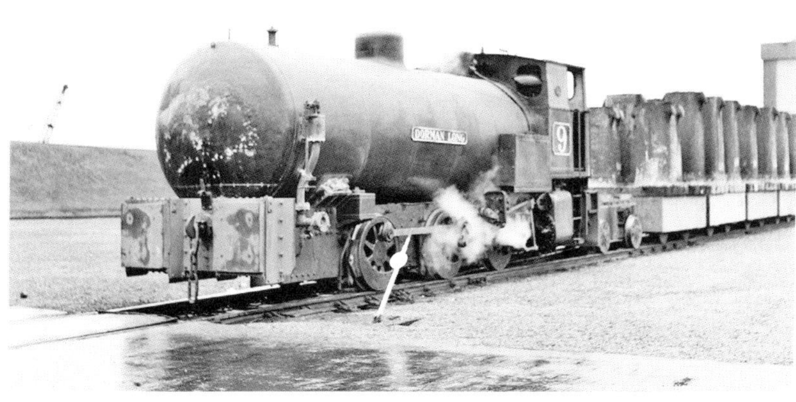

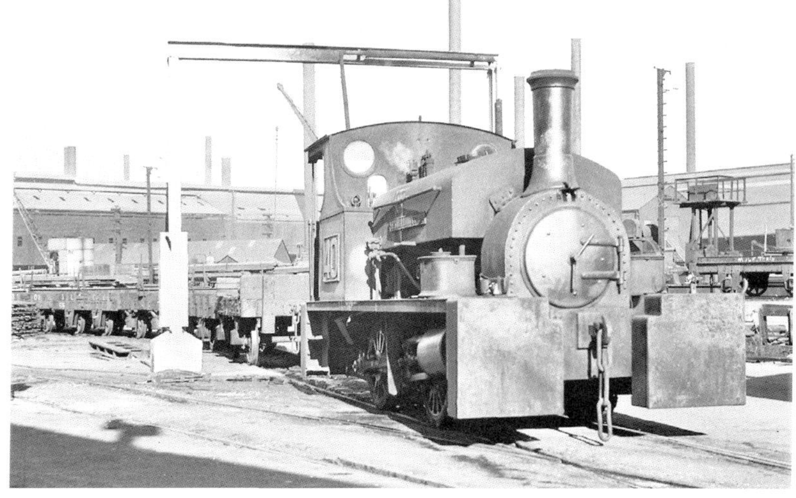

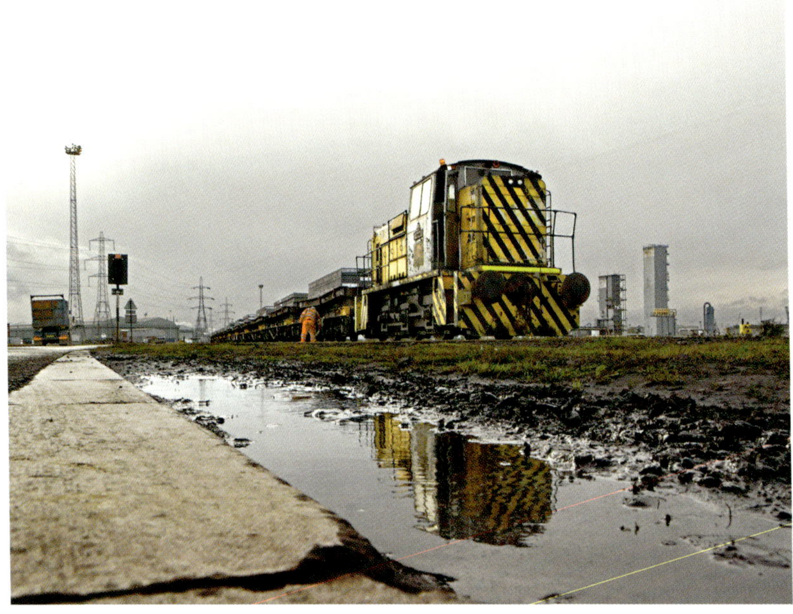

Right: The Teesside works of the BSC employed this extraordinary mobile compressor loco using compressed air transmission. Identified as *MC1*, it was one of three converted in-house, using the frames of former steelworks four-coupled locos built by Peckett and Hawthorn Leslie. *MC1* was a 1958 conversion from a Peckett saddle tank (W/No. 668 of 1897) and was still in use as a compressor on 28 October 1977. (Roy Burt)

Opposite page: During the early, optimistic days of SSI's ownership in October 2012, Di8 class Bo-Bo diesel-electric No. 820 (MaK W/No. 1600.020 of 1996) draws a charged torpedo wagon away from the Redcar blast furnace. They had previously been used for freight traffic in Norway by railway company CargoNet and twenty were constructed in 1996–97 at the Maschinenbau Kiel (MaK) plant in Germany. GB Railfreight purchased ten for the Redcar contract and they were used until SSI (UK) Ltd went into liquidation in October 2015, subsequently being transferred to British Steel Scunthorpe, after temporary storage at Tees Dock (*see page 9*). (Author)

The Teesside steelworks, established by Dorman Long in the 1870s, stretched along the south bank of the River Tees between Middlesbrough and Redcar. At its height there were around ninety blast furnaces within a 10-mile radius. By the late 1970s, under the nationalised BSC, only one survived. Despite the contraction, Corus' Lackenby integrated plant became the largest supplier of quality steel slab in the world, using iron produced in the Redcar blast furnace. The rail network ran from the Redcar blast furnace to Lackenby and the South Bank coke ovens. From 2006 it was connected to PD Ports at Tees Dock. The closures in 2015 ended around a century and a half of steelmaking on Teesside. Today, only the Beam Mill and some support services operate on a much reduced scale at Lackenby.

Left: The days of the General Electric (GECT) locos were almost over in 2012, with the influx of the more powerful imported Di8 Class locos, which took over the torpedo wagon transfers and other duties. GB Railfreight-operated GECT six-wheel diesel-electric No. 266 *Sherriffs* (W/No. 5463 of 1977), fitted with train air brake and three-link coupling fitments especially for these duties, positions a slab train in the exchange 'grid' at Lackenby on 31 October 2012. The closure of the Redcar plant of SSI (UK) Ltd was devastating news for the region and scenes such as this are now no more. (Author)

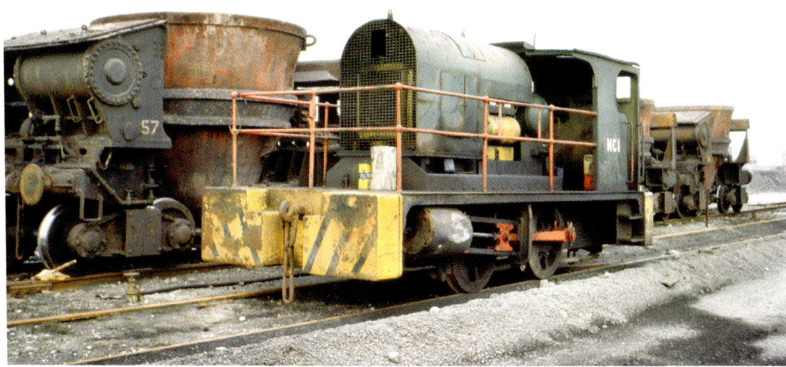

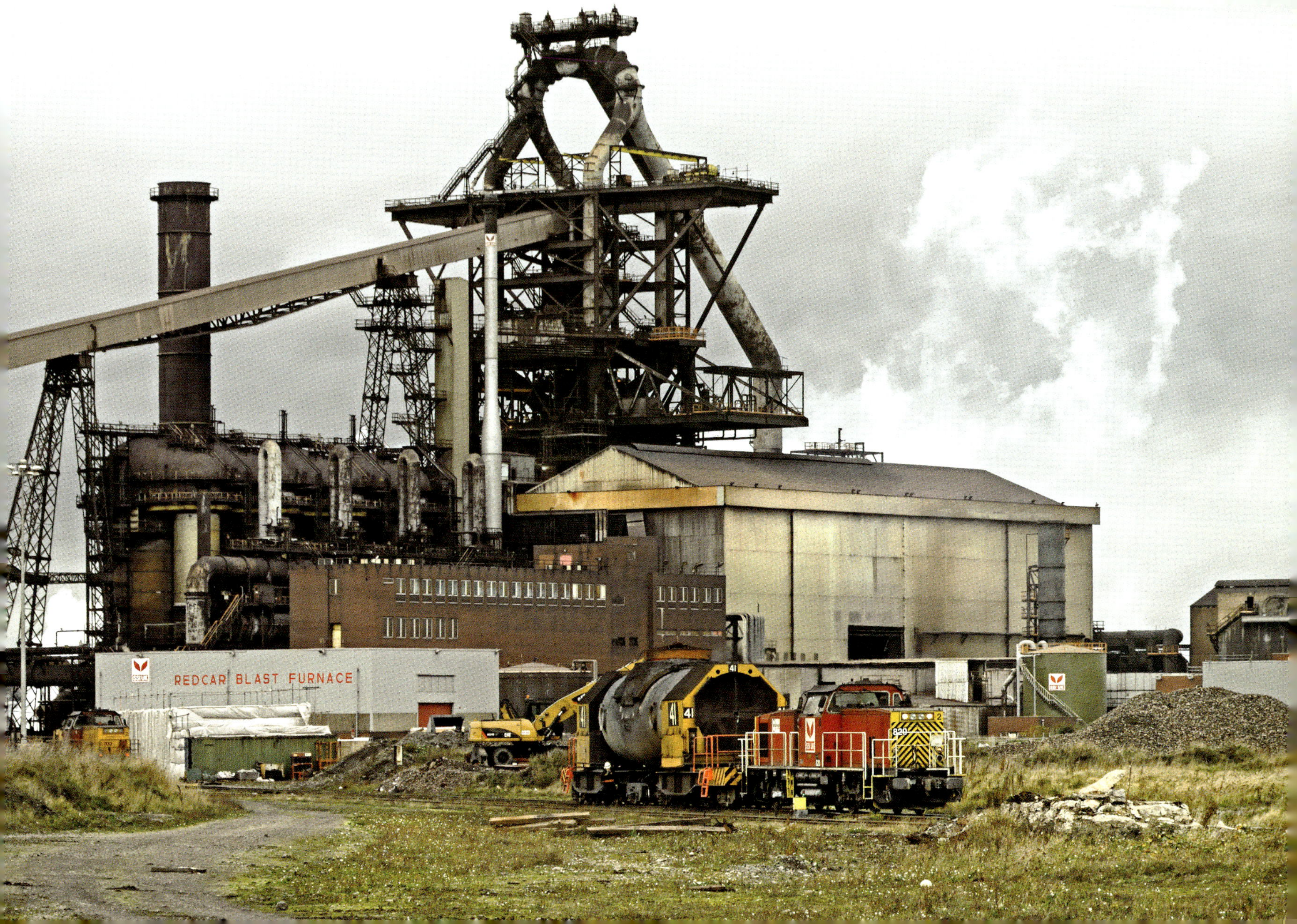

REDCAR BLAST FURNACE
41

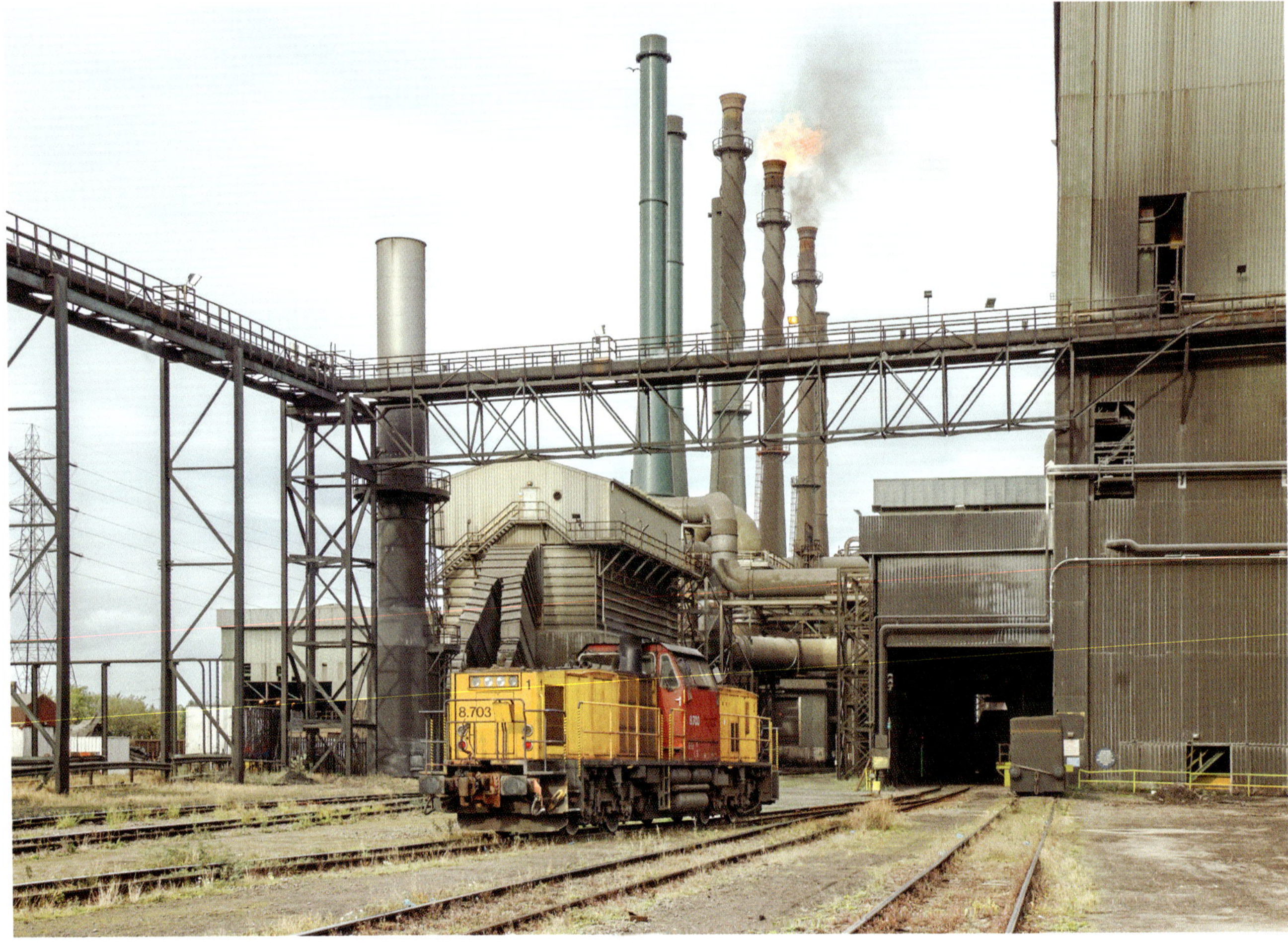

Di8 Class Bo-Bo diesel-electric 8.703 (MaK W/No. 1600.003 of 1996) adds a splash of colour to the otherwise drab industrial surroundings of the BOS Plant as it moves out of the hot metal annex at Tata's (previously Corus) Lackenby steelworks in October 2012, soon after the commissioning of the locos there. (Author)

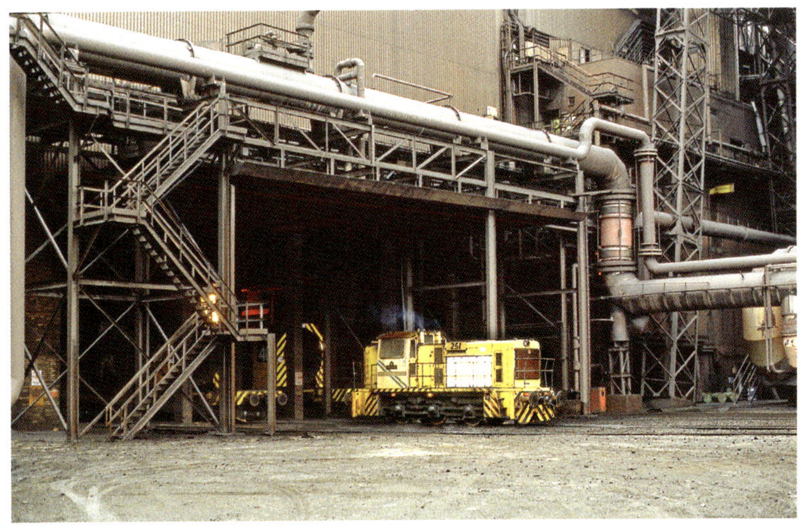

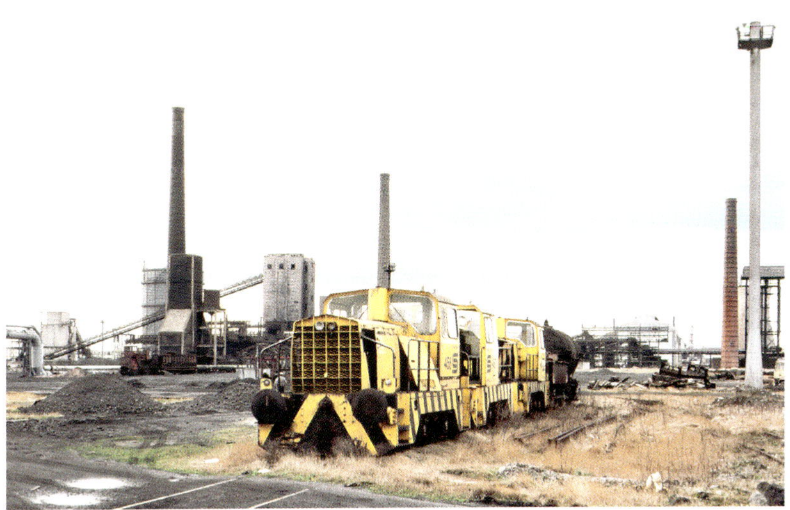

Above: On 3 July 1992, General Electric six-wheel diesel-electric No. 251 *Walter Urwin* (W/No. 5414 of 1976) with its torpedo wagon being charged at Redcar blast furnace.

Above right: Lackenby was not the only casualty in the region; the BSC Hartlepool works, opened in August 1960, stands silent on 18 March 1983, with Thomas Hill four-wheel diesel-hydraulics Nos 456 (W/No. 259C of 1975, rebuild of Sentinel No. 10041 of 1960), 457 (W/No. 260C of 1975, rebuild of Sentinel No. 1011 of 1959) and 455 (W/No. 258C of 1975, rebuild of Sentinel No. 10001 of 1959) standing idle. (Roy Burt)

Right: On 3 July 1992, British Steel's remote radio-controlled General Electric six-wheel diesel-electrics Nos 257 *North Skelton* (W/No. 5426 of 1977) and 252 *Boulby* (W/No. 5415 of 1976) stand in the rain between shunting duties at the BOS Plant, while (*above right*) No. 251 *Walter Urwin* (W/No. 5414 of 1976), the first of the 1970s order supplied from the Vulcan Works to Lackenby, waits for its torpedo wagon to be loaded at Redcar blast furnace before taking the consignment on to the BOS Plant at Lackenby. (Both author)

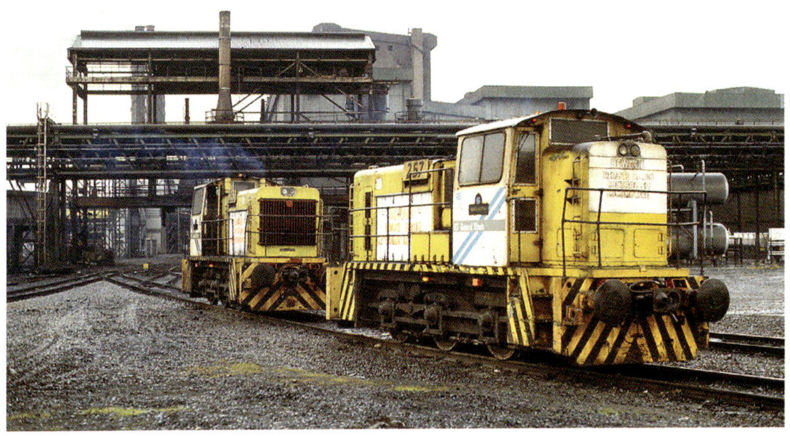

7

SCRAP

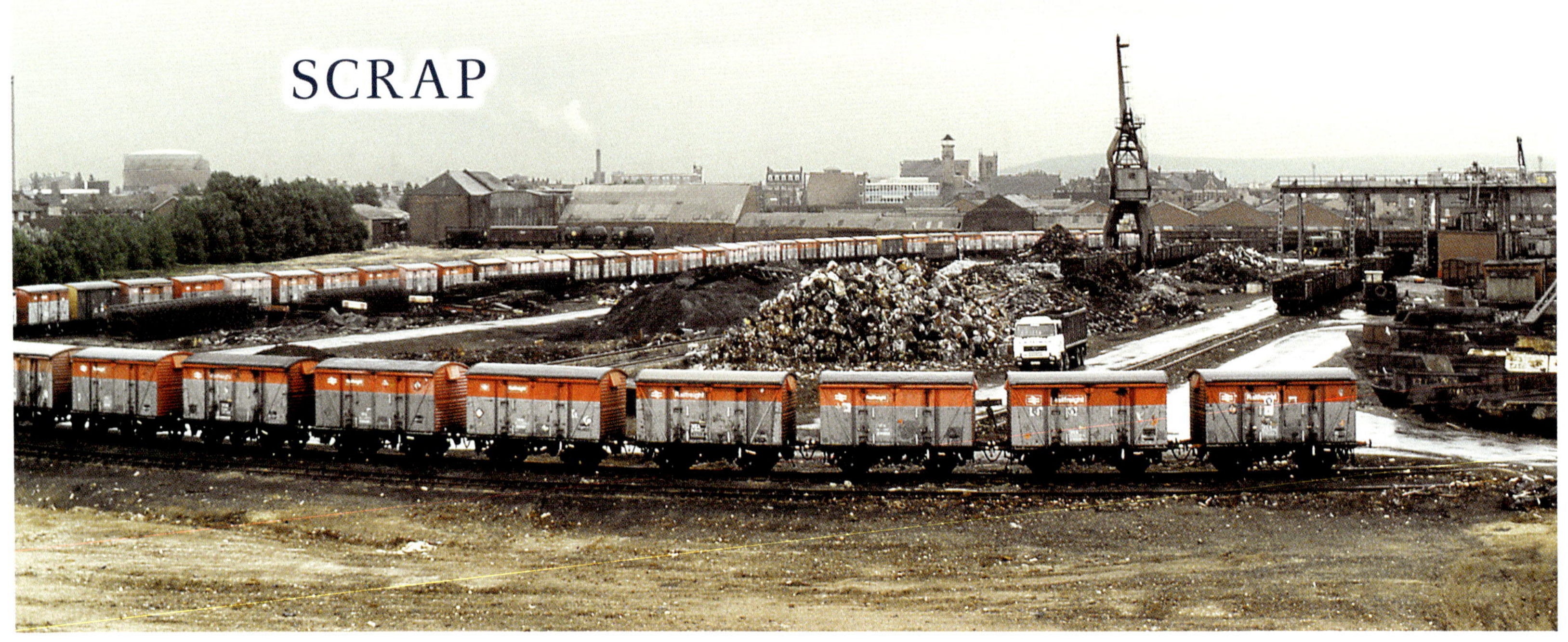

A panoramic view of T. J. Thomson's Millfield scrapyard at Stockton-on-Tees in July 1992. Beneath the gantry to the right can just be discerned the green-liveried Thomas Hill Vanguard four-wheel diesel-hydraulic *Helen* (W/No. 264V of 1976), one of four active locos to be found at the yard at this time, which was fully stocked with former BR vans for disposal. The 'VEA' ventilated van was a traditional BR wagon design, refurbished and air-brake fitted in the early 1980s for the use of customers who were unable to work with the longer wheelbase of newer design wagons. No fewer than 550 were converted, and they were to be seen countrywide on 'Speedlink' trains as well as ad hoc military workings, including conveying explosive material. A decline in Ministry of Defence requirements post-Cold War led to most of the fleet being withdrawn in the early 1990s, with just a handful finding further use in BR departmental service, but many survived in internal use at army bases. At least forty-seven vans awaiting disposal can be counted in this scene. T. J. Thomson's scrap metal business, one of the country's leading metal processors, had been handling scrap since the 1930s, and in the 1970s was Western Europe's largest processor of scrap metal. Many former main line locos and rolling stock were processed over the years, but these operations ceased at its 55-acre Millfield site in February 2017, when their industrial shunting locos were either cut up or sold on into preservation and part of the vast site given over to new housing development. (Author)

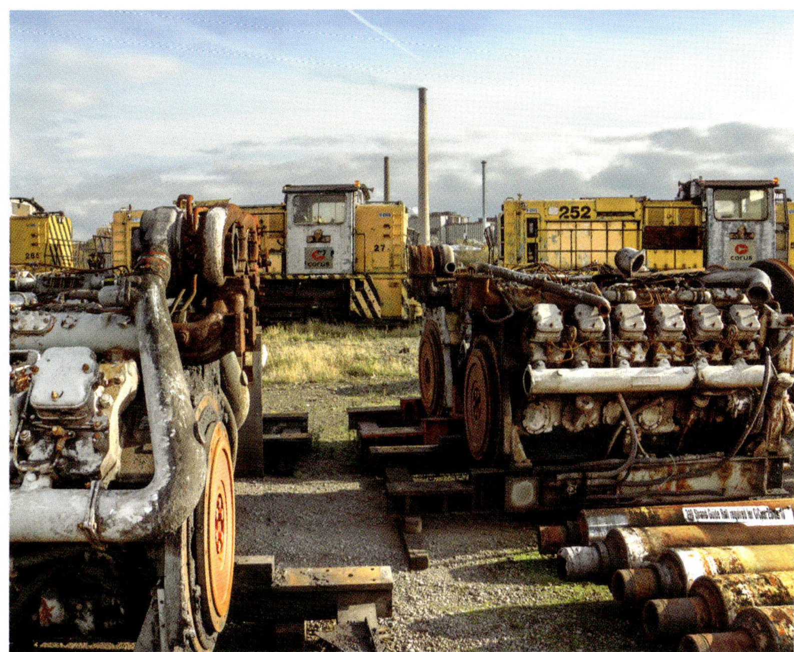

Left: The Tata Steel Europe (formerly Corus Teesside Cast Products) Lackenby loco 'graveyard' in October 2012. In addition to the discarded Dorman 12QT twelve-cylinder power units, Nos 265 *Roseberry* (W/No. 5462 of 1977), 276 *Spawood* (W.No. 5474 of 1978) and 252 *Boulby* (W/No. 5415 of 1976), all with nameplates removed, were three out of a total of fifteen General Electric Vulcan Foundry 1970s-built 750 hp six-wheel diesel-electric locos dumped outside the Lackenby Loco Shop, facing an uncertain future. (Author)

Right: The skeletal remains of Robert Stephenson & Hawthorns 0-4-0 saddle tank *Stella No. 2* (W/No. 7799 of 1954) meeting its fate at Norwood Coking Plant, Gateshead, on 24 August 1971. Next in line to be similarly dealt with was Andrew Barclay No. 92 (*see page 56*). (Author)

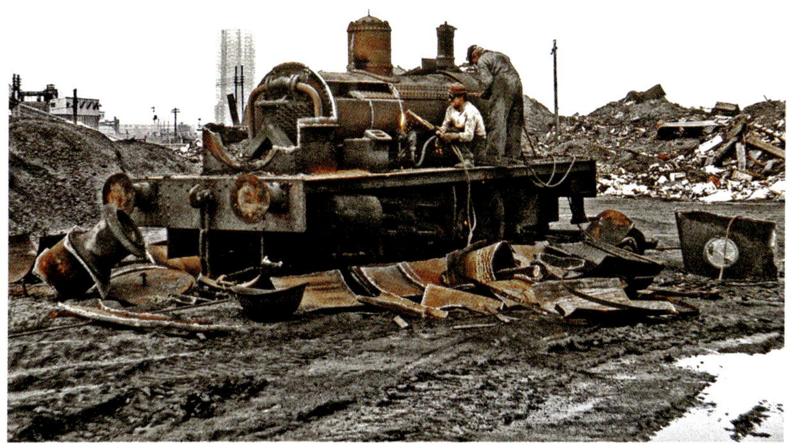

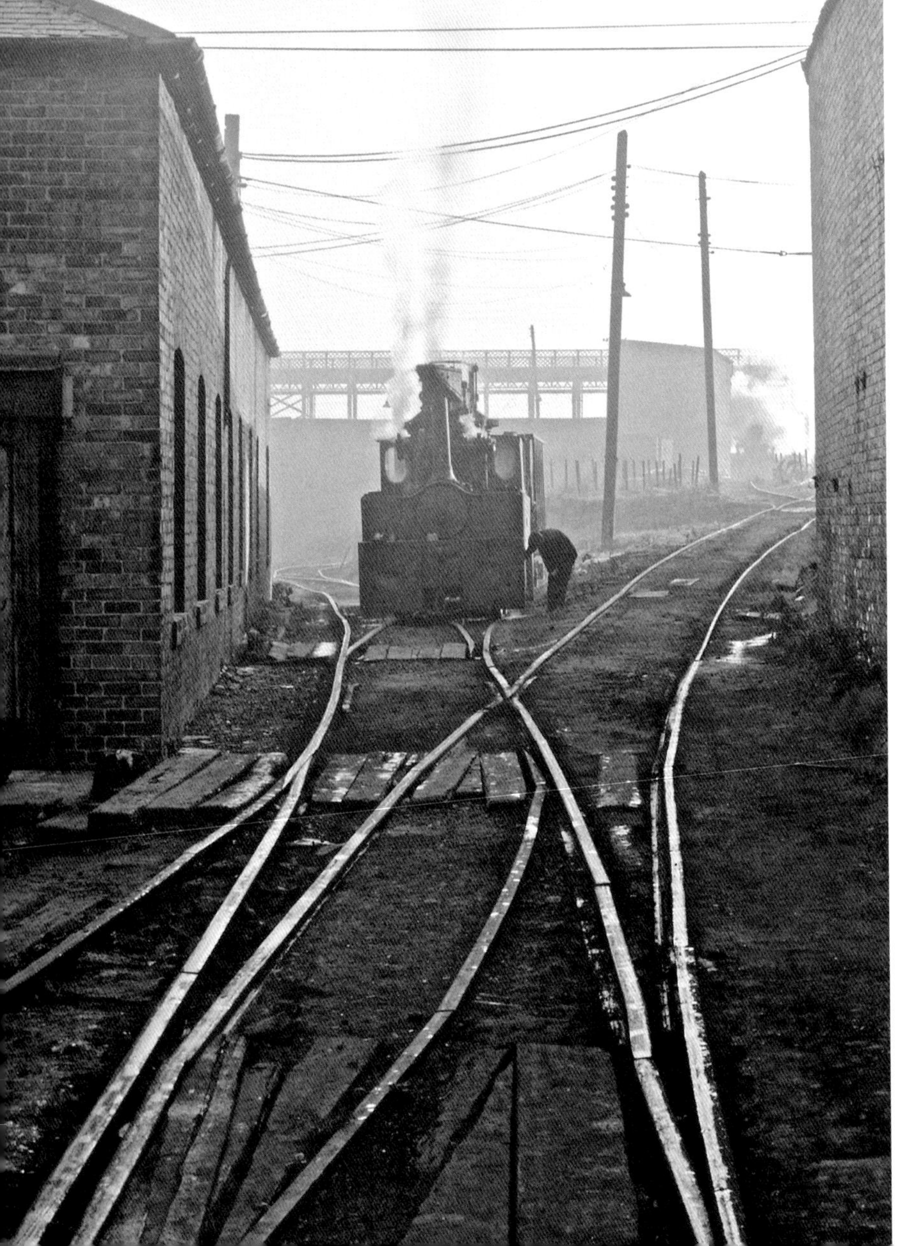

8

DOXFORD'S SHIPYARD

Sunderland was once regarded as the largest shipbuilding town in the world, with a history dating back to the fourteenth century. The industrial revolution saw shipbuilding on the River Wear peak by 1850, with the first iron-hulled collier launched in 1852. One company, owned by William Doxford, a timber merchant in the 1830s, prospered remarkably during this period. His first yard, opened in 1841 at Coxgreen, soon outgrew its size and William Doxford relocated to a larger site in Pallion, covering some 33 acres. This was eventually served by sidings from the Sunderland–Durham railway line, east of Pallion station, and a zig-zag of lines down the hillside into the yard on the bank of the River Wear. Five shipbuilding berths were constructed and in 1872 the first of several orders was received from the Admiralty. The original West Yard was replaced in 1902 by the East Yard, equipped with three larger berths and lofty overhead gantry cranes. The shipyard of William Doxford & Sons Ltd (and subsequently the Doxford & Sunderland Shipbuilding & Engineering Co. Ltd) was well known within industrial railway enthusiast circles for its unique fleet of its surviving Newcastle-built 0-4-0 crane tanks, with their distinctively large block 'dumb' buffers. From 1902 the company had purchased no fewer than eleven crane tanks, all bearing Sunderland district names. The first five, all purchased from new and all built by Hawthorn Leslie, were delivered to Doxford's shipyard between 1902 and 1906, and were named *Pallion, Deptford, Wear, Hylton,* and *Millfield.* These were followed by a solitary Andrew Barclay product, *Grindon,* purchased in 1912. All had 12 x 15-inch outside cylinders, a modified version of Joy's valve gear, and a steam-operated jib able to slew through 360 degrees, worked by an integral two-cylinder engine. The fixed hooks on the jib provided a maximum safe working load of 2 tons on the front hook, 3 tons on the middle and 4 tons on the rear hook, as painted beneath each lifting point on the jib. The final batch, *Roker, Hendon, Southwick* and *Millfield* (the original 1906 *Millfield* having been scrapped in 1938), were supplied new during the busy period of the Second World War, when the shipbuilding company launched some seventy-five ships, as well as manufacturing marine engines. Helping with the war effort around the yard, these locos came from Hawthorn Leslie's successors, Robert Stephenson & Hawthorns Ltd, between 1940 and 1942, except for just one pre-owned 1903-built Hawthorn Leslie, *Brownie*, which was purchased from the shipbuilding arm of the locomotive builder in 1940. Subsequently, four of the earlier crane tanks were converted to conventional 0-4-0 tanks, but all were scrapped over an extended period. The other conventional loco was a pre-owned Peckett 0-4-0 saddle tank, *General*, purchased from Morris Motors in Cowley via dealer T. W. Ward in April 1951. This replaced an older Peckett of the same name, which had been purchased new in 1899, and was subsequently cut up. The 'conventional' locos were used for shunting the high level plate yard and for working traffic to and from the exchange sidings. *General* survived, along with all four 1940s-built crane tanks – *Roker*, *Hendon*, *Southwick* and *Millfield*, plus the original *Pallion*, first purchased in 1902 – right up until rail traffic ceased in 1971. *Pallion* and *General* were eventually scrapped, despite thwarted preservation attempts, but the other four crane tanks have survived. During the post-war years up until 1966, some 123 ships of all sizes were launched from the Pallion shipyard, but following several company mergers and takeovers the yard's fortunes, by then boasting a new all-weather yard, had sadly declined. The shipyard struggled on until 1988, when the last ship was launched, upon the completion of an order of fifteen Danish ferries, the first being built from 1986. The yard was by then one of the last private shipbuilding yards in Sunderland. The former shipbuilding site remains today, and is still in commercial industrial use.

Opposite page: The crane tank locos of Doxford & Sons Ltd were held in very high regard at the Pallion shipyard and were extremely versatile machines. Their short wheelbase proved invaluable in negotiating the challenging track on the site (in all amounting to around 13 miles of track), thus allowing ease of access to many parts of the yard, where extremely tight curves were to be found in abundance. Not only could the locos carry out conventional shunting of flat wagons, they could also lift from either side and carry components to wherever required on site. On a winter's morning in 1970, Robert Stephenson & Hawthorns 0-4-0 crane tank *Hendon* (*W/No. 7007 of 1940*) receives attention near the loco shed prior to undertaking its day's duties. The loco shed is just visible to the right, beneath the Queen Alexandra Bridge. Also visible is the incline, which was the start of the zig-zag of lines to the BR exchange sidings at the top of the hill. (Tony Brown)

Above & below right: On the same morning as the picture opposite, Robert Stephenson & Hawthorns 0-4-0 crane tank *Millfield* (W/No. 7070 of 1942) was captured prior to commencing its shipyard lifting and transport duties, with one of its brass nameplates being polished by its caring driver/crane operator. (Tony Brown)

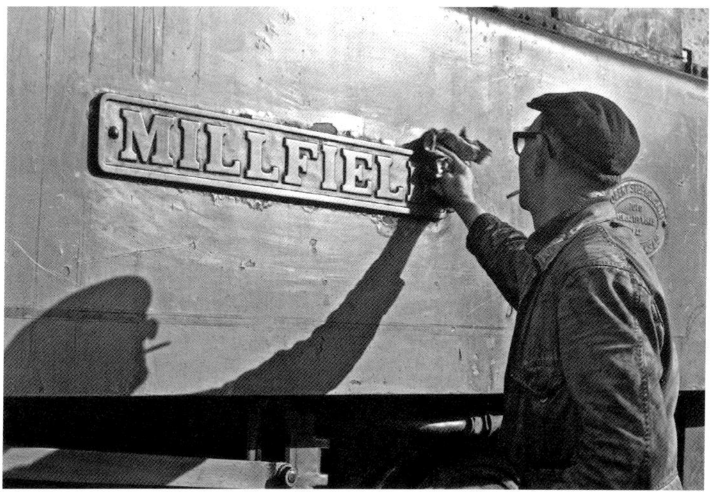

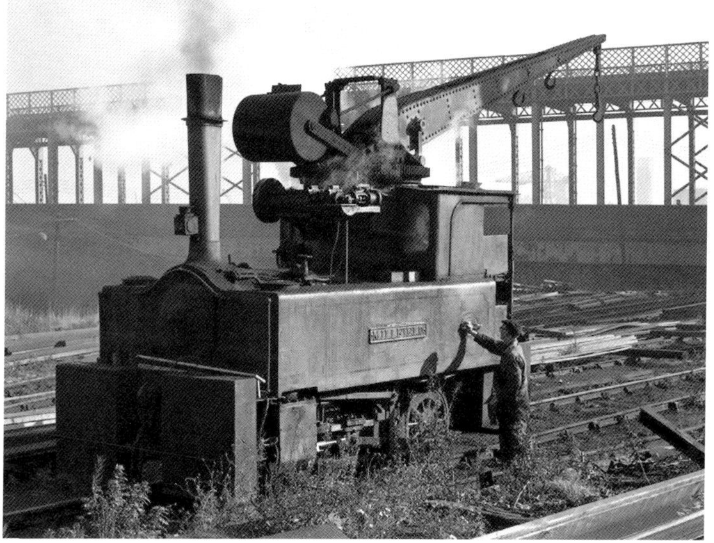

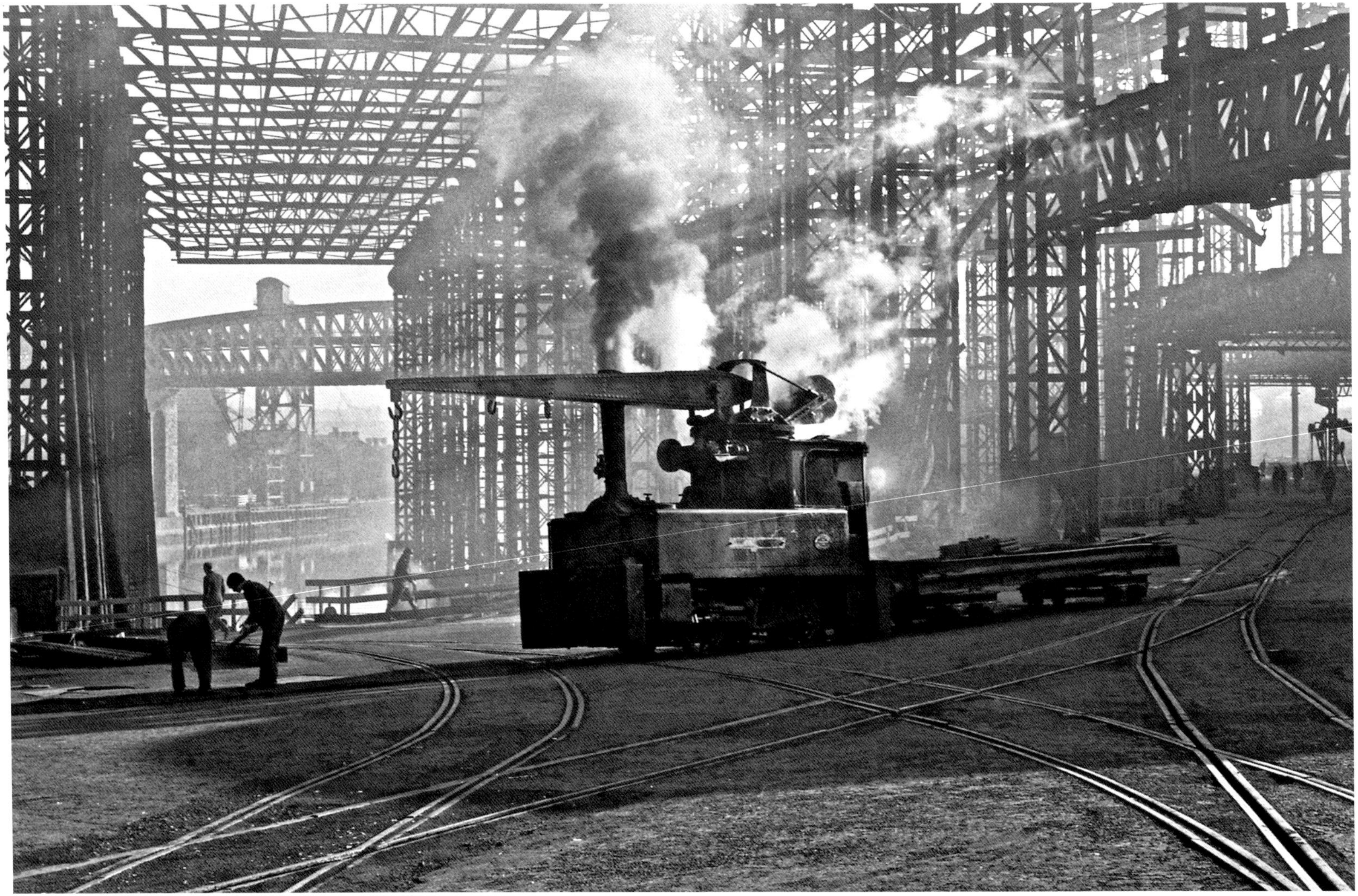

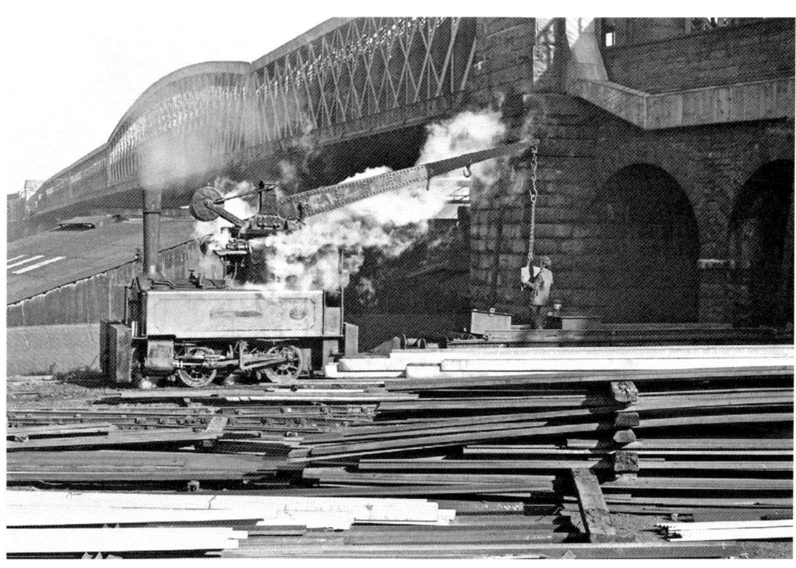

Opposite page: The crane tanks' versatility is well demonstrated in these two 1970s scenes of Robert Stephenson & Hawthorns *Southwick* (W/No. 7069 of 1942), by then devoid of its nameplates, beneath the gantries heading for the prefabrication shops with a loaded twin bogie flat wagon and (*above*) lifting steel sections. The sharp radius curves of the embedded trackwork about the shipyard can be fully appreciated in the atmospheric scene on the opposite page. (Both Tony Brown)

Right: *Millfield* lifting steel plate at the Pallion shipyard in 1967. (Jon Marsh)

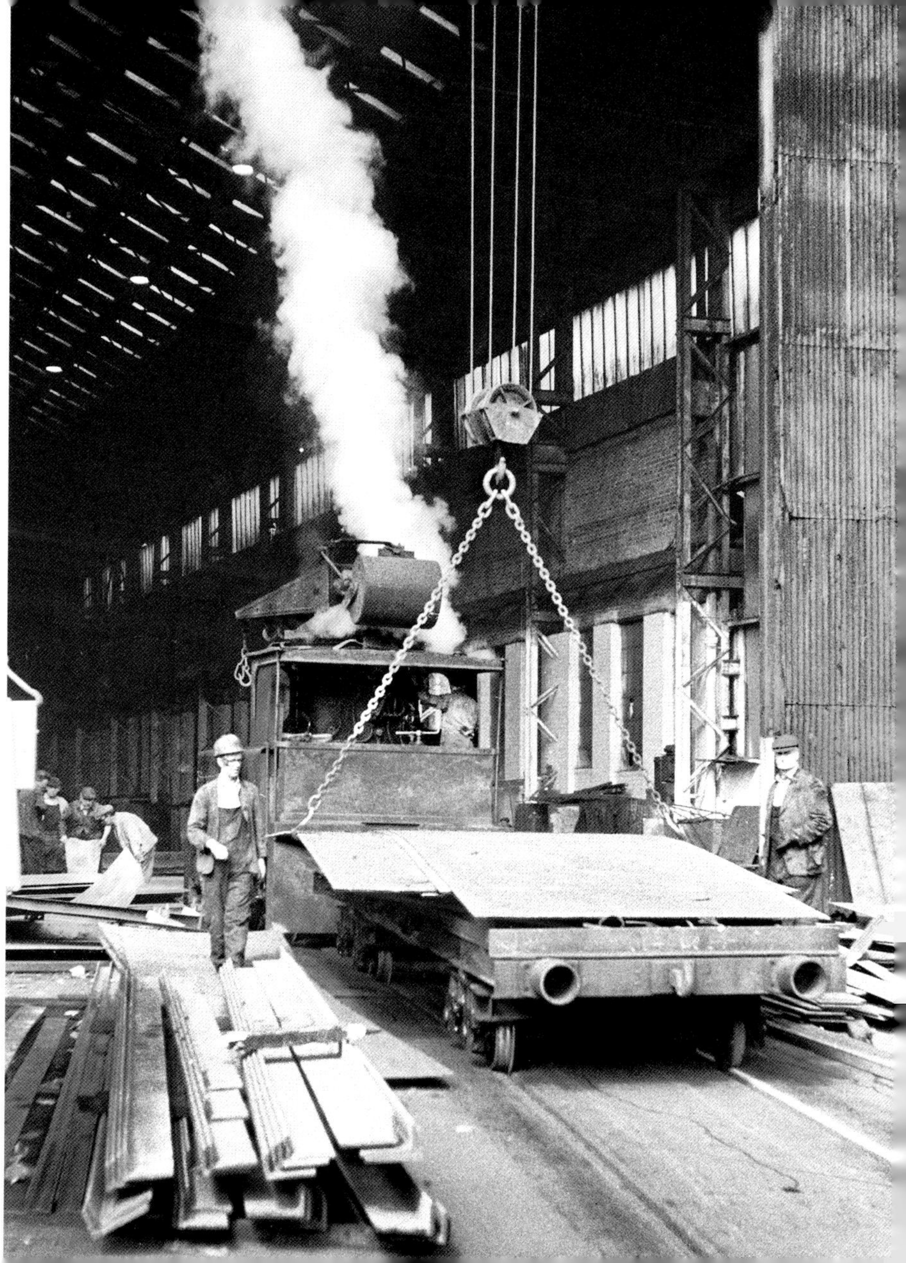

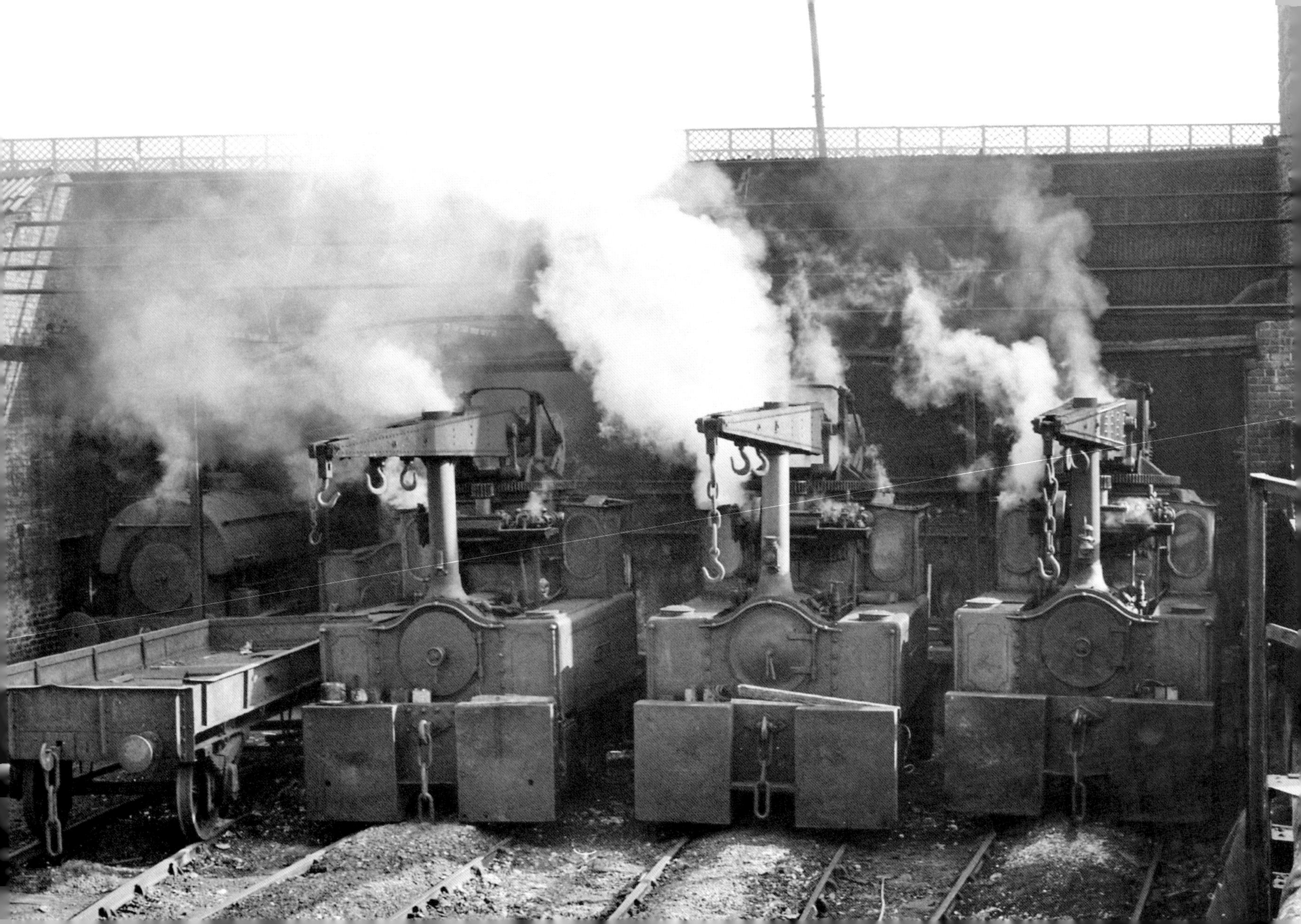

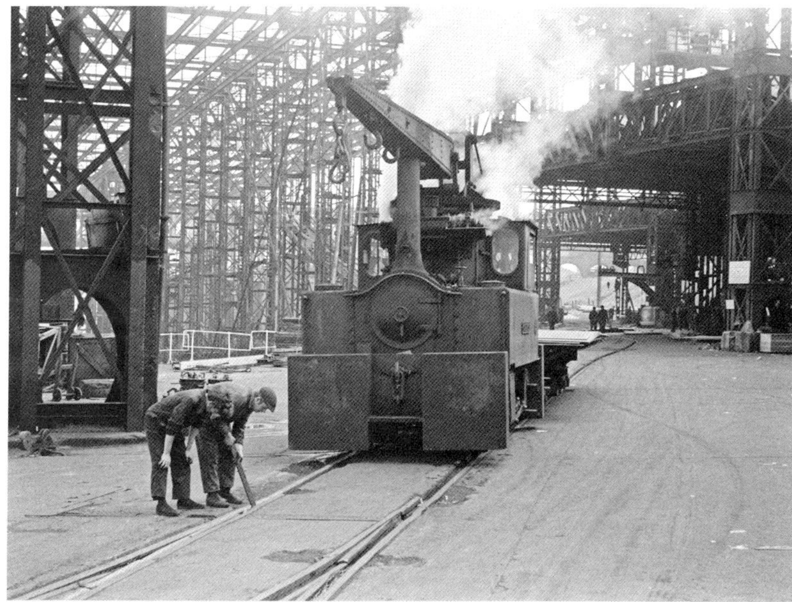

Opposite page: An atmospheric Doxford loco shed scene on an early morning in 1970, overshadowed by the double-deck Queen Alexandra Bridge, with road traffic beneath and the railway deck on the top; the latter actually fell into disuse in the 1920s. Peckett 0-4-0 saddle tank *General* (W/No. 2029 of 1944) and crane tanks (left to right) *Hendon, Millfield and Southwick* stand in the by then dilapidated five-road loco shed. Each road is just long enough to accommodate one loco under what would once have provided adequate protection from the elements. (Tony Brown)

Left: During a 1967 visit to the shipyard, an obstruction is cleared away to enable the points to be changed and for *Millfield* to proceed on its way with its bogie flat wagon of steel plate. (Jon Marsh)

Below: Inside the vast prefabrication shop at the shipyard complex in 1970 there is a veritable hive of activity, as the once-named *Southwick* looks on, ready to undertake one of the many routine tasks that was expected of it during its daily routine. Within two years such a scene, even then unimaginable to many in the 1970s, would be consigned to the history books. We are truly indebted to those photographers who captured these scenes for us to enjoy for posterity. (Tony Brown)

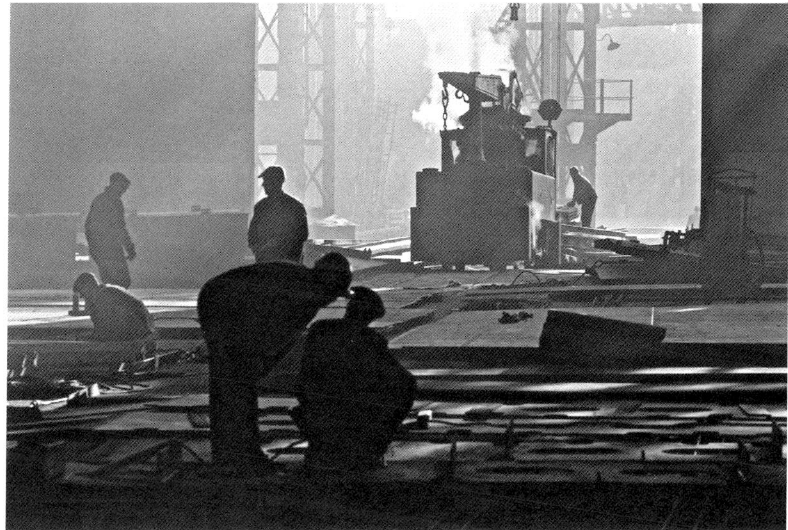

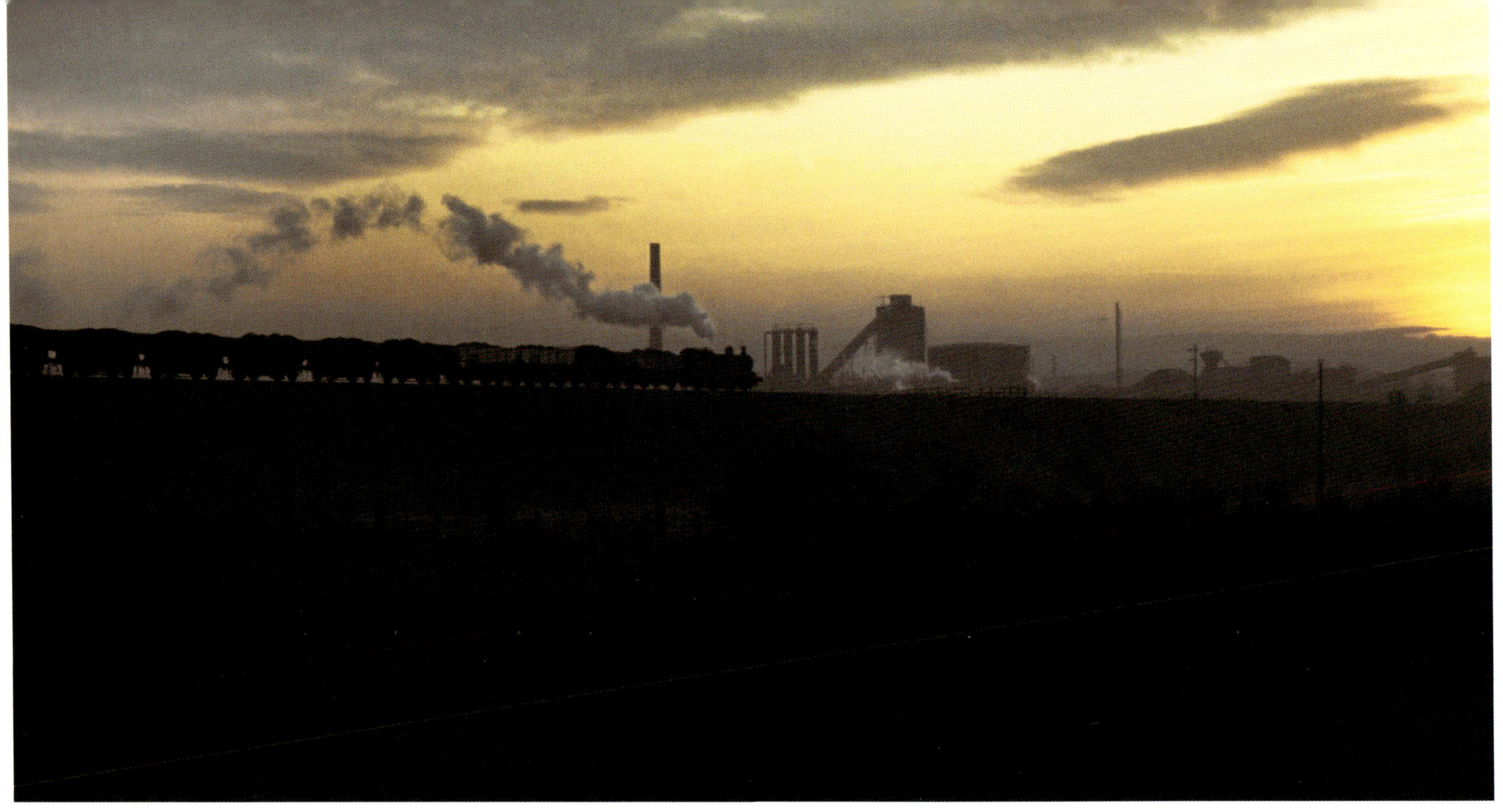

Viewed from Stott's Pasture near Shiney Row, with the Lambton 'D' coke works in full swing beyond at Burnmoor, a 'Lambton Tank' descends Junction Bank at sunset in charge of loaded BR hopper wagons for Penshaw exchange sidings. These were the final hours for steam on the Lambton Railway, in early February 1969 – a magical railway system affectionately known as 'Philly'. The familiar melodious hooters of the 'Lambton Tanks', so synonymous with the area, were to be heard no more sounding out and being carried on the wind around Philadelphia. (Jon Marsh)